To my dear friend Chris

"Keep the Faith"

Forever a Babe

Growing Up With Manchester United

Tom Clare (signature)

Tom Clare

Contact the author: tomclare@comcast.net

Cover design by Paul Windridge

Foreword

The period from 1945 to 1958 will always remain etched in my heart. It had a pronounced effect upon my life, though I also look back on a time of happy and carefree days. During those years, my grandfather instilled into me a love for Manchester United Football Club. It is a love that still burns brightly today. I grew up alongside the emerging young team that became famously known as the Busby Babes. They were unique: so young, so vibrant, so talented, so approachable and so accessible. There was a special bond between all three elements – the club, the players and the fans. Their ultimate tragedy left a deep scar upon a whole generation.

Writing this book has been a long and emotional journey. It began as the dream of my late wife, Paula, who gave me the love, belief and inspiration to write these memories. Yes, they are sentimental, and they are emotional, and I make no apologies for that. My wife, Cheryl, carried on where Paula left off. Without Cheryl's love and total support this book could never have been completed.

I would like to thank the many members of Internet football forums who have encouraged me, and have waited patiently to see this book completed: 606 Substitute; Manchester United Supporters Trust; Red News; Red Café; United Lounge; and Big Soccer.

I am indebted to Tony Smith for his patience, advice, tenacity and professionalism in being my guide along this journey. My thanks go to Amit Basu whose eagle eyes reviewed the final draft. I am very grateful to Paul Windridge for designing the wonderful book cover.

Tom Clare
Houston, Texas
March 2009

Contents

Preface

In April 2003, I first came across the BBC's '606' sports website, which had a discussion forum for each professional football club in Britain. Naturally, I joined the Manchester United forum, and initially just enjoyed browsing through the United-related topics. The names of the forum users brought a smile to my face: Dutch Aaron, Ian Freeman, Xavier, St. Inebrius, Red Tom, No One Famous, Rin Tin Tin's Dog Snowy, William Prunier, Ged The Red, Kevin Mott, Laughing Sale Red, Republic of Mancunia, Red In t'Head, Mark Barton, Ian Clarke, Sharks With Freakin' Laser Beams Attached to Them, There's A Guy Down Our Chip Shop Who Swears He's Pelvis, Farooq ... to name just a few.

My contribution to the forum began when a young Arsenal fan posed a question about Duncan Edwards. Initially, there was little response to this query, so I decided to answer. My reply provoked considerable feedback, and so inspired me to write a number of further pieces about Manchester United, particularly around my memories of the 1950s and the Munich Air Disaster. I saw it as a way to educate (in the most helpful way) younger fans in the great history of Manchester United. By this time several generations, those who had begun to follow United from the late 1960s to the 1990s, had no personal recollections of the Busby Babes and the Munich tragedy.

Unfortunately the 606 forum had a number of shortcomings. First, any contribution of more than 500 words was immediately 'pulled' by the forum's moderators, and disappeared from view almost as soon as it had appeared. Thus a number of my pieces were consigned to the cyber dustbin before they were seen. Despite protestations the moderators refused to budge on this rule. A second problem was that members of any of the club-specific forums had access to all the other forums, and quite often online warfare would break out between rival fans. This was a particular problem on the Manchester United forum, which would be 'spammed' by non-United supporters – multiple copies of a 'spam' post would cause the message board to be locked, preventing genuine users from gaining access. Again, despite protestations, nothing seemed to happen to alleviate the problem. It felt like the inmates were running the asylum! A third problem was with the moderators themselves, as it was more than obvious they had a certain bias where Manchester United was concerned! On a number of occasions, the moderators themselves posed questions to the Manchester United forum, knowing these would cause dissent, and would provoke outbursts from United members. Any complaints made by the Manchester United forum members seemed to go unanswered, or were just arbitrarily dismissed.

For a while people tried to make the best of a bad situation. It was a sad state of affairs, as there were some excellent discussions between forum members, and several people from other clubs' forums would join in – it was always interesting to hear intelligent views from outside the Manchester United perspective. I did manage to post a number of pieces outlining the events that led up to the Munich tragedy, and again there was a significant amount of feedback. Some I remember with much fondness. 'Back Row', a fervent Newcastle United fan, wrote to me posing some wonderful questions, especially about Eric Cantona and his effect on Manchester United. 'Rasputin', an Everton fan, was another who took an interest in the Munich posts, along with 'Gooner Pride', an Arsenal fan. Unfortunately, there were also some truly nasty responses from non-United fans. These really should have been dealt with immediately by the moderators, but the fact that they weren't came as no real surprise. It was obvious that this state of affairs could not continue if the forum were to survive with any credibility and respectability.

On 29 May 2003, Aaron Carter, a stalwart of the Manchester United forum, decided to take matters into his own hands. That particular day saw the straw that broke the camel's back, after the 606 Manchester United forum was 'spammed' on several occasions, and became locked for most of the day. Aaron formed his own 'breakaway' United message board on Yahoo, naming it '606 Substitute', and immediately some familiar names began to desert the BBC's 606 Manchester United forum. Although advertising of other websites was forbidden on the 606 forums, little cryptic messages began to appear on the United forum. These messages didn't take much working out, and were in fact directions to Aaron Carter's new 606 Substitute site. Soon most decent members of the 606 Manchester United forum had made their way to 606 Substitute, which became a home-from-home for all of us. No spamming, no unwelcome intruders, and moderated by members. It proved to be idyllic.

The quality of the postings was tremendous, and the camaraderie was incredible, as was the diversity of places from which they came: Australia, Canada, USA, Hong Kong, Germany, Belgium, France, Denmark, Norway, Venezuela, as well as all points within the United Kingdom. Most of my writings were purely historical pieces, and the response to these pieces from 606 Substitute members prompted the idea for this book. There was so much encouragement from everybody, and I think it is true to say that 606 Substitute has become something of a family.

In August 2003, I returned to England from my home in Houston, Texas to attend my mother's funeral. On my last night in England I met Aaron Carter and Ian Freeman in the Duke of Wellington pub, near Waterloo Station in London. This pub would become a regular meeting place for '606 Subbers' in the years to come. As time progressed pseudonyms on an Internet message board soon became real people with real names, as regular meetings took place in both London and Manchester. Aaron Carter, Nick Midgeley, Jeremy Griffiths, Graham Tully, Charlie Haydar, Tom Chamley, Graham Wilde, David Fyles, David Jacobi, Paul Wharton, Paul Boland and Steve Morrisroe were just some of the names I came to know.

In February 2004 my wife, Paula, and I were in Manchester visiting relatives and friends. I had arranged to meet a number '606 Subbers' one Friday evening in the Woodheys Club in Sale. Earlier I had been in contact with Mike Thomas, who runs the two wonderful websites, munich58.co.uk and duncan-edwards.co.uk, in honour of United's team of the 1950s and its greatest player. My main aim was for members of 606 Substitute, as a group, to lay a wreath beneath the Munich memorial plaque at Old Trafford, prior to the game against Southampton – the nearest home game to the Munich anniversary date. We met as a group on the Saturday morning, and it was on this occasion that I also met Mike, and his lovely partner Elaine, for the first time. The wreath was duly laid, the match attended, and afterwards we went for dinner. It had been the first 'formal' meeting of 606 Substitute members, and was a huge success.

For some time I had toyed with the idea of organising a dinner for 606 Sub members, and although a lot of hard work would be required to make it happen, I thought that given enough support it would be well worth the effort. Upon my return to Houston, I sounded out the membership of the forum, and there was enough interest for me to book the function room at the Woodheys Club, with United and Scotland legend, Paddy Crerand, agreeing to be our first guest speaker.

The first annual dinner of the 606 Substitute group, on Friday, 23 April 2004 was attended by 23 members and 14 guests, who had travelled from the USA and Canada, from their homes around Europe, and from across the UK. It was a pleasure to meet Charlie Haydar (from Ottawa, Canada), Andy Smith (from St. John's in Newfoundland), Graham Wilde, Nick Midgeley, Paul Boland, John White (who had arrived from Belgium) and Ian Clarke. The evening was a tremendous success, and the following morning, after breakfasting on buttered Anadins, a large party left the hotel to attend the Manchester United versus Liverpool league game at Old Trafford. Although United lost 1-0, it in no way spoiled a wonderful weekend.

They say that from little acorns, oak trees grow. Each year now, on the Friday before Manchester United's last home game of the season, the 606 Substitute group meets for its annual dinner in the Manchester area. The number attending has increased with each passing year, and now we have more than 80 present, with a good number arriving from overseas. There is diversity amongst the members in age, race, gender, outlook, and location, and I would like to think that the annual dinner has helped bond friendships that will last for a lifetime.

The enthusiasm of the 606 Substitute members was a significant contributory factor in inspiring the writing of this book. I have constantly been encouraged to put my memories into print. I must also mention similar encouragement from members of the Manchester United Supporters' Trust. However, this project was also the dream of my late wife, Paula, carried on by my wife Cheryl. Without their inspiration, love and total support this book could never have been completed.

When I started to write this book in earnest, I wanted it to be a little different from run of the mill football trivia books. It will concentrate upon my childhood days, and particularly the period between 1950 and 1959, when the flames for my love of Manchester United were ignited and then fanned. As well as conveying my love for my football club, and for the game of football itself, I hope that I can also bring to the reader a picture life growing up in the city of Manchester in the immediate aftermath of World War II.

Introduction: Heading Home to Manchester

The Commemoration Service began at 2.45 in the afternoon. I was inside the Manchester Suite, underneath Manchester United's huge North Stand at the Old Trafford stadium. The date was Wednesday, 6 February 2008. Over 800 people were present in that long, narrow room, and as I looked around I saw that the majority were of my age group – between 55 and 65 years old.

A children's choir had opened the service, singing a hymn that depicted the path of life. Reverend John K. Boyers, Manchester United's club chaplain then read his opening eulogy. You could hear a pin drop as his voice, in a solemn, deep tone resonated down the room. The service was being televised live to a world-wide audience, and on the large monitors, placed at regular intervals along the walls, we could see pictures of thousands of people gathered outside the stadium underneath the Munich plaque. They too were taking in every word spoken by Reverend Boyers, whose voice was transmitted through loudspeakers that were strategically placed above the gathered crowd.

At 3 o'clock precisely, Gary Neville, the Manchester United club captain, took his place on the rostrum alongside Reverend Boyers. The rotund clergyman, resplendent in purple and white robes, lit the Munich Candle which stood in the centre of a plinth, surrounded by 23 small crystal candle holders. Handing the lighted taper to Neville, he began to read out the Roll of Honour: the names of the 23 people who had perished in the Munich Air Disaster on Thursday, 6 February 1958. He began with the name of the club captain, and continued alphabetically, "Roger Byrne ... Geoff Bent ... Eddie Colman ..." his voice never faltering. As each name was called out, Gary Neville's trembling hand lit one of the candles, encased in those small, but beautiful, crystal holders, each inscribed with a victim's name. Underneath each name was inscribed, "Munich, February 6th 1958".

With each name my emotions began to take their toll. Tears ran down my cheeks, and I saw that I was not alone. Old men wept unashamedly together. The memories, the pain, the anguish, the gut-wrenching feeling of sad loss, all returned for each and every one. For me, and for all of my generation, whenever we think of that sad, fateful day in early February 1958, it is always the same, and always will be.

At precisely four minutes past three o'clock, the last name - that of Willie Satinoff – was read out. His candle was lit, and there followed a minute of silent remembrance. Both inside that room and outside on the stadium forecourt not a sound was heard nor uttered. Tears flowed so freely. It was such a moving, poignant, emotional moment, and one that will stay with me for the rest of my days. As the clock hands had moved to four minutes past three, it was exactly 50 years since the moment of that terrible accident in Munich, Germany.

* * *

On Friday, 1 February 2008, I had boarded a Continental Airlines Boeing 777 at Houston's George Bush International Airport. Embedded into the back of the seat in front of me was a video console, showing our route to London. I relaxed and began to read Sir Bobby Charlton's book, "My Manchester United Years". The main reason for my journey back to the city of my birth was to attend the 50th anniversary commemorations of the Munich Air Disaster at my beloved Old Trafford ground on the following Wednesday.

The sixth day of February in 1958 is a date that is ingrained in my mind, but also chiselled deep into my heart. It is a date that has had a profound and significant effect upon my life, and there was certainly nowhere else in this whole wide world that I was going to be at four minutes past three on that date in 2008, other than at Old Trafford, Manchester. I have witnessed many things, suffered personal anguish and tragedy, but that day in 1958, and the events that happened at the end of a slush filled runway in the Bavarian capital, has lived with me ever since. It will never ever go away. For me, and the many thousands of Manchester United supporters of my generation that are still alive, the memories of that terrible day 50 years ago are still all so vivid, all so clear, and are cemented within us. The scar that has been left behind has never healed – and it never will. We will carry it with us until we draw our final breath.

As my aircraft sped through the night, I lay thinking about the years that had led up to the Munich tragedy. All too clearly, the ghosts of my past returned. My thoughts went back to all those balmy days, and all those great games I had watched that wonderful Manchester United team play. Memories flooded back with a strange kind of warmth as I remembered the emergence of a team of boys who would capture the nation's hearts and imagination. They were the seed, the blossoming flower, and the inspiration of my young life. It was to be the very first love affair of my life. As most first loves generally do, it was to end in heartache, but it was a love that would last a lifetime.

In my early years, my grandfather had nurtured into me a love of everything that was Manchester United. From the early 1950s I became besotted with the team and the club. Nothing else was so important to me. And now, as my flight passed the north-eastern seaboard of the United States, over Canada's Newfoundland, and on across the Atlantic Ocean, my thoughts turned to the happy days of my boyhood watching a fine team take shape, sharing their triumphs, the pain of their losses, and ultimately their tragedy. I felt so proud that I had been there to see them win their first Football League championship in 1956, and I also felt so proud to have been there at the start of their dream to conquer Europe

That dream had begun in September 1956, when Manchester United became the first English club to appear in the new European Champion Clubs' Cup competition. The tournament had been founded by UEFA in the previous season, 1955/56, having been inspired by Gabriel Hanot, a French journalist, and the French sporting newspaper, *L'Equipe*. Sixteen European football champions had come together in the inaugural competition, although Chelsea, the English First Division champions in 1955, did not take part. The Football League had pressured Chelsea into declining the invitation, just as the Football Association had kept England out of the World Cup in its inaugural years. This short sighted and parochial attitude was typical of the administration in both governing bodies of the English game at that time.

In 1956, Manchester United became First Division champions, and their forward-thinking manager, Matt Busby, was determined to take United, and future English champions, into this prestigious competition. Busby persuaded the Manchester United directors to stand firm behind him as he argued his case with the game's administrators, who eventually relented with a strict proviso. European Cup games were played on Wednesday afternoons or evenings, and United were under the threat of dire repercussions should they fail to fulfill a league fixture following a midweek European game.

I was just 12 years old at the time, and had followed United for as long as I could remember. Great anticipation was felt by all United fans, who would see their young team compete against the best in Europe. At that time many of those clubs were completely unheard of in Britain, where there was very little coverage of European football in the media.

By 1956, Matt Busby had assembled the youngest team ever to win the Football League, with an average age of just 22 years. Busby had formulated a youth policy when taking over as manager of Manchester United in 1945, and although it had taken some years to come to fruition, the Busby Babes, as they had been affectionately nicknamed by some astute journalist, had romped away with the 1955/56 league championship by an astonishing 11 points. This was a team that captured the imagination of the nation with their exuberant youthfulness and the exciting brand of attacking football they played. The manager now wanted his young team to play and test themselves against the finest in Europe.

Prior to the new European Cup competition being founded, European competition for British clubs had been mainly in the form of friendly matches against top teams from behind the Iron Curtain. Moscow Dynamo and Moscow Spartak had visited Britain, as had Honved, the great Hungarian side, and Red Star Belgrade from Yugoslavia. Although these games had drawn large attendances, with intense media interest, by no stretch of the imagination could they be regarded as genuine competition – they were mainly prestige and goodwill matches. And so when it came, the European experience of 1956/57 was a joy to behold.

By April 1957, our young United team was in the running to win an unprecedented treble of titles – Football League championship, FA Cup, and European Cup. Although United eventually fell to the might and experience of Real Madrid in the semi-final of the European Cup, the team won the First Division championship again, and only lost the FA Cup final to Aston Villa due, I believe, to one of the most cynical, pre-meditated acts of violence that I have ever witnessed in a football match, which resulted in United's goalkeeper, Ray Wood, being incapacitated for most of the game. However, the spark had lit the flame, and after some disappointment at the end of that 1956/57 campaign, season 1957/58 could not come quickly enough for the manager, players and spectators alike – and it was the European Cup, and the prospect of competing for the treble once more, that really whetted everybody's appetite!

The treble had become a sort of Holy Grail for Manchester United, and in the years to follow it would become a dream for all English league champions. Only one club, Liverpool, came close to achieving this dream, ironically only denied in 1977 by Manchester United's 2-1 victory in the FA Cup final at Wembley. Liverpool had already won the league championship, and a few days after the FA Cup final won the European Champions' Cup with a 3-1 victory over Borussia Monchengladbach of West Germany in the Olympic Stadium in Rome. Liverpool had been favourites to lift the famous old FA Cup trophy at Wembley, but another youthful United side rose to the occasion in that final, and also had a little lady luck on their side. It was with tremendous elation that United were able to end Liverpool's treble dream. Liverpool were to win a further four European champions' crowns, but always, the treble has eluded them. For Manchester United, that Holy Grail was finally to be achieved in 1999 on a balmy May evening in the Catalan capital of Barcelona – but that is another story!

In February 2008, as I flew 'home' over the Atlantic Ocean, my thoughts turned to where it had all begun for me. I went back to my very earliest days, when my family lived in Royle Street in Chorlton-upon-Medlock, Manchester. How was it that I had come to follow Manchester United and not Manchester City, or any other local club? Where, when, and how had this burning allegiance to this great club been ignited?

This then is my story of how it all came about, of how those early years following the greatest club in the world fired my passion for my beloved Manchester United. These are my recollections of the major events of that period, events that shaped Manchester United's history, and events that shaped my life.

Times Before Football

The city of Manchester that we see today in the early 21st century bears little resemblance to the Manchester I was born into, just weeks before the end of the Second World War. Likewise, the Manchester United that we see today bears little or no resemblance to the club that was resurrected from the dereliction and destruction of war in 1945. Today, whenever I return home to the city of my birth, and to the Old Trafford football ground, my initial reaction is of nostalgic recollection. The ghosts of years past come flooding back in myriad different memories. It staggers me today when I sit back and take in the changes that have taken place since my childhood, both in the city of Manchester and at Manchester United Football Club.

I do think it is important to relate my immediate family history, from the time of the potato famine in Ireland in 1845, and my great-great-grandfather, one Michael Clare. The family's roots on my father's side were originally in the village of Ballanahinch in the Connemara area of County Galway in the west of Ireland. Michael was born around the time of Queen Victoria's accession to the British throne, the beginning of the longest reign of any British monarch. On my mother's side, the Whelan roots go back to County Tipperary, and it is interesting to note that both the Clare and Whelan families left the Emerald Isle at more or less the same time, and for the same reasons. According to the eminent historian David Fitzpatrick, Ireland during the 19th century "was a land which most people wanted to leave", and this was never truer than during the terrible period of the potato famine.

By 1845, Ireland was inhabited by some eight million people, with the majority of them wretchedly poor, trying to eke out some kind of decent living on tiny plots of land, and totally dependent on each year's potato crop. It was a hard and harsh existence, and hunger was a common visitor over the years to the peasant families who existed in this manner. There had been warnings of things to come, with partial failures in the potato crop in previous years. Perhaps it was because those partial failures were of limited duration, and confined to a small number of counties, that the warnings were more or less ignored.

The year of 1845 changed all that, as more than half the Irish potato crop failed. What caused the crop to fail? Nothing more than a fungus which made the potato plants rot in the ground. This fungus was first noticed when it destroyed crops on the eastern seaboard of the United States of America in 1842. In the early summer of 1845 the fungus reappeared in England, and in the late summer of that same year it was reported in Ireland, first in Wexford and then in Waterford. It spread so rapidly that in the latter half of 1845 more than half of the Irish potato crop failed, and the following year, 1846, saw a total failure of the Irish potato crop.

The effect on the Irish population was devastating, especially, for the peasants. Unused to a cash economy, most of them worked for a landlord, and in return were given a small plot of land upon which to grow the potatoes which would sustain them. With the destruction of the potato crop the landlords began to suffer economically, and many faced ruin. In turn, the starving peasants were evicted in their thousands from their primitive homes and small plots of land. Many of these poor unfortunates had large families, and the starvation was accompanied by outbreaks of typhoid and relapsing fever, which became known as 'famine fever'. In addition to this, there were widespread outbreaks of scurvy and dysentery, and also cholera.

Conditions in Ireland at this time were desperate, and there was much social unrest. It is no surprise, therefore, that many heads of families saw their only hope of survival was to leave the homes and the land that they loved behind them, and to emigrate. Thousands made the long and hazardous sea journeys to Australia and North America, and thousands also perished along those routes. Thousands more decided to leave Ireland, but only to make the short journey across the Irish Sea to England, and the main entry point into this country was the port of Liverpool in Lancashire. This was my great, great grandfather, Michael's choice. After the trek east across central Ireland, Michael and his wife arrived in Dublin in 1848, and after spending a short while in that city, were lucky to find passage on a small sailing vessel that took them over the Irish Sea to the difficult and crowded social conditions they encountered in Liverpool. They had little or no savings and no possessions – in effect they had nothing more than the poor clothes on their backs.

Michael and his wife eventually made their way eastwards to Manchester. To a large extent, Victorian Manchester was an inhospitable place, especially for immigrants, no matter what nationality they were. The reality of life in Britain at that time was that the rich had better food and conditions, while the poor were always struggling for their very existence. Manchester had in fact risen rapidly from obscurity. By the mid-19th century, Britain was irrevocably committed to becoming primarily an industrialised, urban society. Towns expanded further into the countryside, swallowing fields and farms, and turning what were once villages, into suburbs.

Manchester became the centre of the nation's cotton industry, with its famous damp climate conducive to cotton manufacture. Industrialisation forged ahead at great speed, as Manchester became established as one of Britain's premier commercial cities. Manchester was close to the Atlantic port of Liverpool, gateway to America's cottonfields, and an export route for Manchester's manufactured goods, along with the North Sea port of Hull. The world's first commercial railway had connected Manchester and Liverpool in 1830, as by 1894 the Manchester Ship Canal, which extended inland some 30 miles from the Mersey estuary, was open to sea-going vessels – inland Manchester was now an ocean port. Power sources throughout the Manchester region were plentiful, and the mills and factories were driven by steam engines fuelled from the Lancashire coalfield. Manchester over the previous century had also become the hub for a great canal network which linked it to all parts of the country, including the ports of Liverpool and Hull. So Manchester was able to receive raw materials into the city from all over the country, then export quality manufactured goods back out through those same systems and exit points. It was these systems, plus the massive technological innovation of that period, which contributed to the early prosperity and growth of Manchester as a city.

Through this growth and change, Manchester and its surrounding towns generated much of Britain's wealth. It was a period when mass production methods were gradually introduced but, most of the prosperity unfortunately lay beyond the hands of Manchester's residents. The working class people, such as my great-great-grandfather Michael, who actually produced that wealth, lived, worked and died in conditions that today would beggar belief. The inner city areas of Manchester, particularly Ancoats, Chorlton- upon-Medlock, Hulme, and Ardwick, saw an influx of immigrants seeking work and accommodation. Irish and Italian immigrants congregated in the Ancoats area, which was probably the poorest and most deprived area of the city. In Ancoats these immigrants formed the largest section of the vast casual labour force that was available to employers – as casual labour they worked terribly long hours when trade was good, but in harder times found themselves the first to be laid off. This situation was to last for 100 years or more.

These inner city areas were nothing more than slums, and consisted largely of back to back terraced houses. They were built without any kind of regulation, and usually by an employer. The houses were built to cram as many as possible into the space available. The houses were of poor quality, and would quickly fall into disrepair. They were extremely damp and were built without double-bricked walls. In the cold, wet winters, rain would leach through the thin walls, and in the summers the dampness rose up those walls. There were no sanitation services and there was no privacy. Most of these dwellings were overcrowded, and people who worked shifts shared beds. It was not uncommon – as contemporary census records will testify – to find ten or 12 people sharing a single bedroom. The sanitary arrangements were primitive, and again it was not uncommon for as many as 100 of these dwellings to share a single 'privy', usually a deep hole dug in the corner of a yard, or what was termed a 'midden', which was a heap against a wall. The employer-landlords seldom made any kind of effort to relieve these problems. Families even lived in the cellars of these dwellings, and frequently the overflow from the middens spread into these cellars. It came as no surprise that there were serious public health problems in these poor communities.

Given the rapid industrialisation of the city, the air was unclean. The thousands of factory chimneys and coal-burning domestic buildings meant that Manchester was permanently under a pall of smoke. Cholera, pulmonary tuberculosis and upper respiratory ailments were all too common, and there was a high rate of infant mortality. Poor wages, impossibly long working hours, dangerous and unsanitary working conditions, poor housing and no health provision were all major contributors to a high mortality rate in the slum inner city areas of Manchester. Put simply, the wealthier people who could afford to away from the poorest quarters, or even outside the city itself, lived much longer than the poor workers who were exploited by their employers, and who needed to live close by their places of employment.

Great-great-grandfather Michael eked out an existence for himself and his wife in and around the Ancoats enclave. Michael worked as cotton mill hand in one of the imposing mills that dominated the Ancoats area. In 1859, a new arrival in Michael's family was a son, who was christened John, and who would be my great-grandfather. It was a harsh existence trying to bring up a family in such circumstances, so it was no surprise that during the late 1860s Michael began to ail badly, and suffered for the next few years. In 1876 Michael passed away, the victim of tuberculosis.

John Clare turned out to be a bright child, and at the age of 13 managed to find employment in one of the nearby cotton mills. Some years later, there was a mutual attraction between John and a young girl by the name of Sarah Jane Brown, who worked in that same mill. These two young people were married on 22 June 1879 at the relatively new Roman Catholic church of St. Michael, in George Leigh Street,

Ancoats. Sarah had become pregnant with their first child Elizabeth Ann before they were married, and Elizabeth was born in December of that same year. Having a child outside wedlock in those days carried a great stigma, especially for the mother, and so it was that there was a hastily arranged marriage.

Times were hard for the young couple, and as they sought to make ends meet on John's meagre mill wages after Elizabeth's birth, Sarah supplemented their earnings by returning to the mill on what was termed 'piece work'. This meant she was paid by the number of cotton items that she could process each working day. In those dark days before welfare provision, there was no sick pay – if you could not work, then you did not get paid. Employers were ruthless in adhering to this practice. Again, it was a harsh existence in horrible conditions. As was normal back then, families tended to be large in number and the Clares were no exception to the rule. Fortunately for them, for ten years after the birth of Elizabeth they had no further children, and did in fact begin to enjoy a period of reasonable growth, being able to better themselves slightly. But between the years 1891 and 1900, Sarah gave birth to five more children, and it is here that my story really begins with the birth of my grandfather, Thomas Clare, the oldest of those latter five children, who arrived on this earth on 27 January 1891. The story of our special relationship comes early in this narrative.

Royle Street, Chorlton-upon-Medlock

I was born at 5.44 in the morning of Sunday, 28 April 1945 into the downstairs front room of a dingy, two up, two down, damp and musty, dark-brick terraced house. I was the second son, and also the second child, of Tommy and Olive Clare of number 14 Royle Street, Chorlton-upon-Medlock, Manchester. Chorlton-upon-Medlock at that time was a small, run down urban area, just a mile to the south-east of the war-torn city centre.

Like most of the inner city areas of Manchester, Chorlton-upon-Medlock was characterised by row upon row of small, uniform terraced houses, with tiny, smoky chimneys. These buildings could never be called anything other than slums. For the most part, the families that inhabited these squalid abodes were second, third and fourth generation families of Irish and Scottish immigrants, who had been unable to escape the poverty trap bequeathed to them by their forbears. The properties were owned mostly by unscrupulous landlords, who exploited these unfortunate victims of circumstance, and evictions and 'moonlight flits' were commonplace.

Our house was no different to thousands of others throughout the inner city. Upstairs there was a front bedroom and a back bedroom; downstairs, a front parlour and a back utility room that served as a kitchen, dining room and living room. There was also a cellar, which housed a coal chute, and a room running off it that was supposed to be a laundry room. A stone 'dolly tub' was in the far corner of the cellar room for laundry purposes, but few, if any, were ever used. The toilet was outside in the back yard, and during the night, or through the long winter months, the trip had to be navigated in darkness. Like the rest of these dwellings, our house had no electricity; gas lamps were the order of the day, but only in the two downstairs rooms. The gas meter was in the cellar, and as I grew older I would have the job of going down and putting a penny into the slot to replenish the gas supply. The upstairs rooms, and the room down in the cellar, had to be lit by candlelight.

There was only one water tap in the whole house and that provided cold water only. We had a small gas stove for cooking, and our house was heated throughout by an open coal fire in our utility room downstairs.

Number 14 Royle Street still holds myriad memories, and those memories have remained undimmed with the passage of time. It was my home in my formative years – I learned about life there that's for sure. To show that house to anybody in this modern era would, I am sure, see them recoil in horror, because by today's standards it would be classed as uninhabitable, and would certainly be condemned by public health, housing and building inspectors.

Chorlton-upon-Medlock was quite a notorious area in the 1940s and 1950s, and I certainly witnessed things during my childhood that I would hate for any child to see today. It was a harsh existence for families, and for people as individuals. Prostitutes plied their trade freely, both day and night, and they were not too fussy where they entertained their clients. Mostly it was in the back alleyways between the rows of terraced houses. During the evenings they would congregate in groups on street corners, soliciting for clients. The evenings would see drunks roaming the area, and physical violence was often perpetrated by, and upon, these people. An area with such notoriety attracted a wide range of people, from those that we termed 'money people' to the 'down and outs'.

To say that weekends were lively back then would be an understatement of huge proportions. For all the area's poverty, the pubs in Chorlton-upon-Medlock were always full at weekends, at lunchtimes and during the evenings. Pubs licensing hours meant they would open from 11am till 3pm, and then again from 5.30pm till 10.30pm; Sunday hours were from noon till 2pm, and 7pm till 10.30pm. Problems arose after closing time when people were full of ale. It is no exaggeration to say that on a Saturday evening it was commonplace to see two or three fist-fights outside a pub at the same time.

People lived on their wits, and there were several well known local characters who survived by dubious means. 'Jimmy the Dip' was a local pickpocket who mostly looked for victims in the city centre. 'Scotch Dave' was a local hard nut, a thief who would steal to order. 'Billy One Ball' was a local pimp who was loathed by most in the area. 'Stuttering Charlie' was another who survived by thieving, and even today must rank as the ugliest man that I have ever come across. Dick Hazzard and Johnny Grandin operated as fences for the thieves. 'Fraser' was a local character who always dressed in morning suit and a bowler hat, but in reality was a 'con man'. It was a tough area, but that was the lot life threw at you, and families had to deal with it, or sink into despair and oblivion – unfortunately for a lot of families that did happen.

The era into which I was born was undoubtedly harsh, immediately after the cessation of hostilities in World War II. Britain was ravaged by bomb damage, and was economically stretched. There were food shortages that necessitated rationing, and for most young kids growing up, luxuries were now-commonplace things like eggs, cheese, meat, bread, sugar and even sweets – they were all on ration. Wages were low, and most mums took on cleaning jobs, or any other employ they could find, just to supplement the family income. Many dads were unemployed and turned to 'totting', as 'rag and bone' was known back then. They would go round pushing a hand cart, collecting almost anything they could – used clothing, metal, unwanted household goods or appliances, and would take what they obtained to the scrap merchants for 'weighing in'. It was recycling, post-war style!

Most streets in the inner city area had suffered from German bomb damage. Where houses had been leveled, the area of ground that was left was covered with cinders, and it was on these surfaces that, as children, we played together. Gradually, the cinders would crumble from the constant treading down, and would eventually harden into a surface. These small bomb sites were known as 'crofts'.

Most people with regular employment worked in cotton manufacture and light engineering, putting in long hours. At around four o'clock in the morning, in both summer and winter, there would be the sound of the rat-tat-tatting of the knocker-up's claw on the upstairs windows of the terraced houses. The job of the knocker-up was, of course, to go round the houses, making sure that people would wake for work. His long wooden pole had a claw attachment at one end, which would be tapped on the upstairs window until there was an acknowledgement from a person inside. For carrying out this early morning routine, the knocker-up charged the princely sum of three-pence per house per week from his regular round. Between 5am and 5.30am, you would begin to hear the familiar tread of feet on the cobbled stones as people began to leave for work, and the noise of this slight pitter-patter of feet would build to a crescendo as those on shift work rushed to make their 6am start time. It would then become quiet again until after 7am, when the non-factory people would leave their homes to begin their working day. Various times of the day were signalled with the blowing of sirens from the various factory smoke stacks in the area: 7am, noon, 1pm, 5pm and 5.30pm. There were families in the local area whose lives were organised throughout the day by those sirens.

Without doubt, it was the mothers who kept the families together. Fathers would try and find work of any kind, and those that did worked long, long, hours for meagre recompense. Those that did not, and I have to admit there were many in the Chorlton-upon-Medlock area who had no intention of working, would find solace in different practices – drinking in the pubs being the main one. There were also many families upon whom fate had cast a dark shadow, when the main breadwinner had gone away to serve his country during the war, and had not returned. Some of these mothers were left with four, five or six children to bring up, and had to ensure that there was food on the table and a roof over the their heads – in some cases desperate people had to do desperate things. Some of the more 'fly by night' fathers became well known to the local constabulary, and it wasn't unusual to hear that some of them had 'gone away on holiday' for a while, once again leaving the mothers to bear the hardship of bringing up the family.

But for all the doom and gloom, and the harshness of that period, there was also a good deal of sunshine. The communities were very closely knit, and that closeness even remains to the present day among families whose friendships were formed generations ago. There was a spirit of sharing among the poorer people of Chorlton-upon-Medlock, and when a family got into genuine difficulty there was a pulling together for them. Relatives and neighbours would help in whatever ways they could, providing clothing, food and even a few pennies wherever possible.

To illustrate this, the winter of 1947 was particularly long and harsh in the north of England. Fuel for fires was in short supply, and under ration as fuel was also required for industry to help with the regeneration of the economy. In such cold conditions those terraced houses were death traps, especially for vulnerable young children and the elderly. So a group of men from the Royle Street families, my father among them, hatched a plan to ensure that those families survived intact throughout that harsh winter. They made sure that families had enough solid fuel to burn in their fireplaces, that solid fuel being wood. These men would go out at night with handcarts, and walk to the more affluent areas of the city, where they removed wooden doors from the back yards of premises and homes. Living next door to our house, at number 16 Royle Street, was an Irish family by the name of Broderick. Old man Broderick was in his 60s but made his living from selling firewood, and had a shed not a block away in Back Grosvenor Street. Even for him, the harsh winter of that year had made things difficult, as his wood supply dried up. But being part of our community, he was ever-willing to help, and the wood supply that was obtained in the darkness of those nights found its way to his wood shed, where before light of day it became victim of a huge electric saw, and was made into manageable bundles that could be burnt in a fireplace. The bundles were evenly distributed amongst the families each day.

Those men also removed nameplates from front doors of commercial premises in both the local area and city centre. Most of these nameplates were made of metal, particularly brass, but they were screwed on to large wooden boards either attached to the front door, or bolted onto the adjacent wall. The men removed these nameplates, and once back at Broderick's they would unscrew the metal plate from the wood, which would then be sawn up. The metal plates went somewhere else. My father had an old school friend, the son of a Polish immigrant family named Bolger. The name apparently had been shortened to Bolger from Bolgekititz, and Charlie, their youngest son, had started up in business just after the war as a scrap metal merchant. His premises (which would play a part in my learning of the Munich disaster some years later) were on Fairfield Street, close to London Road railway station on the edge of the city centre. Dad knew Charlie pretty well, and he, together with Bob Taylor from number 12 next door, would haul the metal plates on a hand cart over to Bolger's scrap yard for 'weighing in'. No questions were asked by either party. Father and Bob would leave the premises with an amount of cash, which again was distributed evenly amongst the families when they returned to Royle Street. I'm more than certain that they were never ever given the 'going rate' for the metal plates, but then with no questions being asked they were never going to complain. Obviously, the metal plates were melted down at Bolger's and then moved on. The men took a lot of risks doing what they did, and on several occasions had skirmishes with the local police. Fortunately for them all it never resulted in any of them having their collars felt!

Dad was also innovative in the home during this period. Our living room adjoined Broderick's on one side and Taylor's on the other. Dad worked out where Broderick's fireplace would be, and was aware that Taylor's fireplace adjoined Dolly Murphy's at number 10, so was of no use. Surreptitiously, Dad removed two bricks from the bottom of the wall adjoining Broderick's living room, just where their fireplace was. Each evening, Dad would remove those two bricks from that wall, and some of the heat from the Broderick's fire would find its way into our living room. It was several years later that Broderick found out what Dad had done.

In most families there was someone who had mastered the art of playing a musical instrument, and on balmy summer evenings, especially after the pubs had locked their doors; it was not uncommon to hear impromptu concerts going on in the street. My mother and father had beautiful singing voices. Mother was a fine soprano and had sung with the Manchester Schools Girls' Choir, while Dad had a wonderful tenor voice, and was to sing professionally in future years. The street concerts were a joy to behold as barber shop groups, individuals, and duets all performed. It wasn't unusual for people who lived in the surrounding streets to find their way round and sit until the early hours of the morning listening to the talents of our families.

Football – A Wonderful Discovery

My earliest memory is of my 3rd birthday, on 28 April 1948. Even today, I can remember vividly my mum giving me my birthday card with a large figure 3, carried by a large brown teddy bear which was emblazoned upon it. I sat at the table tearing open the envelope, and then opening my birthday present which was – surprise, surprise – a small ball. Just one week later would come my first experience of the game of football.

On the day in question, the living room was full of adults, and the air was thick with smoke and the pungent smell of tobacco. By full of adults, I mean my dad and mum; Mr. Broderick, the Irishman from number 16 next door; Bob Taylor our other next-door neighbour from number 12; and old Henry Connell from across the road at number 15. It was Saturday, 5 May 1948, just a week after my 3rd birthday. As was normal in those days, the men had returned from the pub after a lunchtime drink, this time a little earlier than usual. The pub in this case was The City, on the corner of Royle Street and Rusholme Road, a red tiled building owned by the Walker's Warrington Brewery, and whose licensees were Annie and Jack White. It was a short forty yard walk from the pub's steps to our front door. The men had been quite boisterous when they entered the house, and at Dad's command Mum had already made sandwiches for them all, while the big black kettle was simmering away on the hob, next to the coal fire which heated the house, ready to make a large pot of strong tea.

I could never understand what the white haired, stooped old man named Broderick ever said in his Cork twang, but I do recall that he always spoke so fast, in a high-pitched, whiny voice, and that he was always very excitable. Bob Taylor had a smoker's cough, and was known by the nickname of 'Coughing Bob' throughout the neighbourhood. He always had a cigarette between his lips, and his fingers were stained dark brown by the nicotine of the thousands of weeds that had passed through his knurled, wrinkled fingers. Henry

Connell was the quiet one, a tiny man with grey hair, who always wore a collarless shirt, with a stud hanging out of the button hole. They made a motley crowd, and poor Mum was regularly put to the test back then because Dad was forever bringing different people back to the house with him after a drinking session in the pub. It was a practice that continued throughout his lifetime, and which tested Mum's patience many times throughout the years.

Even though I was so young, I sensed that there was something different about this particular day. All of them seemed to be so excited, an excitement that even transmitted itself to Mum. Dad was busy at the wireless on the old carved, wooden dresser against the main wall of the living room. He was busy attaching the accumulator to it. My brother had been dispatched to the bicycle shop on Brunswick Street earlier that morning with the old accumulator, and the order to replace it with a new one. He had grumbled all the way as we walked up Temple Street, first because he had to take me with him, and secondly because there was acid leaking from the terminals. Dad had wanted to make sure that the wireless was in good working order for the afternoon. Dad connected the terminals, and the radio crackled into life. The men drew their chairs into a half circle as they huddled around the radio, and then just before 3pm it began. Little did I realise that this moment would be the start of a love affair, and a passion that has lasted more than fifty years. The source of the excitement was, of course, the BBC radio commentary of the 1948 FA Cup final between Manchester United and Blackpool.

I remember an awful lot of cursing that afternoon, and a great deal of cheering as well. It was the first time in my life that I really heard the names of Carey and Aston, of Pearson and Rowley, and of Blackpool's great Stanleys – Matthews and Mortensen. United prevailed by four goals to two, after being 2-1 down at half-time, and it came to be remembered as one of the finest FA Cup finals ever played. After the match was over, my dad tried to get me to shout "Up United!" – But it would only come out as "Up Noo Nited!" The men seemed to get a lot of laughter from hearing me constantly repeating these words, but I didn't mind because as they left the house, they pressed farthings, and halfpennies and pennies into my little hand.

'Noo Nited' had been ignited inside me. My granddad then took over the task of educating me about Manchester United. He was a dyed in the wool Manchester United supporter, and he made sure that his second grandson was going to take more than a passing interest in the club. My elder brother, Peter, although interested in football, had a lethargic attitude towards the game, and he could take it or leave it. Not me! My appetite for Manchester United had been whetted, even at such an early age.

A Grand Old Man and Football Mentor

The coals in the grate of the old fireplace burned brightly, casting a shimmering light through the compact parlour room in my grandfather's terraced house in Naylor Street, Miles Platting, a Manchester suburb less than a mile to the north of the city centre. Seated upon his lap, my small head rested upon his shoulder, and I felt safe and secure with his arm around my waist. Gentle movements swayed the old rocking chair on which we sat. The shadows on the walls danced in tune with the rhythmical movements of the rocking chair and the flickering light from the fire. The only sounds to be heard were the ticking of the old clock up on the wall and the squeak of the old chair. I felt so happy and contented as I looked up into his round smiling face, his brow and cheeks wrinkled by the passage of time, and his hair and eyelashes as white as the driven snow. I could see the love that he had for me in his piercing blue eyes, as he looked down upon me. "Tell me again, Granddad", I whispered. And his quiet but lilting voice soothed me as he began his stories once again.

This scenario was repeated in his home on many Sunday evenings throughout my early years. From being five years old I would sit with him, and as the years passed and I became too tall and heavy for him to hold me, I would sit in the armchair opposite. I recall all of those times with so much fondness, so much love, and so much affection, and also with so much gratitude. My grandfather's influence upon my life was enormous. His word was sacrosanct to me. I adored just being with him, and the adoration that I had for him has never ceased throughout my life. He taught me so much.

Although I had an older brother, Peter, Granddad really did dote upon me. My early recollections of him are from when I could have been no more than three or four years old, when my mother would take my brother and me to visit him on Sundays. It was a ritual through the early days of my childhood. On the odd occasion my father would share the duty, but those times were all too infrequent. Many was the time that after an hour of the visit, Mum would leave with Peter, and return home to see to my father's needs, and she'd come back, well into the evening, to collect me. I look back on those days with so much pleasure because it was from here that the bond between my grandfather and I was forged. With me upon his knee, and as he sipped from a large mug of tea, he would regale me with tales of United's history. He had such a litany of names to recall, and a staggering mental library of stories about his beloved club. As I grew older, and understood things more clearly, his explanation of those events would become more detailed. I never grew tired of listening to him. I thirsted upon his knowledge, and he was never too tired to transfer that knowledge to me. Time and again I would sit there in awe of him, asking him to "tell me again Granddad!" He never refused, and had such patience. The seed was planted by him, and he saw the root and flower grow as he instilled his love of the game of football, and particularly the love of Manchester United, into me. And not only about Manchester United, but also about people, life, and how to live it. His benchmark has been the one that I have always strived to reach in my own life.

My grandfather was Tom Clare, the son of Sarah and John Clare. He was born in William Street, Ancoats on 21 January 1891. Ancoats was still very much a slum area at the time of Granddad's birth. Without doubt, as well as being Manchester's first industrial suburb, it was still the mortality black spot of the city. However, during the last decade of that 19th century, concerns for the welfare of the poorer inner city communities started to be addressed. Long overdue regulations concerning housing conditions, building standards, sanitation, and health issues were introduced. Water provision, public taps, laundries and wash houses began to appear. New sewers and sewage treatment plants were built. However, probably the most important thing to happen was the appointment of Manchester's very first Medical Officer of Health. Upon appointment, one of his first actions was to close down virtually all of the city's cellar dwellings. Gradually the health and well-being of the poorer people began to improve, but the main threat still came from the backyard middens, insect borne germs, poor food hygiene, and a very poor food diet. Unfortunately, many of the middens and privies were still in existence into the early decades of the 20th century. But as far as Granddad's childhood was concerned, conditions were certainly a little better than they had been for his parents.

Football in England was in its formative years at the time of Granddad's birth. The Newton Heath Football Club, which had been founded in 1878, played just a short distance from his home in Ancoats. Since their inception, Newton Heath had played their home games on North Road, Newton Heath (today it is known as Northampton Road in Monsall, and a school now stands on the original site), but just two years into his life Newton Heath moved to a new ground at Bank Street in the Clayton area of Manchester, again not too far from Ancoats.

Granddad attended St. Patrick's school in Livesey Street, Collyhurst – yes, the same school that produced Nobby Stiles and Brian Kidd. As a young boy he grew up in and around the streets of Ancoats, Collyhurst, Miles Platting, and Newton Heath. He found and developed a love for the game of football, and would play whenever time would allow. In the autumn of 1899, together with a few of his friends, he started to travel to Clayton to watch Newton Heath. Grandfather was to tell me in later years that the very first game he saw Newton Heath play was at Bank Street, against Port Vale. He was hooked on football from that day on, and so attended games on a regular basis, walking with his young friends to and from the matches played at Bank Street. Although Newton Heath were then in the Second Division of the Football League, and forever feeling the pinch financially, this in no way lessened the young boy's passion for his team. He was not to know that it was the beginning of a love affair that would last for some 67 years, until he passed away in October 1966.

Any aspirations he had about playing the game unfortunately came to a cruel end when he was just 11 years old. His father, John, was employed by a local delivery company that carried goods all around the city. Most of the manufacturers in Manchester used such delivery companies to send their goods to destinations in the Manchester area, and to the city's main rail and shipping terminals. The delivery companies had fleets of horse drawn carts, and John Clare was employed as a driver. He would take his sons, including young Thomas, with him during the school holidays. On one such day, during the summer of 1902, he was delivering goods to a company in Sackville Street, close to Manchester city centre. The children started to play near one of the horses, and for some reason the horse became agitated. When Granddad went to investigate, taking hold of the horse's bridle, it kicked out, shattering Grandfather's right leg. The leg was not set properly at the hospital, and the legacy for the rest of his life was that he walked with a slight limp, with a drag of the foot. Sporting physical activity on a competitive scale was never possible for him after that, but his physical disability would never dampen his love of the game of football, or that of his club.

His love of Manchester United knew no bounds. When he first started following his team as an eight year old boy, they were still called Newton Heath. Just three years later, on 28 April 1902 (ironically, the same day and month as my own birthday), the club was renamed Manchester United. As I sat on his lap in that old rocking chair all those years later, this was one of the earliest stories he would tell me. Although Newton Heath became Manchester United when he was still quite young, he was able to recall the event, though it was only when he got a little older that he really learned the full details.

He would explain to me, in that softly-spoken voice of his, that the club was stone broke in 1902, and that they owed out a tremendous amount of money. The creditors were more than ready to close the club down. Most of them were contractors, and were owed payment for refurbishment work which had already been carried out on the club's Bank Street ground. The debt, apparently, was almost £3,000 – an enormous amount in 1902, and it was little wonder that the club was in grave financial difficulties.

His story told of the events which led up to a shareholders' meeting being held in April 1902 at a place named New Islington Hall, in Ancoats, very close to Grandfather's home, and he explained to me the significance of this meeting in the history of what would become the biggest football club in the world.

In 1901, the Newton Heath club had held a Grand Bazaar in St. James's Hall in central Manchester. The event was held over four consecutive days, with the aim of raising funds to ease the club's precarious financial situation. For all the hard work that was put into organising the event, it proved to be an abject failure, and at the end of the fourth day very little had been raised. The club captain, Harry Stafford, had been in attendance throughout, and had worked tirelessly on the club's behalf. Stafford was the owner of a huge St. Bernard dog, and he had attached a small biscuit barrel to the dog's collar into which people were asked to place their pennies. On the last day of the bazaar, the dog apparently became disoriented and wandered away from the hall. Finding itself lost, it eventually wandered into a city centre pub, managed by a man named Mr. Thomas, but owned by a Mr. J.H. Davies, a local brewery owner and businessman with a gift for making money. Mr. Thomas kept the dog for a day or two, and later showed it to Mr. Davies upon one of his visits to his hostelry. Davies was quite taken by the beautiful St. Bernard dog, so began to make enquiries as to who its owner could be. Those enquiries led him eventually to Harry Stafford. By this time, Mr. Davies had developed a strong liking for the dog and he wanted to keep it as a birthday present for his young daughter. Upon meeting Stafford, he duly negotiated the purchase of the animal. That meeting was to prove fateful, as the men developed a strong friendship which led to Mr. Davies installing Stafford as the licensee in one of his other pubs in central Manchester.

The bazaar failed to raise any significant monies that would help ease the burden on the financially stricken football club, and soon the creditors again came knocking on the door. As the club somehow muddled through the remaining months of 1901, bankruptcy and closure looked to be inevitable, and only a brave man would have forecast that Newton Heath would be playing League football the following season.

At the shareholders' meeting on 28 April 1902, all was seemingly lost, and Newton Heath were heading for extinction. That is until Stafford, who was there in attendance, stood up towards the end of the meeting and explained that he himself was ready to invest £500 in the club. Not only that, but he knew of four others who were willing to do the very same thing. The shareholders in attendance were dumbstruck, but happy to see that here was the man who knew the men who would be the very saviours of Newton Heath Football Club, and who would give it the firm financial platform that it needed. The other four men committed to invest in the club were none other than J.H. Davies, Mr. J. Taylor, Mr. W. Deakin, and Mr. J. Brown, all local businessmen. That shareholder's meeting suddenly became hyperactive with enthusiasm and it was here, just a little later in the proceedings, that Louis Rocca stood up and proposed that the name of the club be changed from Newton Heath to Manchester United. That motion was passed unanimously, and so began a bright new era which for the very first time would put the name of Manchester United at the forefront of English football.

The stories that my grandfather related to me so many times during the early years of my life used to enthrall and captivate me so much. The way he told them painted a vivid picture in my young head, and I always wanted to know more. Each week he would pull me onto his lap and ask, "Which story shall we go through this week, Tush?" (Tush was the affectionate nickname he had for me, and which he called me by throughout his life. Nobody else ever used that name for me, and it was a mark of the special bond between the two of us.)

I find it so enthralling to think that my grandfather actually attended matches at the old Bank Street ground, and that he was at Old Trafford on 19 February 1910, the day the very first game was played on what would become hallowed turf. He saw Ernest Magnall become the first real manager of United the year after the historic shareholder's meeting of 1902, and he told me that Magnall was the first man to really organise the club. He really rated Magnall, and on the playing front regarded him as the man who brought United forward, and out of the depths of football obscurity.

As a manager, he reckoned that Magnall was as good as Matt Busby. In our conversations he used to always tell me just how good Magnall was, particularly at negotiation. Ernest Magnall apparently had great foresight, and would always play his cards close to his chest. He was not one for letting people know what he was about to do, and this included the people at United. One example Granddad gave of Magnall's strength of character concerned United's signing of the 'Welsh Wizard', Billy Meredith, and just a short time later, Sandy Turnbull, Herbert Burgess, George Livingstone, and Jimmy Bannister, all from Manchester City.

There had been general unrest in the game from a player's point of view from around the time Magnall became United's manager until the formation of the Players' Union several years later. Most top players were only earning three pounds a week in the season and only two pounds in the summer. Attendances were rising fast, and teams played regularly in front of crowds of 35,000 and more. The players were agitating for a greater share of the revenues they were generating. Rumours began to abound of 'under the counter payments' to players by their clubs, and it was no surprise that in 1905 the Football Association began to investigate these rumours. Just three years earlier the FA had investigated similar rumours, and both Harry Stafford, and the new United secretary, James West, received four year bans in 1903 having been found guilty on charges of financial impropriety.

In 1905 several clubs came under very close scrutiny, United again being one of them. Fortunately, this time they were found to be clean, but sadly for Manchester City, the Consultative Committee at the FA found them not only guilty of making illegal payments to their players, but also of making illegal payments in their transfer dealings. A number of their directors were suspended for several years. Then they were hit with a further bombshell when Meredith was found guilty of trying to fix a match against Aston Villa, allegedly offering money to a

Villa player to make sure that they lost the game. It was a messy business, with Meredith always professing that he had in fact been acting on behalf of the club. Nonetheless, the FA suspended him for three years. Meredith became something of a nuisance to City, as contrary to the rules of his suspension he would make appearances at the club demanding money. City eventually put him on the transfer list in May 1906, and it was then that Ernie Magnall stepped in and signed him for United for £500, even though his suspension still had almost two years to run.

At the end of that same month, even more trouble surfaced at City. They were once again found to be paying players illegally, and 17 players were suspended for six months, and banned from ever playing for City again. The City directors were in a quandary, but made these players available for sale, notifying other League clubs that there would be an auction for their registrations, to be held in the Queen's Hotel, Piccadilly, Manchester in the first week of June 1906. On the night of the auction, as officials and managers of the various clubs took their seats in the hotel lounge, Ernie Magnall was seen to appear from out of a back room. What those other clubs did not know was that Ernie Magnall had been in touch with the City directors some days before, and had received permission to speak to the players that he wanted to sign before the auction began. Magnall took the cream of the players that were up for sale, and as he left that back room inside his pocket were signed contracts for Turnbull, Burgess, Livingstone, and Bannister. He had once again trumped his rivals.

It rounded off a great period for United – just weeks before the club at last gained promotion to the elite First Division of the Football League, finishing as runners-up to Bristol City in the Second Division. Obviously, the signing of the five City players had been part of Magnall's planning for the next five years or more.

It amazes me even today just how much my grandfather knew about the early days of the club. When floodlights were being installed at football grounds in the 1950, he told me of an attempt to stage a floodlit match at Bank Street some time around 1908. Apparently it was a benefit match for Harry Stafford, who had come to the end of his playing career. United wanted to reward him for his loyal and long service to the club, and a game was arranged against Manchester City. What type of lighting was provided I do not know, but he would laugh heartily as he explained that there was a strong wind during the game, and a number of the lights faded. Eventually, the game became farcical for both players and spectators alike, and was abandoned by the referee.

I learned that with the imminent financial crisis over, following Davies's rescue, the club provided regular support to local charities, particularly by donating gate receipts from public practice matches to local hospitals, with the amount taken at the gate being matched by Mr. Davies, the United Chairman, from his own pocket. I could never see a situation like that happening in today's modern game. However, Davies was not all sweetness and light – he was in fact a very tough businessman. He was married to Amy Tate, the daughter of Henry Tate, who together with a Mr. Lyle built up a sugar refining business, and whose product later became a household name. Although Davies did bring the financial stability to the club, there were stories (never proved) that he also rewarded players with cash payments.

Eventually, they moved from Bank Street to Old Trafford, and this was Mr. Davies's grand idea. Granddad believed it was an essential step, as Bank Street was fast becoming a liability to the club. Because of United's first successes Bank Street could not hold the number of supporters that had begun to increase rapidly. On the big match days against the top teams, it is estimated that there was half as many shut outside the ground as there were inside watching the match. It was too small to accommodate a successful team and a growing fan base. The playing surface was nothing more than a dirt patch and during any inclement weather would quickly turn into a mud patch. A better surface for the players to perform upon was badly needed.

Once again J.H. Davies proved what an astute business man he was. He was chairman of the Manchester Brewery Company, and it was this company that bought the land upon which Old Trafford was built.

After purchase, the brewery company leased the land to the club. Davies had great foresight, and he engaged the services of Archibald Leitch, the architect responsible for some of Britain's most iconic football grounds, including Goodison Park and Ibrox. There was some debate as to how many fans the new Old Trafford should be able to accommodate, and the initial plans that were drawn up for the stadium were on a grand scale. It was eventually decided that 80,000 should be the ground capacity – at that time an enormous figure to plan for.

In 1894, the Manchester Ship Canal had opened and the inland port of Manchester lay less than half a mile to the north of the proposed new stadium. The construction of this facility created thousands of jobs. Just two years later, in 1896, a consortium named the Trafford Park Syndicate bought land from Sir Humphrey de Trafford that lay to the north west of the proposed stadium site. The Trafford Park Syndicate used this land to build what became the largest industrial estate in Europe. Companies like British Westinghouse Electric and Manufacturing Company (later to become Metropolitan Vickers), W.T. Glover's, and the new Ford Motor Company, were enticed to build their factories there. The area became a hive of industry, with the close proximity of the docks being crucial to local trade and industry. The arrival of these companies created thousands of jobs in Trafford Park – and it was this that interested J.H. Davies.

Not many years before, Saturdays became only a working half day with most workers finishing between noon and 2pm. The factories of Trafford Park provided a ready made audience as far as Davies was concerned, with Saturday afternoon football offering the workers some rest, relaxation and entertainment after the rigours of a hard week's work, and he hoped they would fill the terraces of the beautiful new stadium. My grandfather recalled that when Old Trafford was finally ready for Manchester United it was without doubt the premier stadium in the British Isles – and it had cost £60,000.

Grandfather left school in 1905 when he was just 14 years of age, and found work in one of the multitude of cotton mills in the Ancoats area of Manchester. He was happy, and his life was carefree. In the 1907/08 season, when he was just 17 years of age, he saw United win their very first league championship, and he was overjoyed. He rejoiced in the style of this gifted and entertaining United team, and the spirit with which they played the game. He so loved that team, with its immortal half-back line of Duckworth, Roberts and Bell. He saw all the other great United players of the era – Harry Moger, Billy Meredith, Georgie Wall, Sandy Turnbull, Harold Halse, Dick Stacey, Enoch 'Knocker' West, Herbert Burgess, George Livingstone, Jimmy Bannister to name just a few.

In what would become a United blueprint, this was a free scoring side which notched 81 goals in 38 league games that season, with 19 being contributed by the little left winger, George Wall, about whom Granddad enthused. Three other forwards also reached double figures in league games: Sandy Turnbull netted 25, Jimmy Turnbull scored ten, and legendary right winger Billy Meredith added ten of his own. It could well have been more, because after defeating Everton 3-1 at Goodison Park on 8 April 1908, and so securing the First Division championship, there were still six league games to play. But with the title claimed, only one more game was won, and that was on the season's last day. Granddad told me that after the Everton game United had eased off, and did not play with their usual zip and vigour. Even so, the nine point gap between United as champions and the season's runners-up was the largest since the inaugural season of the Football League in 1889, when Preston North End put an 11 point difference between themselves and Aston Villa.

As a young teenager in the first decade of the 20th century, my grandfather began to take an active interest in the trades union movement and in local party politics in Manchester. I have no doubt that he was influenced by his father and by his older brother, Ged, both being staunch socialists, trade unionists and card-carrying members of the Labour Party. It is not surprising when you consider the family background, and it will come as no surprise that Granddad was keen to tell me about the formation of the Players' Union, and the part that the Manchester United men played in it.

The Players' Union was led by men such as Meredith and Sandy Turnbull. Initially, the Football Association had recognised the union, but this recognition was rescinded when the union affiliated itself the Federation of Trade Unions. The FA, the Football League and the clubs feared that the Federation could interfere in the running of the game, and dissipate the power of the governing bodies.

The authorities ordered all players to revoke their registrations with the Players' Union, under threat of a lifelong suspension, and under threat of having their club registrations cancelled – in other words, being thrown out of work. The players at United, all 30 of them, did actually suffer suspension by the FA, and were forced to stay away from Old Trafford. They had to train at the Manchester Athletic Club in Fallowfield, where the famous photograph of 'The Outcasts' team was taken.

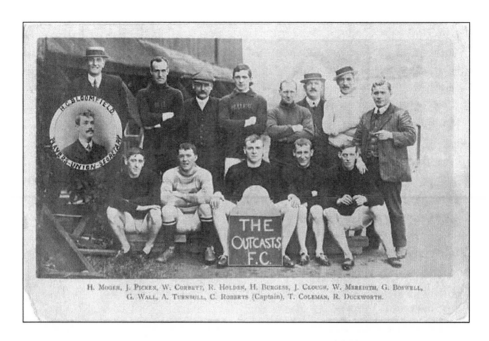

H. Moger, J. Picken, W. Corbett, R. Holden, H. Burgess, J. Clough, W. Meredith, G. Boswell,
G. Wall, A. Turnbull, C. Roberts (Captain), T. Coleman, R. Duckworth.

Charlie Roberts and Billy Meredith were stalwarts in the negotiations that ensued, and in urging the players to stand firm against the demands which were being made being made upon them. It was a situation that caused the start of the 1909/10 season to be put in jeopardy, but fortunately common sense prevailed. On the evening before the season's first games a compromise was reached. The union duly became officially recognised, and all suspensions were lifted. Granddad said that this was such an important thing as far as the players were concerned, but they would have to wait another 50 years before the maximum wage limit was abolished, and even longer before they would have freedom of contract.

My grandfather was just 18 in 1909 when he travelled to London to watch Manchester United win the FA Cup for the first time in their history. United beat Bristol City by 1-0 at Crystal Palace, with a goal from Sandy Turnbull. He left Manchester by rail early on the Saturday morning, arriving in London some time towards noon. From there he went by bus out to Crystal palace, where the final was to be played.

Granddad told me that the United players, who had travelled down to London the day before, had caught the bus from the same place. With the Cup won, a very happy 18 year old made his way back to Manchester, where he arrived late on the Saturday evening.

The victorious team returned to huge crowds at Manchester's Central Station, where a band played *See the Conquering Hero Comes*. Granddad saw the procession that took the team via Manchester Town Hall to the Bank Street ground, from where there was a torchlit procession to a celebratory dinner at the Midland Hotel. It was an extraordinary event.

Two years later, in 1911, United won the First Division championship for the second time, but this heralded a downturn in the team's fortunes. Players were getting past their best, especially the famed half-back line, and there is no doubt that the departure of Ernest Magnall in 1912 began the period into fading obscurity. As I was to find out many years later, it was Magnall's departure to Manchester City that was the root cause of my grandfather's intense dislike for Manchester City. Given what had happened around illegal payments in earlier years, he was more than convinced something underhand had gone on. He told me that Magnall had been coerced into joining United's fierce local rivals, and that it could only have been some kind of huge financial inducement that triggered City's coup. Magnall had been tremendous for Manchester United and was responsible for those first successful years. He was also the architect of the formation of the Central League – a league for the reserve teams of northern Football League teams, and one that was so vital to the development of players for more than 85 years.

The years from 1903 to 1911 represented the first real halcyon period in Manchester United's history, and he recalled it with great clarity. He was not know then that it would be many, many years before United tasted further success. Whenever I return to the magnificence that is Old Trafford today, I often sit and think of him, and I'm so proud to know that he was around at the very start of something that has turned out to be so special in both of our lives.

Barson and Spence

It was while working at the cotton mill that my grandfather met Margaret Winifred McCormick, my grandmother. In the staunchly Roman Catholic enclave of Ancoats, with its population of Irish, Italians, Poles and Ukrainians, she carried the stigma of being an illegitimate child. Today nobody would blink an eye, but at that time it was hard for her, and for her mother. In the way of things, my grandparents' own wedding – on 1 June 1912 at the church of Corpus Christi in Varley Street, Miles Platting – was also a rushed affair. Grandma was already pregnant when she walked down the aisle that June afternoon, for in November 1912 she gave birth to a baby girl, my Aunt Mary. My grandparents began their married life in another two up, two down terraced house in Mellor Street, Ancoats. Granddad continued working in the mill, and on 22 July 1914 another child came along, this time a son, my father Thomas.

Just 24 days before the birth of my father, an event in Sarajevo had a catastrophic domino effect which plunged the world into a war, the horrors of which had never been seen before. On 28 June 1914, Archduke Franz Ferdinand, the heir to the Austro-Hungarian throne, was assassinated by a Serbian group known as the 'Black Hand'. The assassination set off a remarkable chain of events, and what should have been a strictly limited confrontation between Austro-Hungary and Serbia, escalated into the First World War.

It was incredible that such a minor event (if you can call an assassination a minor event) should trigger off such a chain of events that would culminate in a war that would cost so many millions of lives. Britain lost the cream of her youth. My grandfather, like many of his contemporaries, left the mill and enlisted into the Army Service Corps at the beginning of hostilities. Given that he had some disability in his right leg, it was amazing that he was accepted into service. So off he went to do his duty, serving his country in the Great War. Mercifully, though he witnessed all the horrors of the Western Front, he was one of those who came back in one piece, and he left military service at the end of the war in 1918.

Times must have been tough for my grandmother at the outbreak of that war, left behind with two young children to look after. Obviously, witnessing the horrors of war had a big effect on Granddad, and it took him some time to readjust after returning back home. Like his comrades he now had to face the reality of having a family, and a home to look after. On reflection, I think that he never ever really came to terms with it. He never went back to his work in the mill, but in 1919 he began working for the Manchester city council as a general labourer.

The family continued to live in Mellor Street until 1937, when they moved to a terraced house in Naylor Street, Miles Platting. Compared with Mellor Street, this house was a palace. It had electricity, and hot and cold running water.

My grandfather's love for sport survived the war. As well as his love for Manchester United, Grandfather had great affection for Lancashire County Cricket Club, and he played an active role in local amateur and semi-professional football. For years he managed a local pub side, The Smith's Arms from Ancoats, commonly known by the locals as 'The 'Ammer'. The team played on Sunday afternoons in the local parks, and they were highly successful. Granddad's claim to fame, though, and also his pride and joy, was that he was trainer to a very popular local semi-pro side named Manchester North End. He held this role from the mid-1920s until the mid-1930s. North End played at a lovely enclosed ground in the Moston area of Manchester, and they would regularly attract gates of up to 10,000 for their matches. Initially, the club was formed as New Cross in 1922, playing in the Lancashire Combination League, but after just one season they left, changed their name to Manchester North End and, in 1923, joined the more prestigious Cheshire County League. They stayed in this league until September 1939 when the club was disbanded upon the outbreak of war.

The years between the Great War and the Second World War are the most barren in Manchester United's history, and the club fell on desperately hard times. Yet Granddad still gave them his staunch support. After the Great War the team struggled, and were relegated in 1922 when they finished bottom of Division One. I heard tales of players from the 1920s, but two in particular stand out: big Frank Barson, whom Granddad reckoned to be the toughest and most uncompromising player that he ever saw, and Joe Spence, a player he really did love so much.

Frank Barson was the lynchpin of the United team in the 1920s. After United's relegation he was signed from Aston Villa, with whom he had won the FA Cup, and was seen as the man who could lead them back to their former glory. He was an England international, though he played only once for the national side, most likely as result of his fearsome reputation in the game. He served some lengthy suspensions during his career, once for seven months after he clattered an opponent in a game against Fulham. He had begun his career with Barnsley, though they had to wait two months before he could play because he was suspended for being involved in a brawl with Birmingham City players during a pre-season friendly! Before Villa's 1920 FA Cup final the referee, Jack Howcroft, entered the Villa dressing room and warned, "The first wrong move you make Barson, and it's off you go!" Such was his reputation even then.

Barson was built like the proverbial outhouse and that is not surprising given that in his early years he was a blacksmith. As a competitor, he had no equal and took it upon himself to be the team's 'minder'. If he suspected or saw foul play, retribution was the name of his game, and he wasn't averse to letting the referee know beforehand exactly what his intentions were. He was a born leader, and for all of his physical attributes he was more than skillful and was a prodigious header of the ball. Respect of the players around him at Old Trafford was quickly earned as he led from the front. I would imagine that if Barson were playing the game today he would certainly become a cult figure with the United fans. It was not unknown for him to need a police escort from away grounds after games he had played in. Fans of opposing clubs certainly seemed to think that he was a monster, and that he played outside the rules.

It is ironic that one of the inducements United made in an effort to lure the big man was the promise of the licence of a local pub (remember that United's chairman, Mr. Davies, was in the brewing business) if he led the club back into the top division. Within three seasons the target was achieved, and the said licence was promptly handed over. The pub in question was the George and Dragon (apt given Barson's stature as a fighter and battler) on Ardwick Green, close to the place where I was born. But Barson lasted just an hour as a licencee: unable to endure the attention that came his way, he handed the keys of the pub to a barman and walked out, never to set foot in the place again.

Under Barson's leadership, 1924/25 saw United regain their First Division status by finishing as runners-up to Leicester City in the Second Division. They held their own in their first season back amongst the elite, finishing ninth, and also fought their way to the semi-finals of the FA Cup for the first time since the triumph of 1909. The 1926 semi-final pitted United against arch rivals, Manchester City. City were fighting relegation, and United were considered firm favourites to reach their first ever Wembley final. The roads across the Pennines to Bramall Lane, Sheffield, were crowded on the morning of the match, with a mass exodus of football fans from Manchester to the Yorkshire steel city. Unfortunately for United, as is so often the case in such matches, the favourites were found more than a little wanting, and it was City who won the game by the emphatic scoreline of 3-0. It was a bitter disappointment for Barson as he had looked forward to treading the hallowed Wembley turf, and he was never to get so close again. He had also become a little injury prone, hardly surprising given the nature of his game. Barson left United for Watford at the end of the 1927/28 season after six years of solid service. There was no doubt that he had left his mark on the club and was revered by Manchester United's fans – he left more than his mark on a number of opposing players during that time as well!

Joe Spence was Granddad's favourite player of all time. He measured players by Joe Spence's ability. Spence was certainly a cult figure on the terraces in those far off days, and whenever United were in difficulty the cry would go up, "Give it to Joe!" Initially he was a right winger, though there were periods during his career at United when he played centre forward. He was relatively short in stature, just five feet and eight inches tall, and weighing in at a steady 11 stones and five pounds. But Granddad considered he had the biggest heart around, and that no cause was a lost cause where Joe was concerned. He reckoned that Spence would have run through a brick wall for the benefit of the team had he been asked to.

Joe was from Northumberland, where he played in local football before joining Manchester United and making his debut against Derby County in August 1919. He quickly became a favourite, and it is interesting to note that though he operated mainly on the right flank, in his 15 years with United there were only five seasons when he did not score 10 league goals or more. He would start every game with same three part plan: first test the full back's speed; secondly, move the ball from either foot and go inside and outside the full back to test which was his weaker side; and thirdly, he would charge his opponent just to see how he adapted to the physical side of the game. I was told that Spence had great balance, like Jimmy Delaney, Johnny Berry and George Best, and that he stayed on his feet whenever possible.

Unfortunately for Joe Spence, the quality of players around him at United was not as good as it could have been, and he saw some of the club's toughest times on and off the field during his stay at Old Trafford. History tells us that Joe won a couple of international caps for England, as did Neil McBain, Jack Silcock and Clarence 'Lol' Hilditch, but on and off the field United were once again in decline. It was sad for a player of his ability that Joe never ever lifted silverware whilst at United, and throughout his whole career the only medal he ever won was a Third Division championship medal with Chesterfield in 1936. But Joe Spence won my grandfather's heart, and he would never hear a wrong word said against him. It was his misfortune to be at Old

Trafford during such a time of transition, but in a period when United teams often failed to produce the goods, his entertaining presence was a true highlight. Even today, he remains among the all-time top ten United players in appearances for the club, and his 481 league games gave him a record that stood for 40 years until surpassed by Bill Foulkes. Spence made a total of 510 appearances in all competitions for United during his 14 years, scoring 168 goals.

The Gibson Rescue

Because of his involvement in local sport, my grandfather didn't see as much of United as he would have liked between 1926 and 1934. However, he went to Old Trafford whenever he could and kept his ear to the ground as to what was happening around the club. He told me of the first international match to be played at Old Trafford, when the 50th game between England and Scotland was played there in 1926.

He felt the journey back into obscurity for United began in 1927 when Mr. Davies, the club's benefactor, chairman and president passed away. With Davies at the helm the club was kept from financial trouble, and the club was in the process of buying the freehold of Old Trafford. This was completed after Mr. Davies's death, but on the field the team was beginning to tumble into freefall. In 1926, the manager, J.A. Chapman, was found guilty of wrongdoing by the FA, and the club immediately terminated his contract. Initially 'Lol' Hilditch took over as player-manager, but the task was too great for him. In 1927, on director Harold Hardman's recommendation, Herbert Bamblett took over as manager, and Walter Crickmer began his long association with Manchester United as secretary, a post he would hold until he died on that snowy runway in Munich, Germany in 1958. United fell to 15th in 1927, 18th in 1928, 12th in 1929, and 17th in 1930, and in 1931 were finally relegated for the third time in their history after finishing bottom of the First Division, whereupon Bamblett's tenure as manager was ended.

Louis Rocca and Walter Crickmer took the helm on the playing side for a short period. There was supporter unrest and financial hardship for the club, while in the wider world there was recession brought about by the Wall Street Crash of 1930. Unemployment was high and money tight. Unfortunately Manchester United, now in dire straits, had to ask for the mortgage interest on their freehold payments to be suspended; they were unable to meet their liabilities, including the players' wages. It was déjà-vu – 1902 all over again.

James Gibson was born on 21 October 1877, just a year before the Newton Heath Football Club was formed. His family was reasonably wealthy due to his father's flourishing uniform manufacturing business, and they owned a large house closed to the city centre. As a young boy, James was interested in how the family business ran, but tragedy struck when he was just 14 years old. Both his parents were struck down by fatal illnesses leaving James, the eldest child, with his brother and sister. The three Gibson children went to live with their grandparents, but just as some normality resumed both their grandparents also passed away.

The Gibson children were taken under the wing of their mother's brother, Michael Fell, who was a successful corn merchant. James took employment with his uncle and was able to learn those aspects of business that allowed him to rise to the top. His uncle recognised James's qualities, and was not slow to promote the young Gibson into positions of responsibility. There developed a deep and loving respect for each other and as James gained in experience and responsibility, he also became more ambitious. He was inquisitive, thrived on hard work, and was always willing to learn. However, he had a penchant for sales, and this really was his forte.

Just after the turn of the 20th century, with his uncle's blessing, he decided to strike out on his own. He had never forgotten the uniform manufacturing business that had made his late father so successful, and it was into this that he applied his energy and skills. Buying a small factory building close to Manchester city centre, and using contacts that he knew from his father's time, he was able quickly to grow his uniform business. The business developed in part by supplying military uniforms during the Great War, after which James Gibson was a highly successful and respected businessman within Manchester's commercial circles.

After the war Gibson had to find new ways of developing his business, and he moved into the manufacture of uniforms for tram drivers and conductors, having been able to impress this idea upon city corporations throughout Britain. He took on two more partners and they moved into larger premises, just off Oldham Road, in the New Cross area close to Ancoats. For a while there was nothing but success, but in the late 1920s during a period of financial slump throughout the world, the business did come under pressure. One of the partners died, and the other decided to sell his share. Gibson bought out the shares, and being the dedicated man that he was, kept the business stable and withstood the slump in trade.

In 1931/32 United was in a perilous position with falling gate revenues, a lapsed mortgage on the ground, bank credit facilities withdrawn, players' wage payments uncertain and the club on the verge of being unable to fulfill its fixtures.

As J.H. Davies stepped into the breach in 1902, now James Gibson answered the club's call. My grandfather told me that a man by the name of Lintott, a journalist, approached James Gibson to ask him to help rescue Manchester United. Mr. Gibson at that time had no interest in football, but he was a businessman of great resolve, skilled at restoring failed businesses to financial stability. He loved a challenge, and Lintott put it to him that he could be the saviour of what could be a very successful club. Whatever was said by Lintott during his meeting with Mr. Gibson, it stimulated the businessman's interest and he told Lintott that he would be interested in meeting with the United board to discuss his potential involvement with the club.

He met with a man named Mr. Lawton, who was then chairman of the United, and also with Walter Crickmer, the club secretary. Gibson asked first to see club's most recent balance sheet, and what he found horrified him. The club was in debt to the tune of £26,000 and was losing an estimated £2,000 pounds a month. Even he, shrewd businessman that he was, knew that he could not turn this situation around quickly. Initially he got the club through the first month, enabling the players and the staff to be paid. He laid out the plans that he hoped would save the club. There was some resistance to his proposals from the United Board, but backed by the fans Gibson won the day and saw the club through the Christmas period of 1931. It was not until the end of January 1932 that he formally took over the club, but he had by this time won the backing of the United fans, and they had faith and confidence in him. All the existing directors resigned, and he formed a new board comprising men that he knew and trusted. He gave personal guarantees to the bank of over £40,000 and used his own money to ensure a transfer fund. Both the public and the players responded to the firm leadership that James Gibson provided. Gates increased, and from looking certainties for relegation at the end of December 1931, the team finished twelfth in Division Two at the end of the 1931/32 season. Disaster had once again been averted, as it had been in 1902, and another unsung hero etched his family's name into the history of Manchester United.

In 1935 Granddad gave up active participation at Manchester North End, and he became a season ticket holder at Old Trafford. United were still in the Second Division but Mr. Gibson had been able to secure the services of Scott Duncan as manager in 1932. Scott Duncan had enjoyed success with the unfashionable Cowdenbeath club in Scotland, and it was on his shoulders that the United Board and fans placed their trust. It was an uphill battle at first, and considerable money was spent on new players. There was turbulence, but Granddad maintained that United had good people 'inside' the club, and this was to be proved correct when they climbed out of the Second Division in 1936. The elation of regaining First Division status was, however, to be very short-lived because they were relegated back to Division Two after just one season. It certainly wasn't a time for the fainthearted. In November 1937, Scott Duncan dropped a bombshell by asking to leave the club so he could go and manage non-league Ipswich Town.

Despite Duncan's departure, United still managed to secure promotion back to the First Division by finishing runners–up in the Second Division, four points behind the champions Aston Villa. It was dear old Walter Crickmer, aided by Louis Rocca, who took charge of team affairs, and it was a great credit to them that they achieved promotion that season. Things were starting to happen at Old Trafford and players like Johnny Carey, Jack Rowley, Allenby Chilton and Stan Pearson had arrived at the club. In 1938/39 Crickmer managed to keep the team in mid-table of the First Division. However, war clouds were again on the horizon, and football would have to take a back seat for the next six years. Those years were to be so bitter-sweet for my grandfather.

Wartime – Romance and Heartache

Hitler's march into Poland in the summer of 1939 culminated in an ultimatum from the British government that failing a withdrawal by 3 September, Britain would consider itself at war with Germany. The ultimatum was ignored, and Britain was once again plunged into the hardship of war, just 21 years after the Great War had ended. This time Grandfather was classed as too old to serve in the forces, but he was allowed to take an Air Raid Patrol Warden's job, and like everything else he did in life, he took to it with gusto. He worked long hours, and they did take their toll on him.

By the summer of 1939, my father had started to see a young girl named Mary Olive Whelan. He had been introduced to her through a close friend's association, and later marriage, to Olive's sister Alice. The Whelans were a local family from the Ancoats area. It was a large family. Lizzie Ellen and Billy Whelan had eight daughters (including Alice and Olive) and two sons. The family lived in Jersey Street Dwellings in Ancoats, a quadrangle of apartments in four storeys. The Whelan family was well known around the Ancoats area, mainly for the parent's drinking escapades. Billy was a retired service pensioner, having been invalided out of the army in 1906, and had held no job of real means since. Lizzie Ellen just bore the children. Money was always tight, and they would pawn anything and everything to satisfy their drinking habits. It was a tough life for their children, in hard times, and one by one as they reached some element of maturity the Whelan children would leave home at the first opportunity.

On 31 March 1940, my parents were married at the Manchester Register Office. She was just 18 years of age and my father was 25. Their courtship had been relatively brief, and my grandfather was not very happy about the relationship. Olive was a protestant, while my grandparents were staunch practising Catholics, and they were and were horrified that their only son would be married outside the Catholic church. Once again in the family history, the marriage was rushed because Olive was pregnant, and on 6 September 1940 my brother, Peter, was born in a little two up, two down terraced house in Rodney Street, Ancoats.

The relationship between my father and frandfather was always stormy, and this never ceased until my grandfather passed away in 1966. They both had very stubborn streaks and there was little give and take between the two of them, and never any compromise. Grandfather would have done so much for us as a family if only my father had allowed him. He would always say he didn't want, nor need, his father's charity. Because of this, in later years, we as a family suffered. For the first 18 months of my parents' marriage, Granddad could not bring himself to speak with my mother, and he virtually made her an outcast. She could not be present in his house when he was there. But Grandmother Margaret, after the initial shock, warmed to her new grandson and would go to see my mother daily, making sure that both her and her new born baby were fine and not in need.

My father had been called up to serve in the Army in early 1941 and joined the East Lancashire Regiment. After basic training he was billeted in Liverpool awaiting movement overseas. The unit was in the Fazackerly area of the city. Liverpool was a regular target for the German bombers, and it was on one of the nights when the Germans targeted the area that my father's billets suffered bombing. They were destroyed and there was a heavy loss of life. For two days after that raid, my father was on the missing persons' list and Mum, Grandmother, Grandfather and my father's sister Mary feared the worst. Even then Granddad showed no compassion towards his daughter-in-law. It was a horrible situation for Mum to find herself in. Just 19 years of age, with a baby who wasn't even a year old, a father-in-law who treated her as an outcast, and now the prospect of losing her husband looming forever large, with little or no money to depend upon.

On the morning of the third day after that bombing raid, my father was found alive in a hospital in Liverpool. He had suffered severe shell shock and had lost his speech and memory. He suffered a nervous breakdown which led to his discharge from the service some months later. While in the hospital, it was only after the effects of his injuries began to wear off that the doctors were able to establish his identity. The news was passed on immediately to my mother who in turn was able to go around to my grandparent's house and give them the good news. Father came home just a few weeks later. However, further tragedy was just around the corner for them.

Towards the end of 1941 Grandmother Margaret was diagnosed with breast cancer. This was a body blow to my grandfather and my father. My father's sister, Mary, was still living at home, but worked at the Avro aircraft factory in Chadderton (where half of the Lancaster bombers produced for the war were built). It was my mother who stepped forward to look after Grandmother while Mary and her father carried on working each day. As well as nursing Grandmother, she looked after her own household, and eventually Grandfather thawed somewhat and began a dialogue with his daughter-in-law. It was tiring for her, and this was something that Granddad was never to forget. From then on he warmed to her, and for the rest of his life he loved her so much. Sadly, on 22 July 1942 Grandma passed away – she was just short of her fiftieth birthday.

The effect on my grandfather, my father and his sister was devastating. My father adored his mum, and Granddad was lost without her. Grandmother's death became the cause of even more friction between Granddad and his errant son. Dad thought that Granddad never gave Grandmother the attention she had needed: he considered him too selfish, more interested in his job, politics and sport, to the detriment of his wife and family. He firmly believed this was why Grandma's health deteriorated so rapidly.

In the years after Grandmother's death, Granddad mellowed a great deal, and the bond between him and my mum grew stronger with each passing month. For the next few years, Mum kept home for him and his daughter, Mary, much to the chagrin of my father, who, although he accepted the situation, never ever liked it. Mum even turned to

Catholicism and she was embraced into the Catholic church. She and Dad had a Catholic marriage ceremony in St. Patrick's early in 1945, when she was six months pregnant, carrying me.

By now, Mum and Dad had moved from Rodney Street in Anocats to Royle Street in Chorlton-upon-Medlock. Grandfather had advised him against the move because he knew what that area was like. However my father was slipping into bad habits mainly because of his association with a long time friend who really instigated the move for my father. Our family would remain in the Chorlton-upon Medlock locality for some 16 long years.

Granddad's Latter Days

After the Second World War, Manchester Corporation transferred my grandfather to their Cleansing Department as a senior foreman. Yes, he became a bin-man, a dustman, or to use the official title of his job, a refuse collector. He worked in that department until his retirement in 1956, proud of what he did for a living, and proud of serving his city. In the post-war years, his Labour Party and trades union activity became even more important to him, and occupied much of his time as he lived alone. He developed an amazing huge network of contacts, and seemed to know everybody.

Granddad was saddened by his relationship with my father. As he aged and grew mellow, he tried on several occasions to mend the enormous gulf between them. He felt the need to atone for his own shortcomings in those bygone years. My father would have none of it, and would not accept what he called "charity given with a guilty conscience". In reality, Father's stubbornness and hard-headedness only hurt his own family.

Immediately after the war, the city council in Manchester began to build housing estates just outside the city, especially to the south. The aim was to move families out of the poorer inner city slums into decent accommodation in areas that would provide a better quality of life. It was an enormous project that would last the best part of 25 years. At the outset, Granddad offered help to my father by using his influence with people he knew in the council's housing department. My father declined this offer of help which, had he accepted, would have led to our family being moved into a new council house, and would have given us a far better quality of life. It seems the selfish traits that my grandfather undoubtedly had as a young man were inherited by my father. The simple fact of the matter was that my father was perfectly happy in his own world, living the life he wanted, and living where he wanted. Mum's hopes for the family did not come into it.

Granddad was the epitome of a true sportsman - unless it had anything to do with Manchester City! He had an intense dislike for Manchester City Football Club, and everything associated with it. He told me it was only worth going to Maine Road if Manchester United were playing there or if the place was on fire! City really did bring out the worst in him, and I suspect it went back to all those years in the first decade of the 20th century when City were involved in some underhand dealings regarding illegal payments to players. Notwithstanding this, he did instill into me the ethics of being fair, and of appreciating the other team. He also taught me that winning isn't everything, that your good name is paramount, and that you only get out of life what you put into it. He had a saying, which he repeated time and time again, one that has stayed with me through all the years: "You have to be able to lose, to really know how to win." Confusing? As a youngster it was, but as the years passed I began to understand exactly what he meant.

In 1948 he went to his second FA Cup final – 39 years after attending the 1909 final against Bristol City. The 1948 final against Blackpool – the game that my father and his friends followed on our wireless set – was Granddad's first trip to Wembley stadium. And in the years that followed he taught me of the history and the aura that was Manchester United.

In 1951 he found personal happiness again when he befriended a lady named Mary Smith, and in 1952 they were married. My father vehemently opposed the marriage, and even the relationship. Mary was a wonderful lady who loved Granddad and cared for his every need. Unfortunately, the animosity that my father felt for her never went away.

By the early 1950s I had started going to Old Trafford to watch reserve team matches. Granddad encouraged me, and was always interested to hear what I had to say about games. He greatly enjoyed United's First Division title win in 1952, which came over 40 years after he had last seen them lift that magnificent piece of silverware. As an avid admirer of Matt Busby, he watched his progress closely from the day he was appointed as manager, and was impressed as he put his youth policy into operation immediately after the war. He was also impressed with the people that Matt Busby placed around him, people he knew that he could trust to do their jobs and foster a family spirit within the club. Jimmy Murphy as assistant manager, Tom Curry, Bert Whalley and Billy Inglis as coaches, and Joe Armstrong as head of scouting. Busby was happy with the Manchester United board with whom he was able to work closely. They did have their differences at various times, but those differences never lasted for too long. There were rumblings in the boardroom after he started to dismantle the 1952 championship winning team, but he was able to placate them when he told them of the potential of the kids he had in the pipeline, and who were almost ready to break through into first team football. He valued this group of players at over £250,000 which was an enormous amount back in the early 1950s.

Granddad also told me of the staunch ally that Busby had in Harold Hardman, who had taken over the chairmanship following Mr. Gibson's death in 1952. Never was that alliance more valuable than in 1956 when Mr. Hardman backed Busby's request to enter the team into the newly founded European Cup competition. As the years passed I found out that Granddad and Matt Busby actually became very good friends. Granddad was a lifelong friend of Paddy McGrath who owned the Cromford Club, which was situated off Market Street in Manchester's city centre. Paddy was also a close friend of Busby's. Most Saturday evenings would find my Granddad in Paddy's company so it was there that he would share the company of the great man.

In November of 1953 he went down to Wembley again, to watch England play Hungary in a friendly international game. England had never been beaten at Wembley by a foreign international team at this time, but this match was to change all that, and change the direction and whole outlook of the British game. Years later I was able to talk to him about that game, and he spoke so highly of that great Magyar side. He said that they were a team that was so together, so coordinated, that they were like a troupe of ballet dancers. Although Ferenc Puskas took the plaudits and rave notices in that game, he maintained that it was Bozsic, Koscsis, and Hidegkuti who did the real damage. Apparently they pulled the England defenders all over the place with their speed and movement, and from what he told me, England got off lightly with a 6-3 defeat! This statement was reinforced in May 1954 when, just prior to the 1954 World Cup in Switzerland, England played a return fixture with Hungary in Budapest, and were soundly thrashed 7-1.

When the teams had emerged from the tunnel in the game at Wembley, people gasped at what they saw. The Hungarians wore a vastly different playing kit, and their boots were like ballet slippers according to Granddad. They wore lace-up shirts without collars, which were made of a lightweight material (as were their socks). It was those boots that the spectators found eye-catching, and before a ball was kicked most were of the opinion that these 'fairies' were in for a drubbing. Their attitude was well and truly turned in the first half hour, as they sat there in awed silence as England trailed by 4-1. England looked just what they were – cumbersome and more akin to selling platers had they been race horses!

I sat with Granddad in his little parlour, in his terraced house in Naylor Street, in the summer of 1954, watching my first World Cup final on a little 14 inch, black and white television. He loved the football that the great Hungarian team of that era played, but funnily enough, he tipped the Germans in the final.

I recall his excitement at the emergence of the Busby Babes, and his admiration for what United were doing as a club. He loved watching the youth teams of that time, and like us all, eulogized about the 'big fella' – Duncan Edwards. As those Babes really began to emerge in the 1954/55 season, Granddad maintained that apart from Duncan the three other most influential players were Byrne, Whelan, and Viollet. He was overjoyed at the championship win of 1956, and with the style in which it was achieved. He was delighted to watch United make an immediate impact on their first European adventure, and in the March 1957 he travelled to Madrid for the first leg of the European Cup semi-final. Upon his return he raved about what he had seen.

Real (meaning 'Royal' in Spanish) came from the up-market Charmartin district of Madrid. In 1955 their magnificent Charmartin Stadium had been renamed after their club president Santiago Bernabeu. The Bernabeu Stadium was such an imposing sight, and made the best English grounds look decidedly second rate. It was built of white concrete and stone – tier upon tier seeming to reach up to the heavens. There was room for some 135,000 fans inside this splendid arena, and on the big match days it was a throbbing, incandescent mob of football humanity.

Granddad told me that Real was a club in the truest sense of the word, and that the huge Charmartin complex housed restaurants, a library, concert hall, trophy museum and drawing rooms, all lavishly equipped with the finest furniture and were bedecked by flowing crystal chandeliers. Outside the main stadium he told me there were wonderful facilities for swimming, track and field, pelota and tennis, and that Spain's Wimbledon tennis champion, Manuel Santana, learned his game in that complex. But Granddad claimed not just to have seen the finest stadium and team in the world, but also the finest player – Alfredo Di Stefano. His disappointment at defeat to Real Madrid that year did not fester long because he reckoned that United were more than good enough to win the trophy at their next attempt.

May 1957 also saw him back at Wembley for the FA Cup final against Aston Villa, and he returned in anger, with outright condemnation of Peter McParland's outrageous foul on Ray Wood early in the game which cost the Babes the famous and much desired double. Granddad knew Johnny Dixon, the Aston Villa captain who had family in Manchester, and just a few weeks later he really took Dixon to task about the incident when they met at a function in Manchester.

In May 1957, when United had retained the First Division title again, he was so optimistic at the team's progress and the fact that they now had a year's experience of European football under their belt. As the 1957/58 season unfolded, he was buoyant about United's chances of landing the treble and really did want the team to meet Real Madrid once again. He travelled over to Dalymont Park in Dublin to watch the first game of that season's European campaign against Shamrock Rovers. He loved going over to Ireland and he had many friends in Dublin, and upon his returned he raved about Billy Whelan's performance in a game that was won by 6-0. He would not travel to countries that were behind the Iron Curtain as he always thought that they were sinister places, so that trip to Ireland turned out to be his last European football journey. Unfortunately fate decreed that this United side would never reach their dreams, and the tragedy that was Munich took its toll on Granddad. He grieved for those dear boys, as we all did, and on the Sunday after the disaster we both attended Mass at St. Patrick's church in Livesey Street, Collyhurst, and we prayed for those we had lost, and for the well-being of those who had survived. Throughout that Mass, along with hundreds of others, our tears flowed quite freely.

He watched as the club tried to recover from the devastation of the disaster, and he was at Wembley again in 1958 to watch a patched up and inexperienced team lose in the FA Cup final to Bolton Wanderers. Granddad conceded that it was a game too far for that team, and that the emotions of the three months before that final finally took their toll on the young boys that were left. However, despite the despondency and gloom that appeared to be looming over Manchester United, he always maintained that given time there was still a platform for Matt Busby to rebuild the club once again.

In the early 1960s Granddad's health started to fail, but he still found the energy to make it to Old Trafford. He adored Bobby Charlton and always rammed it down my throat that he was the role model to follow. My proudest moment was going to Wembley with him in 1963 for the FA Cup final against Leicester City, the only time in our lives that we actually attended a match together. On the way home that evening, he said, "This is the start of something very, very special". In 1965 he was very sick, as cancer began to ravage his body, but he still saw United lift the championship and he managed to attend quite a number of games at Old Trafford. He loved the type of football that United were playing. George Best was going to be a great player he reckoned, but he didn't think he would be as good as Joe Spence! Denis Law was already a great, but he loved to watch, and talk about, Pat Crerand. He reckoned Paddy was the architect of the team, but that he also had that much needed 'devil' in him that was needed to succeed.

The time I spent with him during my childhood, youth, then early manhood was just so precious. As I enter old age today, my memories of him have never faded nor do they dim. If I close my eyes I can still take myself back to those times and hear his soft, gentle voice, explaining to me all those events that were so important to the history of Manchester United.

Unfortunately, those events are now consigned to history, and are lost to many in the modern era. Although history and nostalgia seem not to matter to some, it is all still so vivid for me. Sadly, on 1 October 1966, Granddad passed away, and when he did a huge void was left in my life. He was such a good man, and he left me with so many, many, happy, happy, memories. He was a man who gave me so much love, so much encouragement, and taught me so much about how to live your life. He also gave me my love of Manchester United. My God, how I loved and how I still miss that dear old man.

Starting School

The families of Royle Street were predominantly of the Catholic faith. The children attended the Holy Family infants' school (behind All Saints, between the Manchester Registrar's Office and the Manchester Ear Hospital), moving on to St. Augustine's junior and senior school. The girls' junior and senior school was on York Street, where the BBC Manchester studios stand today. The boys' junior school was within the Cavendish Church of England School at All Saints, a situation caused by the destruction of the old St. Augustine's boys' school by the German bombers during the war. The senior boys' school consisted of three prefabricated buildings that housed six classrooms; it stood at the junction of York Street and Sydney Street in Chorlton-upon-Medlock, land today occupied by university buildings.

Religion played a large part in family life back then, and the priests had a high profile in the community. The Salvation Army had a citadel on Grosvenor Street, and every Sunday morning their brass band would parade around the streets playing hymns, while their officers collected pennies and encouraged local support. The local Wolf Cub, Boy Scout, and Girl Guide organisations were also housed in the citadel. As children grew up, no matter what their religious denomination, most would spend time in that citadel. St. Luke's CE church and school were on St Luke's Street, round the corner from our house. Across the way from St. Augustine's boys' senior school, and situated at the corner of Sydney Street and York Street, was the Old Garratt Mission. Again, regardless of denomination, most kids in the area spent some time in the mission. The 27th Boys' Brigade unit was to be found at the end of Temple Street, and again lots of the kids would find their way there. Youngsters were attracted to the citadel, the mission, and the Boys' Brigade by the activities that these organisations provided. Apart from offering spiritual learning they would also arrange day trips to the countryside, and to the seaside resorts of Lancashire and north Wales. Musical tuition was also available, and they provided the instruments and tutors. All of these institutions had their own football and netball teams, and they certainly provided an escape from the everyday humdrum of the harsh local life in Chorlton-upon-Medlock.

Those of us attending a Catholic school had to be careful not to let our school teachers, and sometimes even our school friends, know if we attended any of these non-Catholic organisations. It was considered not the done thing, and as far as the parish priest, headmasters and headmistresses were concerned, would lead to our eternal damnation! At the very least you would return home from school with a strongly worded letter, followed by a visit from the parish priest to the family home. Many times my father and the priest had a heated debate about him allowing me and my brother to attend both the Boys' Brigade and Salvation Army organisations. My father's point was that the Catholic Church provided no facilities for youngsters to expend their energies, nor did it stimulate their interests in other than the spiritual side. The parish priest would advise my father that it was not the right way to bring up Catholic children, to which he was always met with the same reply, "If you don't play the game, don't try to make the rules."

For the most part, we were happy young kids, oblivious to the harshness of life at that time, with most families in the same boat. Some families were able to escape from the poverty trap, but they were mostly young people just starting out in life. Their escape route (like that of my Irish forebears, but for different reasons) was emigration, especially to Australia. These emigrants became known as the 'Ten Pound Poms', a reference to the 'Assisted Passage' scheme by which the Australian government would foot the bill for a family's travel, especially for those that had trades people amongst them. The only cost to the families was a single ten pounds payment. Many of my young school friends were to disappear this way. Australia seemed another world away, and to most it was. The Commonwealth countries in those days were as helpful as they could be to their mother country. Once a year each school in Manchester received a supply of foodstuffs which was distributed amongst the families of the children. Each child would be given a parcel that would contain a few tins of meat, fruit and sweets. None was ever refused.

Before I went to school at the age of five I was 'minded' by various people while my mother and father were at work. When I first attended the Holy Family infants' school I came under the watchful eye of Mother Gertrude, a lovely, caring nun whom I will always remember with great fondness. My first crush came at the Holy Family School when I fell in love with my teacher Miss Eagan, a red haired, large bosomed, young Irish lady! I just loved going to school, loved the teachers and the safe environment of having the other children around me; not forgetting the bottle of milk and the marshmallow wafer that we received every morning. The majority of the kids came from poor families, and the teachers gave lots of their time to us – I recall so many happy and good times. Miss Eagan taught us to paint; we were little mites with long handled paint brushes, some with just a few bristles, painting shapes upon newspaper sheets, and then having to explain to her what we had painted – well, even van Gogh first started painting wallflowers! There was an annual school outing to Ainsdale beach, near Southport, which we all looked forward to so much. It was amazing for us to go from the inner city to see the sea, and to play amongst the sand dunes. With our school plays for the nativity, harvest festival and Easter we were all happy in our own little world, oblivious to the struggles of our parents who were raising families in such a deprived area.

At playtimes and lunchtimes as many as twenty or thirty children, five and six years old, would chase a small tennis ball around the school yard, roared on by patients from the wards of the Manchester Ear Hospital which adjoined the school. The wards on the west side of the hospital had balconies that looked out over the school playground, and if the weather was fairly decent, the patients would sit out in the open air and watch the games unfolding down below them. Even at that early stage of lives, we were either 'red' or 'blue', and would divide into those teams in the school yard. It was something that was bred into you. The football bug well and truly devoured me. I would kick anything I could – tin cans, stones – and Mum was always bending my ear about the state of my shoes, as more often than not I would kick the toes out of them. As I had learned to read, I would pick up any reading material about football – newspapers, magazines, comics – I had an insatiable thirst for the game. It didn't matter what it was about, or which club, as long as it concerned football I wanted to read it. Whenever I was at Granddad's home he would ask me which teams played at which grounds, which players played for which teams. If I didn't know the answer, I would make sure I found out before my next visit. Even at such a young age, my knowledge was better than most kids about the game.

Getting to Know Old Trafford

In the autumn of 1950 I was introduced to watching live football. In those days, the various schools throughout Manchester would receive a free allocation of tickets for reserve team matches from both Manchester United and Manchester City. These tickets would be distributed by the schoolteachers in the senior school on a Friday afternoon, together with red bus tokens for the Manchester buses which allowed free travel. My brother, Peter, got hold of a couple of these tickets and a handful of bus tokens, and so took me for my first visit to Old Trafford. I was already hooked on United, but to go and to see a match at Old Trafford – at any level – was more than I could have ever wished for at that age. My brother forever maintained that taking me to Old Trafford was the biggest mistake he ever made in his life! Unlike me, Peter was a boy who at that time could take or leave football. It never consumed him as it did me, and he had many other interests – fishing, music, and cycling to name but a few. After that first visit he never fancied having to chaperone me to matches, but he did always take the tickets and bus tokens that were on offer at school, and he did accompany me to other games for a short while. When he became quite sure that I knew my way to Old Trafford, we came to an agreement. We would leave home together about 11 o'clock on a Saturday morning, walk to All Saints, and then go our separate ways, him to do whatever he wished, and me to Old Trafford. In those days, there was no floodlighting at Old Trafford, and Saturday reserve games would kick off at 2.15pm during the winter months. Peter and I would meet up again around 5.30 and make our way home together, and our parents were never any the wiser!

On my secret trips to Old Trafford, Peter and I would part company at All Saints. I would catch the number 49 bus, and sit with my nose pressed against the window as it trundled its way up Stretford Road. The pavements were always crowded with Saturday shoppers, and in my mind's eye I can still see the local landmarks that became so familiar along the route. Paulden's store at Cambridge Street, Clynne's pub, Braun's pork butcher's, the Fifty Shilling Tailors at Great Jackson Street, the Zion Institute, the Three Legs of Man pub, Burke's Brushes. Then the bus would take the right fork as it entered Trafford Bar at the junctions of Stretford Road, Talbot Road, and Chester Road. Turning into Chester Road, on the left hand side the bus passed the famous old dark-sooted, castellated building that was Henshaw's Intsitute for the Blind, where my father would go for training in woodwork just a few years later. The White City Stadium was further along on the left, a stadium that could hold 25,000 people and which hosted greyhound racing, rugby and athletics; today only its old grand entrance remains, surrounded by a modern retail park. Salford Docks would loom large over to the right. The ocean-going ships of Manchester Liners and the Royal Mail rested majestically at their berths on the various quaysides, their funnels spouting smoke as they prepared to cross the Atlantic to Canada and the United States.

Then the bus would arrive at my alighting point, just past the Trafford pub at Warwick Road. The sheer excitement and thrill of going to Old Trafford has never left me, even to this day. I still get that same delight, that surge, that same expectation I experienced as a young child. More often than not, my arrival at Warwick Road would be over two hours before kick-off, with few people around. I would walk down Warwick Road and over the railway bridge, on whose bricks, blackened with soot and grime, was emblazoned the white painted slogan: 'Ban the A-Bomb – United We Win!' Then I arrived at the brick croft that passed as the forecourt to the ground – you have to remember that it was just a few short years since Old Trafford had reopened after suffering wartime damage from German bombers. Although the stadium had been rebuilt, the service areas all around were virtually non-existent apart from United Road. What is now known as the forecourt, and also the area at the back of the Stretford End, were nothing more than cinders.

For the next 90 minutes or so I would walk round and round the ground – I never got fed up. Everything about Old Trafford used to fascinate me. I would peer through the gaps in the huge wooden gates that used to be opened at three-quarter time to let the crowds out. Everything painted on the walls I would read – admission prices, gate numbers, you name it. Across the canal bridge, the black tower at the Kilvert's lard works used to intrigue me as it stretched high into the sky like some imposing medieval castle. On the opposite side of Warwick Road, on what is today the car park facing the United 'Megastore', was a mineral company named Aerowater – 'mineral' being the word we had for soft fizzy drinks, a phrase that seems to have fallen by the wayside today. Many was the time I slipped quietly into their yard unobserved, and 'nicked' a few drinks from the crates loaded on the back of the parked lorries. I would stand in the middle of United Road and peer up at the two great chimneys which stood atop of buildings in Glover's Cables factory, that loomed so high, and that towered above the stadium like two giant sentries on duty at Buckingham Palace. I would stand against the wall underneath the dressing room windows on the railway side of the stadium, and the smell of liniment would permeate the air – a smell that is still there today! I would walk down the side of the ground by the railway station, watching the steam trains pass by, and I'd watch the players arriving, on foot from Warwick Road. They were besieged by kids for autographs, before disappearing inside the main entrance.

When the turnstiles opened I would be one of the first inside. There were always hordes of kids at reserve team games, and as the seasons went by it was inevitable you would get to know each other. We would have sprint races, up and down the Old Trafford Paddock terracing. A tennis ball would often appear, and we would play football, even on the terraces. We would talk about our favourite players, and dream our dreams, then as kick-off time drew near, we would make our way to our selected vantage points to watch the game. I laugh now as I think of the many times I sat on top of the old concrete dug-out by the players' tunnel. Sometimes during the course of the game I would hang over the top, and peep down to see who was inside. It must have frightened the occupants to death to see this little urchin's face suddenly appear, with its unkempt hair dangling down, and snotty 'candles' upon his top lip! Dear old Billy Inglis, the reserve team trainer, used to scream at me. He would be sat in there, sometimes with Jimmy Murphy for company. Billy would be dressed in his white overall coat, Jimmy in a suit.

As the weeks and years rolled along, I got to know who the players were in the reserves: Jack Crompton, John Aston, Billy Redman, Tommy McNulty, Don Gibson, Mark Jones, Jeff Whitefoot, Harry McShane, Johnny Scott, Noel McFarlane, John Doherty, Eddie Lewis, Lawrie Cassidy, Stan Pearson, Jackie Blanchflower, David Pegg, and a number of others. Opposing reserve teams in those days mainly comprised old pros coming to the end of their careers, and a sprinkling of younger players trying to make their way in the game. I used to love watching these games, as they were so competitive – some of those hardy old pros were tough beggars to say the least. I recognised many of the older players from magazines or newspapers, those who had been dropped from their first teams and were trying to play themselves back into form, or were making their way back into the game after injury. The Central League, in which United reserves played for many years, was in those days certainly no place for the faint hearted. For young players on the way up it was a tough school, but it sorted out the men from the boys, and gave managers and coaches a good insight into the kind of character that these young players had.

After a game we would hang around outside the Old Trafford main entrance. Unlike today there were never any autocratic commissionaires or security men policing the door, and often we would go inside. The area immediately inside those solid wooden doors was quite open, and led to the stairway that went up to the directors' box and to the posh seats in the main stand. If you turned left there was the sliding door which led to the dressing rooms – Mecca for us, young starry eyed kids. Immediately inside the main door was the players' tunnel, a surprisingly steep and narrow concrete ramp that led down and out into the stadium and then onto the pitch. The number of times I ran down that tunnel as a young boy, imagining that I was carrying the ball and leading out my heroes to a full house – Oh! What a dream that used to be. We kids would fight to be first in the line to run down that tunnel, followed by the rest of the 'Ragged Arsed Rangers'! It must have been so funny for the ground staff, who after a game would be tending to the playing surface, replacing divots and forking areas around the goalmouths, to watch this assembly of scruffy street urchins emerging from that old tunnel. They never chastised us or interfered with our innocent play; usually they would just smile, or make a few witty remarks. The kids would wait for the players in the area immediately outside the dressing rooms. If you waited long enough you could even travel home on the same bus with your hero. In those days there was a very close bond between the players and the fans, the community and the club. These days, at every top club, all that has changed. Back then it was such a very rich, fulfilling, and heartwarming experience for fans of all age groups. You felt part of it all, and the club embraced both the fans and their local communities with great warmth.

There have been so many changes in the game since those first visits of mine, and some for the good. But other changes have, in my opinion, caused major damage to the game and its structure. I think it is true to say that today the game has lost its roots in the working class community, and in future years it will be interesting to see what football (and social) historians make of it all. In today's society, youngsters will never enjoy the sheer elation of the freedom that my generation enjoyed. We were free to come and go as we pleased, without supervision, fear, or hindrance to watch our beloved football teams.

Junior School and Family Tragedy

In September 1952, aged 7, I progressed to St. Augustine's junior school, housed as I described in the Cavendish School – still in All Saints, but on the Loxford Street side of the quadrangle. This is where my learning really began, under the stern, but watchful and compassionate, eyes of both Miss Hulme and Mrs. Hawksey. Gone from my daily environment for the rest of my school days was female company, as the girls of my age were transferred to the girls' junior school, which was at the bottom of York Street.

Just a few weeks after I started at 'Gussie's' there was a significant event in our family. On 26 September 26 my mum gave birth to a bouncing baby girl – my sister Margaret Mary, who for some reason has never ever been referred to by either of those names! My parents nicknamed her 'Myra' and that has been the name that she has answered to throughout her life. It was also the beginning of a very sad and troubled time within our family, as my father's health began to deteriorate. His sight quickly began to fail, and he began to have severe stomach problems. Both complaints caused him to undergo major surgery – one operation being pioneering surgery at the time.

As a child I was oblivious to much of this, and I took to junior school with happy and carefree abandon. I had a thirst for learning, and just loved to read. My partners in crime during those long distant days were Gary Poke, Brian Walsh, Peter Cassin, David McGinty, and Philip Watson. Gary and Brian were from more affluent families than Peter, David, Philip and me, but that never put any barriers between us. We were all just so happy and comfortable with each other. We were all football daft, and we all supported Manchester United.

The playground at St. Augustine's junior school was a small rectangular area, separated from the Cavendish school yard by a wall. On two of the walls at opposite ends of our playground there were small painted 'goalposts', and during playtimes it was inevitable that a tennis ball would appear, as if by magic. The lads would divide themselves into two teams, usually United against City, and for the next 15 minutes would burn off their excess energies with a match. Even at such an early age, those games were competitive, and many an argument broke out between the two sets of players. More often than not the argument was whether a goal had been scored, or whether a shot had hit a 'post'. The outcome of many a dispute was a bloody nose for someone, perpetrated before the teacher on playground duty could intervene.

Football consumed our young lives, in school or out. We played the game at any opportunity. It was the same for kids in districts all over the city. We played in the cobbled streets and on waste land, in fact on any space we could. 'Street leagues' were common, and were the breeding ground for many future United and City stars. It was where they honed their early skills, where they developed the toughness both mentally and physically to survive in the professional game.

Playing every hour we could, the teams would expand to as many as 15 a side. No holds were barred. Get stuck in. You learned to look after yourself because often there were kids older than yourself playing in the opposite team. There was no sentiment in these games. It is true to say that most young boys back then were 'footy' daft! We listened in awe to our fathers, grandfathers, uncles, and their friends, as they regaled us with tales of the great managers, players, and clubs of the past, and the great feats they had all accomplished. With a hunger for knowledge of the game, befitting the appetite of a piranha, we read everything we could: comics, books, newspapers, magazines, because in those dear days, apart from the odd radio programme or newsreel clip at the cinema, the written word, and printed picture, was our only way of learning about the game's immediate and past history. None of our families owned television sets because all the houses in those areas were lit by gaslight. Today, I see young kids with the best of everything: replica kits, designer boots, tracksuits, training shoes, shin pads, 'keeper's gloves, and proper footballs. Things do come easily for them. They are saturated with football coverage on the television, and watch as the game is dissected, piece by piece, by people called pundits, some of whom never played the game at a decent standard – and even those that have talk as though football began the day that they started playing.

Today's media coverage is full of sensationalism, bias, untruths, innuendo, and certainly does not concentrate, nor report, on the game itself. This does influence kids' perception of football, and for the most part would have them believe that anything pre-1992 was not worth a mention. I smile to myself because it makes me realise how lucky the kids of my generation were. Not for a minute do I begrudge today's youngsters their material possessions; fair play to them, and, if they fall in love with game, all power to them. But it makes me wonder what will fuel their hunger, their imagination, their passion, and I wonder if they will discover the romance of this great game.

Manchester United became champions of the First Division of the Football League in May 1952, for the first time since 1911. They were top dogs in town. As the new season of 1952/53 began, I entered a period of an innate jealousy for some of my young school friends. I began to hate going into school on Monday mornings, as I knew I would have to listen to kids telling me how they had attended the previous Saturday's match at either Old Trafford or Maine Road. They had been taken to these games by their fathers, and the descriptions of what they had seen would see my eyes turn green with envy.

Home life became tougher as Dad's health began to deteriorate, and this was why he could never take me to a football match. Although a United supporter, Dad was never an Old Trafford regular – he had other interests that came before football. There had never been too much money about in our family, but now there was even less. Dad's absences from work became longer and longer, until in the middle of 1953 when he could no longer work at all. He had serious infections in the corneas of both eyes, and had been attending the Manchester Royal Eye Hospital which adjoins the Manchester Royal Infirmary on Oxford Road. His ophthalmic doctor was a wonderful man by the name of

Doctor F. Stewart-Scott, who was one of the most eminent eye surgeons in Britain at that time. Much of the damage to my father's sight had been caused by his practice as a young boy of putting tobacco juice into his eyes, to make them red and enable him to stay off school.

My father's failing eyesight was a body blow for my mother, and the way she struggled to make ends meet was testament to her love of us all; she showed great determination and resourcefulness to make a go of things. Nothing in the house was wasted, and looking back it is amazing to think that we never went short of food at home. She could make a meal out of almost anything. She mixed and matched, she made and mended our clothes, and while we could never have been called fashionable, we had clothes on our backs and shoes on our feet – sometimes! At times I had exasperated her by kicking the toes out of my shoes, or tredding the stiffeners down on the heels, so much that the stitching came apart. Her solution was to take the studs out of my old football boots, blacken the leather with shoe polish, and send me off to school with those on my feet. Of course my young school mates were always quick to notice, and I would be the source of the day's merriment.

By 1953, my brother Peter had become the first choice senior goalkeeper for Gussie's school team, and I would go along on Saturday mornings to watch him play. He was more than a useful 'keeper, and had he applied himself more he may well have progressed to a higher level than he ever did. He could take or leave football, and I don't think he realised just how good he was, or how good he could have become. I always enjoyed going to watch him play and his team was formidable opposition for any side in those days. They had some really good players, Bobby Murray and Martin Lyons as inside forwards; Micky Burgin the captain and a giant of a centre half; boys who went on to play in the Cheshire County League, which was no mean achievement back then. Peter's team won their league two seasons running, although the only thing that they received for their efforts was a certificate which went to the school – there were no individual medals. In the 1953/54 season they had a tremendous run in the Manchester Senior Schools Shield and by April had progressed to the semi-finals.

The semi-final coincided with the day my father underwent pioneering eye surgery, as Dr. Stewart-Scott attempted corneal grafts in Dad's eyes. There was much optimism; Dad built his hopes up high, as did all the family. We believed that he would regain sight and that he would be able to take a more active part in family life once again. Corneal graft surgery was still very much in its infancy and was nowhere near as sophisticated and successful as it is today. There were risks, but although these were explained to the family, nobody gave failure a thought.

On the morning of the semi-final we were at assembly in the main hall of the school. The headmaster, Mr. Tommy Callaghan, had made arrangements for the boys from the senior school to come across from York Street to watch the game, and once they were all present and settled, he read out a letter, written by my father to the boys of the football team, wishing them all well. Tears fell from my eyes as Mr. Callaghan read Dad's letter, and when he had finished he added his own good wishes, then led prayers for the success of Dad's operation which was just a few hours away.

Mum was at the hospital all day with our baby sister, Myra. The semi-final was being played on the ground of Newton Heath Loco in Newton Heath, which back in those days was Mecca to Manchester's footballing kids. An enclosed, compact ground, with small stands on three sides, and on the field the goals had nets! Today many Manchester United supporters wrongly believe that Newton Heath Loco was the original home of the Newton Heath club which became Manchester United. This is not true. The original Newton Heath ground was on North Road, now Northampton Road, where Moston Brook High School stands today.

It is important to draw the distinction between Newton Heath and Newton Heath Loco. Newton Heath was founded in 1878 by the

Carriage and Wagon Department workers of the Lancashire and Yorkshire railway, hence the club was known for a while as Newton Heath (LYR). Newton Heath Loco, on the other hand, was founded by workers of the Motive Power section of the same railway company, and had their ground at Ceylon Street. For many years, especially in Louis Rocca's day, Manchester United retained close ties with Newton Heath Loco, their former neighbours.

The semi-final was a curtain raiser to the main match: Manchester Catholic Boys versus Sheffield Catholic Boys. I made my way to Newton Heath on the number 82 bus from All Saints, along with my young school friends. It was our first visit to the Loco, and when we got off the bus on Oldham Road in Newton Heath, we were surprised to see so many people making their way into Ceylon Street, where the small ground was situated. Gussie's had been drawn against a Wythenshawe high school, named All Hallows. Our boys had never heard of them and didn't have any fear of them. The little ground began to fill up as kick off time approached, and I stood quite close to the dressing room doors and the steps that led down to the pitch. The door opened, and inside I could see big Mick Burgin in his blue and white striped shirt and white shorts, ball in hand, ready to lead out his team. And behind the skipper, in his mauve goalkeeper's jersey, was my big brother, Peter. It is hard to describe my emotions at that moment, but what I do know is that I felt so proud of him as he walked down those steps and onto the pitch. If I am truly honest, it was a defining moment, as I decided it was going to be goalkeeping for me! I just wanted to follow in his footsteps.

Playing at Newton Heath Loco was a huge experience for youngsters, and one that kids faced with much nervousness. A large crowd; referee and linesmen; and an atmosphere. The game began, and it ebbed and flowed throughout the first half. Gussie's scored first through Bobby Murray, but All Hallows seemed to be a much bigger set of lads, and by half-time they had turned the deficit into a 2-1 lead, with Peter performing some heroics to keep their forwards at bay. It seemed the whole semi-final experience was affecting the boys from the inner-city school. Danny Avery, the sports master had to get to work on them during the break. They emerged from the dressing room once more, and within minutes of the restart Bobby Murray scored a second for Gussie's with a close range header to level the scores. It was a much better performance in the second half, and several times they went close to taking the lead. As the time ticked away, Gussie's boys began to tire, and they were hanging on as All Hallows gained the upper hand. A draw would require a replay – there was no extra time in junior football back then. With just a few minutes to go, calamity! A simple back pass to the 'keeper from his full back. Whether Peter took his eye off the ball, I do not know, but as he went down on one knee to gather the ball it somehow found its way through his legs and into the back of the net. It was heartbreaking. It seemed to knock the stuffing out of his team, so much so that in the dying seconds they conceded a fourth goal.

I waited for him to emerge from the dressing room after the game. When he did, he was red eyed and distraught. His first words were, "How do I tell Dad that we lost?" Most of our school friends stayed on to watch the senior game but we both just wanted to get home. He was inconsolable on the journey back, and I felt so badly for him. He'd played his heart out, done his best, yet he felt that his simple mistake had cost his team the game. As we got closer to home we both became very quiet and I'm sure that we were both thinking about Dad.

The operation on Dad's corneas had taken place that morning, and Mum was at home when we arrived. There was no news on how the operation had gone, as Dad's eyes had to be covered for almost six weeks. The following day, after school, Peter and I were allowed to go and see him. We made the trek along Oxford Road to the Manchester Royal Eye Hospital, reached his ward, and then found him lying in bed with pillows behind his back, and swathes of bandages around his head, covering his eyes. His first question was for Peter: "How did you get on Son?" Reluctantly, Peter told him of the loss. "How did you play?" was his next question. It was so hard for my brother to explain, and once again I felt for him, as he was still so upset about his costly mistake. There were tears in his eyes as he related events to Dad. I told Dad that

Peter had played well, and that his first half performance was terrific. Dad sympathised with my brother, but I was glad that he didn't have to witness the look of disappointment that consumed Peter's face. I still feel that the semi-final game affected Peter for a long time afterwards. He lost his interest in football almost completely after that, and, if my memory is correct, he didn't play another game of competitive football until he went into the forces in 1958.

The six weeks before Dad's bandages came off dragged for us all. Everywhere we went we were asked, "Any news?" Everybody was batting for Dad, and there was so much expectation that he would be able to see properly once again. On the fateful day, Peter and I met each other on the way home from school, and we went into the house to find Mum crying in an armchair. She told us that they had removed Dad's bandages, but he could not see anything. Dr. Stewart-Scott had indicated that the prospects were not good, and he was almost certain that Dad's sight was irrevocably impaired. He would have to be classed as a registered blind person. It was tragic, and a bitter pill to swallow, especially for Mum and after all the hope and expectation.

The surgeon's prognosis was correct. Dad's sight was beyond repair and he was blind. The emotional struggle he experienced after that operation was of enormous proportions, and he was never the same man again. Despite attending Henshaw's Intsitute for the Blind for a number of years, where he attempted to train as a joiner, he could never settle. Just over two years later he decided that, to all intents and purposes, his working life was over. Unfortunately for the family, he then began gradually to look to alcohol as a release from the disappointment and bitterness that had begun to engulf him with each passing day. It was a tragedy; he was just 40 years old.

The Emergence of The Babes

When I attended my first reserve team game at Old Trafford in 1950, I could hardly imagine just what joy, elation and happiness the next seven and a half years would bring me. At the same time, I could never ever have imagined that it would also culminate in such horror, shock and devastation. What began as a wonderful journey on a roller coaster of happiness, ended so abruptly and without any warning whatsoever, and has affected me deeply ever since.

For those young players of Manchester United, the experience of being around the club between 1950 and February 1958 must have enriched their lives enormously. It was such a happy club, with everyone from the chairman and board of directors, down to the tea ladies and laundry girls, playing their part. Manchester United had finally become a real family. As those years passed, everybody, and that included the fans as well, had a feeling of real belonging, of being a part of something that was very, very special. Even as a young boy, I had a gut feeling that something was happening that was a joy to watch. It was something akin to a flower growing from a seed, and then blooming in the warmth of the summer sunshine.

The emergence of such fine talent brought an effervescence to the club. You have to remember that the country was emerging from the shadow and austerity of the Second World War. Rationing was still very much in evidence, even in the mid-1950s. It was common to see young men in military uniforms, even at football matches. Sport was an outlet from the drudgery of normal everyday humdrum life, and those doing their mandatory two years of National Service included many of the country's professional footballers.

Manchester United had finally finished as champions of the Football League in April 1952, the culmination of seven years' hard work by Matt Busby, Jimmy Murphy and the rest of their staff. There had been some near misses in the championship race, as they had finished runners-up on no fewer than four occasions between 1946 and 1951. Although United won the FA Cup in 1948, the league title seemed so elusive to them. Many of the players of that period had begun their careers before the war, and had effectively lost six of their prime football years between 1939 and 1945. John Aston had come through from the Manchester United Junior Athletic Club, which was the colts' team, or MUJACs as they were affectionally called. Stan Pearson, John Anderson and Henry Cockburn had the same United pedigree. Jack Rowley had been signed from Bournemouth, and Louis Rocca had brought over from Dublin a young inside forward by the name of John Carey. Allenby Chilton, originally from Durham, had been on Liverpool's books, and Rocca had managed to persuade him to join United in September 1938. Ironically, he made his debut for United against Charlton Athletic, just 20 hours before war was declared. All these players had lost six years of their United careers by the time normal competitive football was resumed in 1946. They went away and served their country in its time of need.

By the time they had won the 1951/52 championship, the team had grown old. Jack Crompton, Johnny Carey, John Aston, Allenby Chilton, Henry Cockburn, Jack Rowley, and Stan Pearson, were all into their 30s when the 1952/53 season began. But, even throughout that championship winning season, Busby's eyes were on the future, and he was already starting to introduce youngsters into the team. Over the next season and half, he gradually phased out the old guard, and names such as Ray Wood, Tommy McNulty, Bill Foulkes, John Doherty, David Pegg, Mark Jones, Jeff Whitefoot, Eddie Lewis, Billy Redman, Jackie Blanchflower, Duncan Edwards, Dennis Viollet and Albert Scanlon began to appear on the team sheet. It was the dawn of a new and exciting era.

In 1953, Matt Busby signed the Barnsley centre-forward, Tommy Taylor, for a record fee of £29,999. Busby was a canny Scot, and he didn't want to burden Taylor with a £30,000 valuation – an enormous sum back then. Instead he persuaded the Barnsley board to knock one pound off the fee, and he gave that pound to the tea lady who was serving in the boardroom while the deal was being done. It was a smart move.

In the 1952/53, the Football Association introduced a new cup competition for young players under the age of 19 on 1 September each year. It was the birth of the Football Association Youth Challenge Cup. The competition was open to all clubs, both professional and amateur, as long as they were affiliated to the Football Association. For the next five years, the FA Youth Cup became the sole property of Manchester United, an achievement that gave the club as much pride as winning any of the major trophies available at first team level. In that inaugural season the United Youth team was drawn against the minnows of Nantwich Town and won 23-0. It is still competition record, along with United's achievement of playing 43 consecutive matches without defeat.

The FA Youth Cup certainly captured the imagination of the fans. In the first leg of the first final, against Wolverhampton Wanderers at Old Trafford in April 1953, 22,000 supporters turned up to watch Matt Busby's future Babes demolish Stan Cullis's kids by 7-1. The final was over to all intents and purposes, but the following week a crowd of 14,000 turned up at Molyneux to watch the second leg, which finished 2-2. Manchester United's team for the two legged final in that inaugural FA Youth Cup season was: Gordon Clayton; Bryce Fulton, Paddy Kennedy; Eddie Colman, Ronnie Cope, Duncan Edwards; Noel McFarlane, Billy Whelan, Eddie Lewis, David Pegg, and Albert Scanlon. Only one member of that team, Bryce Fulton, failed to make at least one first team appearance in the First Division of the Football League. That final was the marker of things to come.

The 1953/54 season began badly for Manchester United. In the first eight league games United drew five and lost three, including a 2-0 derby defeat against Manchester City at Maine Road. More alarmingly, attendances had begun to fall, and for the fixture against Middlesborough on 9 September, a crowd of just 18,161 was present. Chilton, Aston, Cockburn, Pearson, Rowley, and McShane were still figuring prominently, though they were by now well into their thirties. The team was languishing fourth from the bottom of the First Division. Some directors were beginning to get more than a little restless, and this began to irritate Busby and Murphy. Although he had chairman Harold Hardman's backing, there were rumours of discontent among other directors.

What the doubters failed to see, though, was that below the first team, the younger United sides were doing well, and were packed with emerging talent. This talent was being nurtured, and taught to play a bright, open attacking style of football, with no fears. Junior players were playing in open age leagues, and were holding their own whilst gathering experience. This was no time for impatience, and Hardman was able to stem the unrest amongst fellow directors.

First team results continued to fluctuate, though by late October the team had climbed to mid-table respectability, occupying 13th position with 14 points, 12 points behind the leaders West Bromwich Albion. On 28 October 1953, Manchester United travelled to Scotland to play a friendly game against Kilmarnock, and Busby decided to take along some of his younger players, one of them being the emerging wing half, Duncan Edwards. Early in the match, Henry Cockburn, the veteran international left half, suffered an injury. Before the game it had been agreed that substitutes would be allowed, and so onto the field strode the young colossus, Edwards, to replace him. Duncan was just 17 years old, and had already made one First Division appearance some six months before, when on 4 April he had turned out against Cardiff City in a 4-1 defeat at Old Trafford.

Already playing regularly in the first team was the club's youngest ever debutant, wing half Jeff Whitefoot. At Kilmarnock, Busby also introduced Jackie Blanchflower and Dennis Viollet. The match at Kilmarnock was won, and the youngsters showed up well. Busby decided to give the youngsters a chance in United's next league game, against Huddersfield Town at Leeds Road on Saturday, 31 October 1953, and they came away with a creditable draw 0-0 which left United in 14th position in the league. There was a youthfulness about the team that day, which lined up as follows: Wood; Foulkes, Byrne; Whitefoot, Chilton, Edwards; Berry, Blanchflower, Taylor, Viollet, Rowley. The average age of the team was just 24 years – only Chilton and Rowley were over 30. It was the sign of things to come. That night the Manchester Evening Chronicle reporter Alf Clarke led with the historic headline in the Football Pink: *"Busby's Bouncing Babes Keep All Town Awake"*. Little could he have known that the name 'Busby Babes' would achieve immortality, capturing the imagination of generations of United fans. Over the next few years every football fan in the land would refer to the young United team as the Busby Babes, the name by which they are affectionately know today, and will be forever.

On 7 November 1953, the same team played at Old Trafford against a very experienced Arsenal. Only 28,141 were present to see the youngsters again play well, with 20 year old Jackie Blanchflower

scoring one of the goals in a 2-2 draw. The following week United travelled to Ninian Park to play Cardiff City, who were lying in 8th place in the division. The young United team produced a devastating performance which blitzed a far more experience team, and came home with a 6-1 win. On 21 November, United entertained Blackpool, the FA Cup holders, at Old Trafford. The Blackpool team included such celebrated players as goalkeeper, George Farm, Eddie Shimwell and Tommy Garrett at full back; Ewan Fenton and Harry Johnston, the captain, in the half-backline. But it was the Blackpool forward line that really took the eye, and made Blackpool such a wonderful team to watch: Stanley Mathews, Ernie Taylor, Stan Mortensen, Jackie Mudie, and South African, Bill Perry. A crowd of 49,853 were inside Old Trafford to see the young United team put on another scintillating performance in drubbing Blackpool by 4-1, with centre forward Tommy Taylor netting a hat-trick. This win pushed United up to 8th in the league, from mid-table mediocrity just 4 weeks previously.

The next two fixtures, away to Portsmouth and at home to Sheffield United were drawn,1-1 and 2-2 respectively, lifting United up to 7th position, still 11 points behind the leaders, Wolverhampton Wanderers. On 12 December, United travelled to Chelsea, where they lost 2-1 – their first defeat in seven games dropped them back two places to 9th.

It was now approaching the Christmas period, and United bounced back to beat Liverpool and Sheffield Wednesday, both at Old Trafford. United went nap in both games, winning 5-1 and 5-2, with goals shared between Tommy Taylor (5), Jackie Blanchflower (3), and Dennis Viollet (2). Although the team was playing well, this was not reflected in the gates at Old Trafford: only 26,074 turned up for the Liverpool game, with 27,123 at the Sheffield Wednesday match on the afternoon of Christmas Day. Nevertheless, the two wins propelled the team into 5th position in the league, and it seemed they were about to mount a serious title challenge.

On Boxing Day they won the return fixture with Sheffield Wednesday at Hillsborough by one goal to nil, and this was followed by at 2-1 victory at Newcastle, where almost 56,000 were crammed into St. James's Park to see Bill Foulkes hit the winner. It was his first senior goal, and something of a fluke – a clearance from inside his own half that caught the Newcastle goalkeeper standing on the edge of his penalty area as the ball flew over his head and into the goal.

On 9 January 1954, the team had a rest from league activity, and made the short trip to face Burnley at Turf Moor in the 3rd round of the FA Cup. The game was an eight goal classic, though United lost by 5-3 and went out of the competition. It was a typical January day in East Lancashire, with a strong wind blowing and cold sleet falling throughout the game. It was a fans' delight as the game ebbed and flowed in poor conditions. The young United team, while playing their part, were always chasing the game. United lost more through inexperience than anything else, but it was all part of the young team's learning curve.

The week after the Cup defeat at Burnley, there came another test for the young Babes – a home derby game against Manchester City. Busby rested Jack Rowley, and introduced a youngster in the left wing position: 17 year old David Pegg, who hailed from Doncaster. Pegg had enjoyed a run of 21 games in the 1952/53 season, and had played in the first three games of the current season before losing his place to the ageing winger Harry McShane, who in turn lost his place to Jack Rowley. Since Manchester City's return to the top echelon of English football at the start of the 1951/52 season, United had managed to beat their neighbours only once in five outings. This derby game was to be no different, ending in a 1-1 draw before 46,379 spectators.

The next fixture was against a team which has proved to be Manchester United's nemesis throughout their history: a club residing just 12 miles the north of Old Trafford, namely Bolton Wanderers. They have, and always will be, a tough, physical team to beat. The Bolton team of 1954 was certainly no different, and they steamrollered a young United team by 5-1 in front of 46,663 fans at Old Trafford, the second highest home gate of the season. Once again, it was a step up on the learning curve for the youngsters, who learned that as well as having an abundance of skill, there are games in which you have to prevail in the physical battle before you can express yourselves.

The team got back on the winning trail in the next two games, winning 3-1 at Deepdale against Preston North End, and 2-0 against Tottenham Hotspur at Old Trafford. Ray Wood, who had become the first choice goalkeeper earlier in the season, had picked up an injury against Bolton so the veteran Jack Crompton returned for both these games. Winger Johnny Berry took a knock at Deepdale, so for the Spurs game, Busby introduced another teenager: 19 year old Noel McFarlane (the father of Ross McFarlane who was to have a good career on the European golf circuit), a young Irishman from Bray in County Wicklow. It would turn out to be his only first team appearance for Manchester United. United beat Spurs 2-0, and were still in 6th place, but still trailed the leaders, West Bromwich Albion, by nine points.

Returning to Burnley the following week, Crompton remained in goal, but Berry replaced McFarlane. It didn't matter, as Burnley came out on top to win 2-0. The last game in February took the team to Roker Park, Sunderland, and the largest and most hostile crowd they had seen in their short careers. The youngsters seemed to revel in the atmosphere generated by 58,440 supporters, against a Sunderland team languishing just four places from the bottom of the league. United battled and played their way to a 2-0 victory to stay 6th.

Just one week later came the stiffest test so far for this new team – a visit from Wolverhampton Wanderers, the only team within striking distance of the leaders in the First Division, West Bromwich Albion. Wolves were managed by the autocratic Stan Cullis, who had been a Wolves player before the war. There was intense rivalry between the two managers, with Cullis attempting to emulate Busby's youth policy at Manchester United's. However, the quality of the youngsters in the United junior teams was far better than anything Wolves could muster, as endorsed by results in the FA Youth Cup. Cullis also had a bee in his bonnet about Duncan Edwards signing for Manchester United – he could never understand why the boy from Dudley went to United and not a local club such as Wolves or West Brom. The answer, as we shall see, was quite simple: Duncan didn't want to play for any of them!

At first team level, however, Wolves were a formidable team during that era. They boasted a whole host of international players: Bert Williams in goal; two uncompromising full backs in South African Eddie Stuart and Bill Shorthouse; a half back line of Bill Slater (who would turn out to be the last amateur to play in an FA Cup final when he played for Blackpool in 1951), England captain Billy Wright, and the big blond Ron Flowers. But it was their forward line that packed the punch. They had two fast, tricky wingers in Jimmy Mullen on the left, and the diminutive Johnny Hancocks on the right. Hancocks had to be seen to be believed. He was so small, standing just five feet three inches tall and he wore size three football boots. But this guy was effective, and what a shot he packed in either of those tiny feet. Without any exaggeration at all, Hancocks hit the ball as hard as any player in the history of the game. To illustrate just how effective he was, his career record with Wolves was 378 appearances and 168 goals – a startling striking rate for a wide player in any era, and you have to remember that he played in an era when robustness was the order of the day. For a little man he had tremendous skill, courage, tenacity, and the heart of a lion. Inside Mullen and Hancocks were three players who would all go on to play for England: Peter Broadbent and Dennis Wilshaw as tricky inside forwards, and Roy Swinbourne, a dashing centre forward who knew where the back of the net was. They were a fearsome outfit to play against.

The fixture didn't fire up the imagination of the United supporters, however, and although the attendance was better than many other Saturday home games, only 38,989 were in attendance. United were without vice-captain Roger Byrne, who was away winning his first international cap (beginning a run of 33 consecutive England appearances – some feat back then) for England against Scotland at Hampden Park. Into Byrne's place stepped 26 year old Billy Redman, who had limited first team experience, but had still played enough games in the 1951/52 championship season to collect a medal. The youngsters once again rose to the occasion, beating Wolves 1-0, with a goal from winger Johnny Berry. Wolves were a tremendous scalp for them to claim, and the win pushed United above Bolton Wanderers into 5th place.

The next two games were away against Aston Villa and at home to Huddersfield Town. At Villa Park, United drew 2-2, and went on to beat Hudderfield 3-1 – 40,181 fans turned up for that game, and it seemed that attendances were on the rise. United's faint title aspirations were dashed the following week, on 27 March, with a 3-1 defeat at Highbury. More seriously, United lost the prolific goalscoring centre forward, Tommy Taylor, for the rest of the season. He suffered a knee injury during the game and was nothing more than a limping passenger for most of the second half. For the remainder of the season, Busby elected to bring back the veteran full back John Aston, and play him at centre forward in Taylor's place.

Next up on the fixture list was Cardiff City at home, and Blackpool away. The Cardiff City game was lost 3-2, and once again United lost a very important part of the team when winger Johnny Berry collected an injury that would put him out until the last game of the season. More alarmingly, the gate for the Cardiff match was only 22,832. The game at Blackpool's Bloomfield Road was also lost, 2-0, as the Seasiders gained revenge for their drubbing at Old Trafford earlier in the season. At the top of the table, West Bromwich Albion had reached the FA Cup final, but their league form faltered, allowing Wolves to overtake them to claim top spot. The two defeats had pushed United back into 6th position.

Over the Easter weekend United played three games in four days against Charlton and Portsmouth at Old Trafford, and then away at the Valley in the return fixture against Charlton. On Good Friday, 16 April, Charlton were beaten 2-0 in front of 31,876. The following day United enjoyed another 2-1 win, over Portsmouth, before a gate of 29,663. It was the last home game of the season. Those two wins pushed United back into 5th place, as Wolves led the division by a solitary point from West Bromwich. There was a sparse crowd of 19,111 at Charlton's expansive Valley ground on Easter Monday, where United lost to a single goal. The last game of the season was away to Sheffield United, and United finished on a high note, winning the game 3-1. United finished 4th in the First Division with 48 points, edging out the Lancashire duo of Bolton and Blackpool who had the same points but a worse goal average. The champions were Wolves who ended the campaign four points ahead of local rivals West Bromwich Albion. However, West Brom had some consolation just a week later, collecting the FA Cup at Wembley by beating Preston North End 3-2 in a rather dour and drab final.

For Manchester United it was a season that had begun erratically. But since the game at Huddersfield on 31 October 1953, the young team had acquitted itself well. They had played 27 league games, winning 15, drawing five, and losing seven. The signs were there though that this young team had it in them to do well in First Division football. They played some wonderful football in some of the games. Of the teams who finished above them, they had played Huddersfield Town twice, winning once and drawing once; the games against West Brom had been lost early in the season, but they had beaten Wolves, the eventual champions. Down at Old Trafford, the blue touch paper was being lit. The Babes were growing up, and it wouldn't be too long before this young team came of age.

My First Team Debut

Anticipation, expectation, excitement, happiness, frustration, disappointment, despair, anger, depression – emotions that have, at one time or another, been part of the 'match day drug' throughout my life. Football, to those of us that found a real true love of it, and the 'special love' that is Manchester United, has affected us in so many, different ways. Certainly, it affects our emotions, the way that we think, our rationality, our objectivity, our perception. It affects our calendar, our finances, and most of all, our relationships! Even today, after more than fifty years of going to watch my beloved Manchester United, I still experience the same sensations that I encountered as a nine year old boy attending his first senior match, especially when my journey is taking me to Old Trafford. There have been so many changes in football during my time, and the Old Trafford stadium is unrecognisable from the ground I first entered at the age of five to watch my first reserve game. Following Manchester United is a drug – there is certainly no known cure! It is not something that you can just cast aside like a worn out coat – once you have had the 'experience', it is with you for life. These past fifty years have provided me with a fascinating roller-coaster of a journey, one that has brought me to the pinnacle of happiness, and has also seen me plough the troughs of despair.

My senior journey began on a lovely warm, sunny Wednesday evening. It was 1 September 1954, and the occasion was Manchester United's second home game of the 1954/55 season. For the previous four years I had attended most of the reserve team games that were played at Old Trafford, and many junior and youth games as well. As I was growing up, my schoolmates would tell me how their fathers had taken them to first team matches at Old Trafford or, for the City fans, at Maine Road. To say that it used to get under my skin and make me jealous goes without saying. I was football daft, and United mad! I would read, listen, and watch anything to do with the game. My spare waking hours were spent playing football, anywhere and everywhere that I possibly could.

Hearing my school friends on Monday mornings, as they recounted their tales about the previous Saturday's match, used to hurt me so much, though I would never show that hurt openly. I resented the fact that their fathers could take them to matches, whereas mine could not. In 1952, my dad's sight had started to decline, and by 1954 had gone almost completely. My granddad, to whom I was very close, would never take me along to a match, and there were a number of good reasons for that, which I understood. He lived in another part of the city, and he had his own circle of friends who attended matches with him; plus he sat in the main stand.

Throughout the summer of 1954, all the odd coppers I had accumulated from odd jobs were lovingly and meticulously saved in an old jam jar. Unbeknown to any of my family, I had found a hiding place for this jar behind some bricks in one of the walls in the backyard; I had disguised it well. That season had begun for United with a home game against Portsmouth, which they had lost 1-0, and as usual I had had to listen to my young mates going on about how they had enjoyed their trips to the match. My feelings were so hurt, and I was so desperate to watch United's first team. I was determined that come hell or high water; I was going to attend the next home game. In those days, there was no floodlighting at Old Trafford, and the mid-week games in the early part of the season kicked off at 6.45 in the evening. The next home game happened to be on Wednesday, 1 September 1954, and the opponents were Sheffield Wednesday.

The excitement built up inside me from the Monday of that week, and I formulated a plan in my young head – which, unfortunately, did mean me having to tell a few white lies to Mum and Dad. I told them I would be late home from school on the Wednesday evening as I was going to altar boy training, and then on to the school youth club which was in rooms underneath the Holy Family church, in All Saints. The church is still there today. I told them to expect me home around half past seven, knowing full well that I was going to be much later than this. Before leaving for school that Wednesday morning, I furtively removed the bricks from the wall in the back yard, emptied my jam jar into a small purse that I had, and slipped it into my pocket. One of my chores was to take my young sister to Holy Family school at All Saints each weekday morning, and after leaving her in the school yard, I would make my way over to York Street and St Augustine's boys' senior school, where I had just started my first term. Mum worked in the mornings, but she would collect my sister from the infant's school at half past three in the afternoon. Counting my coppers as I walked with sis to school, I found I had the princely sum of two shillings and fourpence – about 12 pence in today's money.

The classrooms in the senior school consisted of three old prefabricated buildings, with two classrooms in each building. Outside was a small area of playground which opened onto a large concrete rectangle, which was affectionately named 'the big pitch' – a sacrosanct area on which the older boys in the school would play football. As a youngster fresh into the senior side of the school (the junior school was housed over Oxford Road in the Cavendish school building), it was always your ambition to be regarded as good enough at football to be invited to play on 'the big pitch'!

From my classroom in York Street, I could see the huge tower and clock of the Refuge Assurance Company building, rising above the other commercial premises that lined Oxford Street. The excitement building inside me throughout the morning was making knots in my stomach – my mind was solely on going to the match that evening, and my lessons that day were irrelevant. The passing time was like a slow ebbing tide for me, every minute was like an hour as I watched the huge fingers of the Refuge clock turn slowly through every minute of every hour. At three o'clock, at playtime break, I slipped out through the little school gate and into York Street, carried on over Sydney Street, past the Old Garrett Ragged School Mission, then past Duncan and Fosters bakery, and on into Grosvenor Street. I had to be very careful not to bump into my mother who would be going to collect my sister from school at that same time. Turning right, I crossed Oxford Road into Cavendish Street, and on to the bus stop that was across the road from All Saints Park. I stood back and away from the bus stop, hidden in one of the recesses in the black sooted building that was then the Manchester College of Art. Fortunately, the bus that I wanted, the number 49, arrived fairly quickly, and I was able to board it without a problem. After paying my penny ha'penny fare to the conductor, I was at last on my way to Old Trafford, the place of all my dreams.

Even at that young age, I could sense that this was something different – not like attending a reserve team game. The bus meandered its way up Stretford Road past all the familiar landmarks. It must have been around four o'clock when the bus stopped just past the Trafford Pub at Warwick Road. Not too many people were around at that time. Things were a little different back then; there were no street vendors along Warwick Road, there was no souvenir shop, and there was no Manchester United Development Association building. As always, I crossed Chester Road and made my way down Warwick Road, then across the railway bridge. Being at Old Trafford for a first team game for the first time was like finding El Dorado!

First, I walked around the ground. Even though I had attended many reserve, youth, and junior games at the ground, it was always a source of fascination for me. The Scoreboard End, and the Stretford End, were only small terraces back then – the two main features of the ground were the Main Stand (where my granddad sat) and the Popular Side, which was affectionally known as the Glover's Side because of the huge Glover's Cables factory and its two imposing chimneys that were behind. I was able to see which entrance I would be negotiating to get into the ground – and found that the entrance fee was just sevenpence for a junior – about three pence in today's currency. (Interestingly, the adult admission in those days was only one shilling and threepence – about seven pence today.)

I continued around the ground walking past the Stretford End, and then alongside the Main Stand, with the railway to my right. The pedestrian bridge which crosses the railway line at the Stretford End wasn't there in those days (it was built prior to World Cup games taking place at Old Trafford in 1966). As I approached the main entrance, the windows of the dressing rooms were open up above me, and the smell that for me has become associated with Old Trafford permeated the air ... liniment.

I continued on and walked on down past the ticket office and back up Warwick Road to Chester Road. The shop on the corner of what is now Sir Matt Busby Way, facing the Ford dealership was then a grocery shop, and next door was a fish and chip shop. My tummy was telling me I was hungry, so I joined the small queue that had begun to form and bought fish and chips, wrapped up in newspaper, for the sum of sixpence – 3 pence today. I devoured those fish and chips while sitting on the steps of the old Dog and Partridge pub – the site of The Bishop's Blaize today.

As I ate, more and more people were beginning to arrive, and I found it all so exciting and fascinating – this was certainly not like any reserve team match I had attended. After my sumptuous meal I walked back down Warwick Road again, and as I got close to the railway bridge, I could hear music. It was played by a band of four buskers, and there was a one legged man standing with the help of crutches, holding out an old flat cap collecting any donations that the passing fans were willing to give. That band became an integral part of the match day scene at Old Trafford for many years afterwards. I stood on the corner of what is now the Old Trafford forecourt, just past that railway bridge, and saw Jack Rowley, Allenby Chilton, and Stan Pearson walking down Warwick Road chatting to the fans, and passing me as they turned left and walked along the wooden railway fence towards the players' entrance.

The person I was really waiting for was not too long in arriving, and I spotted him as he wheeled down the road on his old bicycle. I couldn't take my eyes off him. The fans were shouting to him as he pedaled along, and he acknowledged them with his shy smile. Duncan was just short of his 18th birthday then, and as he wheeled past me, I took off after him. Down to the old ticket office he went, freewheeled along, and when I got close up to him, I just stood there, absolutely mesmerized by his presence as he lined the kids up and signed their books and pieces of paper. I didn't get his autograph that evening, but it was so thrilling for me just to stand near him. How I idolized that boy. Even at that tender age, he had such a great presence and aura. After signing everybody's books and papers he tied his bicycle to the lamppost by the ticket office with a piece of string from his pocket, and disappeared through the small wooden door.

I made my way round to United Road, and the junior turnstile, and joined the small queue of kids. There was a real buzz around the place now, and I could hear the newspaper sellers pitching their voices. It seemed as though I queued for ages, and I willed the turnstile door to open. When it did there was a big cheer and the click-clack, click-clack of the rotating turnstile could be heard as the gateman quickly attended his duties, and the queue moved along fairly fast. I handed over my sevenpence, and once inside there was the programme seller. I duly parted with fourpence - two pence today – I had my first senior programme in my hand.

The covered enclosure of the Popular Side had a tunnel in line with the half way line. I reached the terraces through that tunnel, and at last I was inside the ground. I stood there momentarily, taking it all in, and for some reason I recall that everything looked much larger to me. The pitch was like a bowling green at this time of the season, and its greenness was accentuated by the background of the dark main stand. The terraces had gangways freshly painted with lines, and the picket fence around the perimeter had also seen a new coat of paint during the summer break. People were already entering the ground from all directions as I made my way down the steps to the front of the terracing on the half way line. I leaned against the wooden perimeter fence, staring directly across the pitch to the players' tunnel. I read through the programme so many times, marvelling at all the information it contained – so different from the reserve team's single page programme that I had become so accustomed to seeing.

Today, those old programmes really paint a picture of times past. It was nothing as grand as the modern glossy magazine; there were adverts for tailors, florists, raincoat manufacturers, boot polish, and dubbin; British Rail advertised its fares for United's next away game. As I looked at the team sheet in the centre pages of the programme, the ground was filling up around me, and the buzz was becoming louder and louder. My stomach churned with the excitement of the whole occasion. A funny little fellow was dressed in a red and white evening suit with tails, and a red and white bowler hat; he was carrying a large red and white umbrella adorned with red and white balloons. While smoking the obligatory cigarette, he began walking around the pitch. From the brim of his bowler hat, red and white painted corks hung down in front of his eyes. I was to find out later that this was Jack Irons, the unofficial Manchester United mascot.

The Beswick Prize Band had arrived, and began to set up on the half way line, over in front of the Main Stand, and they began playing a selection of military marches as the crowd whistled along. Then, just before they formed up to march around the pitch, their lovely young female cornet player, Sylvia Farmer, sang the Judy Garland number, 'Over the Rainbow'. This was all so different for me and I was engrossed. White smoke drifted over the top of the Main Stand opposite me, as a the trains from London Road and Oxford Road stations arrived, their carriages packed with fans, who alighted onto the little platform facing the back of the Main Stand. The smoke formed into white billowing clouds, and as it drifted over the top of the stand it moved so gently downwards, towards the pitch, then dissipated just as quickly as it came.

Even though I had previously been to well-attended Youth Cup games, the ground today filled more than I had ever seen before, and I was just so excited – here I was at last seeing my heroes 'in the flesh'. For the record, a crowd of just 31,317 was in attendance that evening. Five minutes before the 6.15 kick-off there was a feeling of anticipation among the youngsters on the perimeter picket fence. I still remember the people that were stood around us: ordinary working class folk, many still in their work clothes, obviously having come straight from their place of employment. There were four or five miners behind me, their faces a clean white, but around their eyes were signs of the coal dust from their work in the bowels of central Manchester. Yes, there was a coal pit at that time situated in Manchester, not a short walk from the city centre. There were large numbers of servicemen present, dotted throughout the crowd, and resplendent in their uniforms. The majority would have been serving out their obligatory two years of National Service. There were also plenty of females in attendance!

Looking across to the players' tunnel, I could see the team in their red shirts begin to trot out – they were led by skipper Allenby Chilton, and as they came onto the pitch, a huge roar engulfed the ground. In those days, the United team always went to the Scoreboard End to do their 'kick-in'. There was no such thing as a 'warm up' in those days. I looked around and spotted Big Duncan, pushing the ball in a triangle with Jeff Whitefoot and Chilton. I could see Colin Webster, Jackie Blanchflower, Jack Rowley, Denis Viollet and Johnny Berry, all firing balls at Ray Wood, and over in front of the main stand Bill Foulkes and Roger Byrne were passing a ball up and down the line to each other. Jack Froggatt skippered Wednesday that night, in a team that also contained his brother Redfearn, and future United player Albert Quixall.

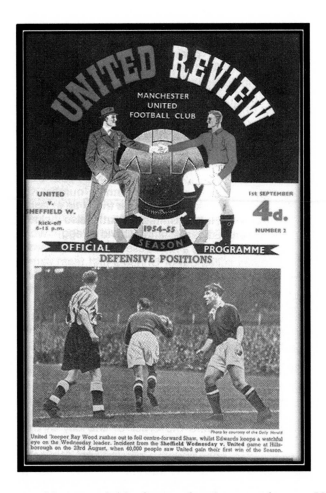

United 'keeper Ray Wood rushes out to foil centre-forward Shaw, whilst Edwards keeps a watchful eye on the Wednesday leader. Incident from the Sheffield Wednesday v. United game at Hillsborough on the 23rd August, when 40,000 people saw United gain their first win of the Season.

The game passed by so quickly for me, but I was so happy. United won 2-0, both goals scored by Dennis Viollet. All too soon it was over, and time to make my way home to face the wrath of my parents. I left the ground and had my first experience of negotiating Warwick Road with thousands of others, as the crowd bottlenecked close to the bridge. At times my feet never touched the ground, and I was carried along by the sheer mass. Once over the railway bridge, the congestion eased just as quickly as it had started, and I made my way to the bus stop where I found lots of 'specials' waiting to be filled. The chatter on the bus was all about the game, and people were smiling as they exchanged their views After getting off the bus at All Saints, I walked home in the twighlight, along Grosvenor Street, wondering what fate was waiting for me – it was shortly after nine o'clock.

I turned into Royle Street, and entered the house. My mum and dad were beside themselves with worry, and had earlier sent my brother out looking for me. I think they were relieved more than anything that I was safely home. Dad was cross with me, no two ways about that, and at first he didn't believe that I had been to the match. It was only when I pulled my creased programme from my pocket and passed it to Mum, that they believed me. Although I got an earful from my parents, I was allowed from that day onwards to attend first team matches at Old Trafford on my own. It was a happy, happy young boy that went to bed that night, and an even happier young boy that proudly related his experiences to his schoolmates the following morning. No longer did I ever feel left out.

It is so interesting to look back on that evening and reflect that out of my original two shillings and fourpence, I had spent threepence on bus fares, sixpence on fish and chips, sevenpence on entrance, and fourpence on a programme – a total of one shilling and eightpence – a total of nine pence in today's money. Oh, that I wish the kids of today had the same opportunity.

That was the beginning of what match day meant to me. Even today, I like to get to the ground relatively early – I still feel that excitement, the expectation, the buzz, the rush of adrenalin. I saw the great Babes team, and the happiness those boys brought to United. I plunged the depths of despair with Munich, and then watched as the club was rebuilt. I experienced the heady days of the mid-1960s, and what I call the period of 'Busby, Best and Bachus'. The European dream was fulfilled on that May evening in 1968, and Matt Busby had achieved his goal. I saw the break up of a great team and the mediocrity that followed, and then the despair of relegation. The candle was lit again by Tommy Docherty, 'The Doc', and I hoped that a new young team was being built, only for it to founder on Doc's infidelity. I watched the years of Sexton, and the boredom, frustration and disappointment that they brought. Ron Atkinson briefly sparked, but again foundered on his own shortsightedness, and finally I watched as Alex Ferguson arrived, and once again the sun has shone, the seeds have grown, the harvest has been reaped, and we were all fulfilled.

Unfortunately, it hasn't always been roses along the way. The off the field politicking, and the direction the club was taken by the Edwards family does hurt and sadden me. Both father and offspring have so much to answer for, not only at Old Trafford, but also (especially in Martin's case) for the commercialisation and direction which football in England has been taken.

We now have an American family that owns Manchester United. I doubt that they will ever feel what the genuine Manchester United fans feel for their beloved club. This family has managed, in such a short space of time, to do what many have tried, but have so spectacularly failed. And that is to systematically destroy and divide what used to be the 'Manchester United Family'. They will never feel what I feel for the Club, their experiences will never mirror mine, nor those of thousands of people like mine. How could they? Even now, four years after their acquisition, they do not understand what Manchester United is all about – and they never will. Certainly, they won't be here forever, but after they have departed, they will never be remembered with reverence and gratitude, as the Davies and Gibson families are. Nor will any of them ever be remembered with the fondness felt for those such as Ernest Magnall, Louis Rocca, Walter Crickmer, Joe Armstrong, Bert Whalley, Tom Curry, Harold Hardman, Billy Inglis, Ted Dalton and Les Olive. The sad thing is that I doubt if they even know who those people are.

Doctor Garrett's Memorial Home

After I had attended Manchester United's match against Sheffield Wednesday in September 1954, I felt on a par with my schoolboy contemporaries. No more would I have to listen to them regaling me with their tales on a Monday morning. I could now go to United's games on my own, without the help of an adult chaperone, so in essence I now felt superior to my school friends!

Just three weeks later, on Saturday 25 September 1954, I made the trip to Maine Road to see a Manchester derby game for the very first time. I had been to Maine Road several times before, but only to watch reserve or schoolboy matches. This was an entirely different kettle of fish, and I was filled with adrenaline for several days before the big match. It was to be the first game I attended with my schoolmate, Brian Walsh. It was hot and sunny, so we walked to the ground, arriving early to take our place on the perimeter wall at the Scoreboard End. A crowd of 54,105 turned up that day to see Manchester City triumph 3-2, but the game has special memories for me for two reasons.

The first reason is that I saw, for the first time, an opposing player who was to become an icon to me – someone on whom I tried to model myself. His name was Bernhard Karl Trautmann, commonly known as Bert, the Manchester City goalkeeper. He was awe-inspiring, and he was the difference between the two teams that sunny afternoon. He had natural blond hair, stood over six feet tall, and had a wonderful physique. His agility had to be seen, and he very rarely hoofed the ball upfield, preferring instead to throw to a player who was in a position to receive, and who could use it more constructively. I couldn't take my eyes off Trautmann, performing just in front of me that afternoon. I was mesmerised.

The second reason was a wonderful goal scored against Trautmann that afternoon. At the time, the young Northern Irishman, Jackie Blanchflower, was a promising inside forward, who had progressed into the United team the previous season, in the famous game at Huddersfield. Midway through the second half, United were 2-1 down against City. They were attacking the Platt Lane end of Maine Road. Blanchflower received the ball in midfield, midway between the half-way line and the edge of the Manchester City penalty area. He had his back to goal, some 35 yards out, when the ball was played in to him. Pirouetting, he unleashed a shot with such venom from his right foot that it flew as straight as an arrow, and over the top of Trautmann's head. Even today, I rate it as one of the greatest derby goals I have ever seen. Still, United lost the game, and losing to City was to become a regular occurrence over the next 12 months.

I was so happy that I was now able to attend first team home games, and I looked forward to Saturdays with so much anticipation. Immediately after the Sheffield Wednesday game I had watched United beat Charlton Athletic, 3-1, when for the first time I saw the famous Charlton goalkeeper Sam Bartram. Sam was another great 'keeper and had a great personality. I remember his vivid ginger hair and huge hands. I was now beginning to see players that I had only seen in newspaper and magazine pictures. They were all so instantly recognisable to me.

On some Saturday mornings, when United were not at home, I would sneak off around lunchtime, and go and stand on the porch steps at the Queen's Hotel, which was on the corner of Piccadilly and Portland Street; the Thistle Hotel now stands on that site. My reason for being there was that the Queen's was used by teams from the south and Midlands who were visiting the North West. They would arrive at the Queen's on the Friday evening before the game, and on Saturday mornings the players would gather in the foyer as they were leaving for the ground where they were to play that afternoon. It was easy for youngsters to get autographs, as there would sometimes be two, or even three, teams staying at the hotel.

The week before my first derby game, I stood in the porch of the Queen's hotel in mid-morning. Through the large wood and glass revolving doors, I could see people gathered in the hotel foyer. With me on the steps were a dozen or more youngsters, all clutching autograph books or soccer annuals. The word was that the Arsenal team was inside – they were due to play Preston North End at Deepdale later that day. Every so often I would go to the revolving door, press my nose against the glass and peer inside. I did this a number of times, until once I saw a tall man beckoning for me to come inside. I was a little timid at first, but after he beckoned me a second time, I pushed through the huge revolving door, and rather sheepishly walked towards the big man. I stood there in front of him shaking like a schoolboy who had been summoned to the school headmaster's study.

The man spoke to me in an accent I hadn't heard before. He asked me to walk across the road to a gentleman's outfitters named Dunne's (it is still there today!) to collect a small package for him. He promised that while I was gone, he would have all the Arsenal team sign my book. I didn't need to be asked twice. Off I ran, pushing hard through those revolving doors, running down the steps of the hotel, and then helter-skelter across Piccadilly. On entering Dunne's, the shop staff looked at me with the utmost suspicion. However, when I told them what it was I had been sent for, the male shop assistant disappeared, then returned with a large, grey flat cap, which he then meticulously wrapped in green and white paper bearing the Dunne's emblem. Once this task was completed, he handed it over to me, and off I went at breakneck speed, back to the Queen's Hotel.

Up the steps I went, not bothering to talk to any of the kids, clutching the small parcel in my hand, and I rushed through those revolving doors. I found the big man and handed the package to him. As I stood in front of him, he reached into his pocket and pulled out a silver half-crown, which he handed to me, smiling, along with my autograph book, duly signed by the whole of the Arsenal team. He thanked me for running his little errand, and I was thrilled as I made my way back outside the hotel. The kids outside were so envious of me, and I now didn't have to wait around to get any autographs. The half-crown was burning a hole in my pocket already – it was like being handed a fortune. The man for whom I had run the errand was none other than Jack Kelsey, the Wales and Arsenal goalkeeper. The flat cap that he had purchased from Dunne's was obviously to be used to keep the sun out of his eyes during the future games that he played.

On another occasion, I was standing waiting for autographs outside the main entrance at Old Trafford, after a reserve team match against Blackpool Reserves, early in the 1954/55 season. A small black-haired man appeared from the doorway and asked me if I would run an errand for him. He wanted me to run down to the United Café which was on Warwick Road (I believe the Development Offices stand on that site today), and with the half-crown he had given to me I was to buy him a packet of 20 Turf cigarettes. Of course I was off like a sprinter, and within five minutes I was back with the cigarettes. I remember correctly the packet cost one shilling and sixpence, and the shilling change was pressed back into my hand by the player, who was none other than Scotland international, Jackie Mudie.

In October 1954 my world came crashing down around me when I learned that I was being sent away from home for six weeks. It broke my heart at the time; I just did not want to go. Nineteen fifty-four was a hard year for my mother, as she struggled to cope and readjust to my father's blindness, while having to raise three children. My brother, Peter, turned 14 years old on 6 September that year, and my sister celebrated her second birthday in that same month. I was in my tenth year, and was a bit of a handful for her, mainly because I was outside playing football most of the time, and never wanted to a game to end.

In 1950, Manchester Education Committee had implemented a scheme whereby children could be sent away to north Wales for a convalescing break of between six and eight weeks. Most of the kids who were sent there inevitably came from the run down, inner city areas. The poor housing conditions which still prevailed meant that many of those inner city children ended up with upper-respiratory problems, and I was no different. The break, away from the poor housing and unclean Manchester air helped enormously. I was sent to a convalescing facility in Conway, called Dr. Garrett's Memorial Home. It was my first time away from home, and the very thought of it, at such a young age, terrified me.

I left Manchester on Tuesday, 19 October 1954. On the previous Saturday, Manchester United were involved in a quite extraordinary Division One game at Chelsea's Stamford Bridge stadium. Chelsea scored five times that afternoon, as an 18 year old debutant amateur by the name of Seamus O'Connell scored a hat-trick! O'Connell was to stay an amateur, playing a total of 17 games for Chelsea, and scoring 11 goals, before returning to the amateur game. He went on to win two FA Amateur Cup winner's medals with Bishop Auckland, and one with Crook Town. But his five goals at Stamford Bridge that day were not enough, as Manchester United scored six! Almost 56,000 spectators were inside the ground to see another hat-trick, this time by Dennis Viollet. Two goals from Tommy Taylor, and one from Jackie Blanchflower, made sure that maximum points went back with the Reds to Manchester.

On the Tuesday, Mum and Dad took me to the Manchester Education Committee offices, at the junction of Jackson's Row and Deansgate in the city centre. I didn't want to go and there were tears and tantrums before Mum finally cajoled me onto the waiting 'charra'. (Charra was the name for a coach in those days, abbreviated from the word charrabang.) It was raining heavily as the charra pulled away and began its four hour journey to north Wales, and I sat with my nose pressed against the window feeling alone and rejected. The bus entered Chester Road and as we passed Warwick Road I could see the Old Trafford stadium momentarily. I wondered if I would ever see it again!

This was all a new strange experience for me. The coach stopped in Chester for what is now termed a 'comfort break', and by this time it had gone dark. I fell asleep and before I knew it I was waking up outside the place that was to be my home for the next six weeks. We were ushered into a large dining room and fed an evening meal of macaroni and cheese before being taken to the dormitories, and put to bed. Our clothes were taken away, and we were given fresh clean pyjamas – something that I had never worn in my life. I cried myself to sleep that night. For the first three days, we were kept on bed rest and this greatly irritated me a lot, making me disruptive, to say the least. I hated having to stay in bed all day and night. But after the third day we were allowed up, and issued with a standard uniform of a grey roll neck sweater, grey short-legged trousers, grey socks and black boots. We were then transferred to a large house, where we were accommodated for the remainder of our stay. The upper half of the house contained the boys' dormitories; the lower half the girls'.

In the evenings mixed activities included learning how to dance, play acting, singing and charades, while daytime activities, indoors and out, kept us all occupied. The housemaster was a wonderful fellow who kept the boys in line, while the housemistress took charge of the girls. We were taken on long walks when the weather was good, and these would inevitably see us climbing the hills above Conway that looked out across Colwyn Bay to Llandduno and the Great Orme. At this time the boxer Randolph Turpin owned a hotel at the top of the Orme. On two or three occasions each week the housemaster would take us to a piece of flat ground not to far from the home, where we would play football. He would use cricket stumps to mark the goals, but for me it was like playing at Wembley! It was a grassy field, and after we had divided into two teams, I would invariably take my place in goal and imagine that I was Bert Trautmann. I just loved those afternoons, and I could throw myself about on the grass keeping the ball out of the goal. I really did enjoy myself, and I must have made an impression, because whenever the teams were being selected, I was always one of the first to be picked.

By the middle of my stay I had settled down, but I always had this nagging fear that I had been sent away and would never return home. Lunchtime was always important, as this was when the mail was given out. I had never received a personal letter in my life before, but two weeks into my stay I finally had that experience. During my stay in Conway I received just two letters from home, written by my mother, and that was the only way that I found out how Manchester United were doing. She would tell me what the results of United's matches from the previous couple of weeks, and tried to reassure me that everything was fine at home. She said that the time would soon pass and I would once more be back at home with her. Sadly, her words at that time never eased my fears.

Tuesday was always a bad day for me, as this was when kids who had come to the end of their stay at Dr. Garrett's would go home. New arrivals would be there for all to see the following morning. I had calculated in my little head that my own departure was due on 30 November, six weeks after I had left Manchester. The night before you were due to leave, your 'uniform clothes' were taken from you just before bedtime, and the clothes that you had arrived in were then placed on a chair at your bedside, ready to be worn on your journey home the following day. If this didn't happen, then you knew you weren't going home. On Monday, 29 November, I was all excited, so sure that I would be leaving the following day. But it was not to be, and I was heartbroken. I had calculated the minimum stay time only, and I realised I could be there for another two weeks.

Although I had enjoyed many of the activities, particularly the walks, hill climbing and football, deep down I resented being there. I got into more than my fair share of scrapes and fights during my stay, and I was often disciplined by the housemaster. A lot of the kids I tangled with were older than me but it made no difference; I wasn't afraid, even though several times I got a beating, which was done out of sight of the nurses and the housemaster. The nurses were all local Welsh girls, and would speak to each other in Welsh; this used to infuriate me because if they didn't want you to hear or know something, they would switch from English into their native tongue. It was also there that I nurtured an intense dislike for macaroni and cheese – it always seemed to be on the menu. Even today I can't stand the stuff!

The majority of the kids who had arrived with me in October duly left for home on 30 November. All that morning I was disruptive, and surly to everybody around me. Even playing football that afternoon did not pacify me, and my mood carried on into the evening. The following morning I had quietened down a little, but it was the afternoon that really took my mind off everything. The housemaster gathered the boys together after lunch, and told us we were being taken to the television room to watch a programme that would be on for most of the afternoon. There were rumblings of unrest among the boys – we wanted to go walking or play football. However, when we were all assembled in the television room, in front of a large projection screen, we were told we were to watch a live football match from Wembley Stadium – England were playing the world champions, West Germany. The rumblings of discontent soon evaporated.

West Germany had won the World Cup in Switzerland the previous summer, while England had been eliminated by Uruguay in the quarter-finals. This was going to be an acid test for them. I made sure I was sat on the front row, with an uninterrupted view of the screen. What an afternoon it turned out to be at Wembley for England, who won convincingly, 3-1, with goals scored by the three inside men, Roy Bentley, Ronnie Allen and Len Shackleton. It was Mathews, Finney and Shackleton who took my eye with their intricate dribbling and ball skills. They tortured the German defence that afternoon. I was elated! England had beaten the world champions, so in my young head surely England were the world champions now? But there was no real consistency from the England team at the time, largely because the side was selected by an FA committee. To illustrate the point, for the next international match against Scotland, in April the following year, the selectors made seven changes to a team that had thrashed the world champions just five months earlier.

On the Monday evening of 7 December 1954, I jumped for joy when I returned from the bathroom to find my own clothes neatly piled upon my bedside chair – I was at last going home. I was so excited, and I don't think that I slept a wink that night; every minute ticked by so slowly for me. At six o'clock the following morning the nurses made sure we were awake and had washed and brushed our teeth. Breakfast was at seven, and eight we were loaded onto the charra for the journey back home to Manchester. My fears had disappeared, and I could not wait to see my mother again. It was around midday when that bus pulled into Jackson's Row in the centre of Manchester, and there she was, waiting for me with my young sister.

Off home we went, where my father was waiting for me. I was so happy to be back home. I caught up with all of the news, and of course United was the most important topic for me. They had been having mixed fortunes while I had been away on convalescence in Wales, winning three games, drawing two, and losing two. However I was delighted to learn that they were in second place in the league, just one point behind the leaders, Wolves. I did have some disappointment, though, when I found out it would be almost three weeks before I would be able to go to another first team game. Still, I was back home, back with my family and friends – I was so happy again!

Derby Days 1955

The year 1955 duly arrived, and there were big changes to be seen in Royle Street, Chorlton-upon-Medlock. On the opposite side of the street, eight families moved out to the Wythenshawe, Brooklands, Benchill and Baguley areas of Manchester. Gone from the streets were the kids that I had grown up with, kids from the Burns, Keogh, Prince, Stretch, McNamara, Bowman, Cleary, and Pearson families. Within days of these families' departures, their houses were demolished. These events gave my mother hope that our family too would be moved to decent housing in a much better locality. Unfortunately it was a false dawn for her, and it would be another five years before her dream was realised. The remainder of the houses that were left in Royle Street were to stand, and remain inhabited, for another 12 years.

My mother's frustration and anger at our housing situation often boiled over, and it used to hurt me to see her so upset. She desperately wanted to get her children away from the locality. There were five of us living in a little two up, two down terraced house, which was in relatively poor repair. My brother was now almost 15 years old, I was ten, and our baby sister was just over two. We needed larger accommodation, especially as my brother was now well into his adolescence, and would be leaving school in the coming July. There was little or no privacy throughout the house. The landlord was a mean little man who had no intention of making any repairs to the property, but would, without fail, be knocking on the front door at six o'clock every Friday evening to collect the rent. This was indicative of the many landlords who owned slum properties in the run down areas of Manchester's inner city. There was little or no legislation to stop them preying on the poor families that occupied their properties. They charged relatively high rents, and non-payment by their tenants was in many cases met with violence. It wasn't until the middle 1960s, when the London landlord, Peter Rackman, was brought to book for enforcing the very same procedures, particularly against immigrants, that new legislation was introduced to stop these horrible practices.

My father had started his rehabilitation as a blind person. He was to be placed in Henshaw's Institute for the Blind at Old Trafford, with the object of training to be a carpenter. He also began taking Braille lessons at the Manchester Institute for the Blind in Deansgate. One of the services the Institute for the Blind provided was free portable radios for blind people, with batteries replaced free of charge. This meant that our old radio could now be abandoned, and there would be no more trips for me to the accumulator shop on Brunswick Street.

The big problem for my mother was that Dad was happy to keep the family where we were. He simply didn't want to move, and it caused a lot of friction. He would not accept his father's offer of help, and my mother used to get upset with this attitude. Dad found it really hard to come to terms with his disability, and he retreated into a world of self-pity. Even though he was receiving help from the various blind institutions and associations, he was of the opinion that there was no other case worse than his own, and he became very, very bitter.

One morning in early January 1955, quite unexpectedly, a few of my classmates and I were told to report to Cavendish School on Loxford Street, All Saints. We had no idea what this was all about. When we arrived, and reported to Mr. Silver, the Cavendish schoolmaster, we were informed that we were about to take our 11 plus examination. We'd had no warning about this, and for most of the party from St. Augustine's, it was coming a year earlier than we had expected. Nonplussed, I threw myself into the examination and felt no nerves, nor any worries. The examinations were held over two days, and we looked upon the exercise as time away from our own classrooms.

On the Manchester United front, Christmas 1954 saw the team lose both games against Aston Villa, following a draw the previous week against Portsmouth – it wasn't good, just one point from six. However, on a very cold New Year's Day in 1955, I made the trek to Old Trafford to see United beat Blackpool by 4-1 to get back on to the winning trail. United were drawn away at Elm Park against Reading in the 3rd round of the FA Cup, where they managed to scrape a 1-1 draw.

The replay was scheduled for the following Wednesday afternoon at Old Trafford. As usual, the draw was made for the next round on the following Monday, and what a plumb it was: Manchester City versus Manchester United - what an incentive for United to win the replay. There were no floodlights at Old Trafford then, so the Reading replay would kick off at 2pm. I made up my mind that I was going to take half a day off school to go and watch, something that would become common practice over the next few years. I never mentioned anything to my parents, or to my brother. At lunchtime, instead of heading off to the school canteen service, which was on Upper Brook Street, I slipped out of school gate unobserved and headed for Old Trafford. It was a bitterly cold day and there were long periods when heavy snow fell throughout the game. United won in a canter by 4-1, but I remember that game for seeing the "Gunner", Jack Rowley, score a goal at the Stretford End with as venomous a shot as you will ever see. The ball never rose much above the ground, but it flew like a rocket, and the Reading goalkeeper did not move until he picked the ball out of the back of the net.

United were due to meet Manchester City in the 4th round of the FA Cup at Maine Road on 19 February. Fate decreed that just a week before they would meet at Old Trafford in a league game, when I was full of excitement at seeing my first derby game on home turf. My enthusiasm transmitted itself to our neighbours in Royle Street, and next door at number 12, Mrs. Betty Taylor began knitting me a red and white scarf. Upon the red and white sections she knitted the names of the United players – red names on the white background, white names on the red background. Just up and across the street at number 15 was a family by the name of Connell. They had a daughter Sally, who by this time was 23 and was a United fan. Sally got hold of an old Air Raid Warden's rattle from her place of work, and painted it red and white before giving it to me. It made an enormous racket, and my parents forbade me to use it in the house. With a new scarf and rattle, I now felt like a proper supporter.

The twelfth of February 1955 is a date I will always remember – for one thing, heavy rain and sleet fell throughout the day. I couldn't wait to get to Old Trafford to watch United gain revenge on our near neighbours. After doing my chores in the morning, there was no hanging about, I was off. I was so full of optimism as I travelled my normal route to the ground, and when I arrived I followed my ritual of walking around and around the outside of the stadium until the turnstiles were opened. That I was soaked to the skin never bothered me at all. Instead of taking up my usual place on the 'Glover's Side', down at the front by the picket fence, because of the rain I decided to stand on one of the crash barriers half way up the stand. This afforded me a great view as the ground began to fill. In this position I was surrounded by adults, and there were a large number of Manchester City fans in the immediate vicinity. There was a lot of good natured banter between the United and City fans, but no animosity. Cigarette smoke permeated the air and there was a lot of talk about the forthcoming Cup tie, to be played at Maine Road the following week. I was brave enough to join in with some of the banter and got my leg pulled unmercifully by the City fans.

When the teams entered the pitch from the tunnel, the heavy rain was still falling and the pitch was a glue pot. My optimism was dampened when play began because Manchester City really did play well, and eventually overpowered the United team. They certainly won the physical battle early, and dominated United, so much so that by half-time (if I recall correctly) City were 3-0 ahead. My heart sank. If there was a bright spark for me, it was in the performance of Bert Trautmann who was magnificent. He stopped anything that came his way, and two saves in particular were from blockbuster shots from Duncan Edwards. City's slick interpassing and movement was too good for United, and everything they fired at goal seemed to go in. The United fans around me were silent, while the City fans were cock-a-hoop.

The second half was no better for the Reds, and City scored twice more. The 5-0 scoreline hurt me immensely. However it could have been much worse, as City also had two second half goals disallowed.

The journey back home was made in silence, and the bottom lip quivered. By the time I got home *Sports Report*, the weekly results service on the BBC Light Programme, was in full swing. Dad had listened to the results and couldn't believe that United had allowed City to trounce them so comprehensively on their own ground. For me it was too much, and the tears erupted as I hated hearing criticism of 'my' team. Going into school on the following Monday was a nightmare for all young United fans, and the kids that supported City were quickly on our case to ram the result down our throats – as they were entitled to do. It did cause some friction in the school playground and there was a coming to blows with a young boy named Michael Carragher because I couldn't take his incessant ribbing. Both of us ended up with bloody noses and a trip to Mr. Faye's office for 'six of the best' for fighting in the school playground.

All that week I couldn't wait for Saturday's FA Cup tie with City to come around. Again I built my enthusiasm and optimism up as the week progressed. Mrs. Taylor had finished my scarf and Sally Connell had finished painting my rattle – I was all set. That Saturday morning was cold as I set off from home to walk to Maine Road. I had my warm topcoat on, but wrapped around my neck my precious scarf served two purposes – keeping me warm and showing my allegiance. The walk took me up to Oxford Road, and then on to Cambridge Street where I turned left and headed down past the Manchester Dental Hospital and on to Lloyd Street. I passed the Robin Hood pub on the left, which was rumoured to be a drinking hole used by the City players, and finally I arrived at Maine Road. This was much different from the league game that I had attended there the previous autumn. There were many, many more people around. Maine Road was a lot bigger than Old Trafford in those days, and it took me time to circumnavigate the ground. It was place I could never get used to, and I felt it had a cold, dreary look.

I took my place in the queue at the Platt Lane End of the ground, and the turnstiles opened earlier than normal. I paid my entrance and ran straight down to the front, immediately behind the Platt Lane End goal. It was a great vantage point. The only seating area in the stadium in those days was away to my left hand side. Like at Old Trafford it was known as the Main Stand, the place where the City season ticket holders religiously took their place. There were three tunnels at intervals alongside that side of the ground and it was from the middle one that the players would eventually emerge. Away to my right hand side was a huge spion kop terrace that arced in a quarter moon shape – it was enormous and uncovered. Straight down the ground behind the opposite goal was the Scoreboard End with its tiny brick scoreboard. I thought that it was vastly inferior to the structure which served the same purpose at my beloved Old Trafford.

The stadium filled steadily and at 2pm the Beswick Prize Band appeared. They alternated between each stadium on Saturdays. Jack Irons, the United mascot, appeared walking around the perimeter of the pitch, pan-faced as insults were hurled at him by the City fans. The crowd grew and grew and grew! It got to the point where the police instructed all the children that were pressed against the wall to climb over the top and sit on the cinder track. The scene was like an army of ants clambering all over some unfortunate prey. I didn't need asking twice, for I was up and over in a flash, and was sat directly behind the goal. Wow! What a view I would have, and how close I was to the players. At five minutes to three there was an enormous roar as Roy Paul, the City captain and Wales international wing half, led his team out onto the pitch. Trotting towards me was Bert Trumann – I was mesmerized and couldn't take my eyes off him. What a presence this man had, and what an effect he had on young schoolboys like me. I watched as the City forwards fired in balls at him: Hayes, Review, and Clarke; it all looked so nonchalantly easy for the big German.

The game kicked off with United attacking the Platt Lane End. It was a far different performance from United from that I had witnessed the week before at Old Trafford. It was united who dominated, but they just couldn't find a way past Trumann. When they eventually did, from a rocket of a shot by Edwards, the ball thumped against the crossbar and rebounded far away and to safety. Trumann was magnificent and he was the difference between the two teams. As is often the case in matches like this, it was the defending team who broke away and scored the first goal – the scorer being Don Revie (who would later manage the notorious Leeds United team of the 1960s, and then the England national team) for City. For all of United's pressure they went in at half-time 1-0 behind. The second half was a repeat of the first, as United pressed and pressed. Midway through the second half there was a flare up inside the centre circle which involved Allenby Chilton, the United skipper and centre half. Whatever happened, I couldn't tell, but the result was that Chilton was sent from the field of play by the referee. Later, I learned it was for what the referee would term "foul and abusive language". It was now a huge uphill task for United, and in the dying minutes of the game as United pressed for an equalizer, once more they were caught by a quick City break. The move ended with Roy Clarke, the City left winger, rolling a simple ball across the goalmouth which allowed Don Revie to score both his and City's second goal. My young heart sank. They hardly had time to restart the game when the referee blew his whistle for full-time. United were once again out of the FA Cup and my heart was broken once more. I had now been present at three derby matches and City had triumphed every time.

The dismissal of the United skipper, Chilton, virtually ended his career at Old Trafford. The week after the FA Cup defeat he was skipper of the team that lost at home to Wolverhampton Wanderers, and for the next two games he was suspended. But the Wolves game proved to be his final first team appearance in the famous red shirt. Mark Jones stepped up from the reserve team to fill his place, and held on to it from that moment on. In the FA Cup tie at Maine Road another United player's first team career also came to an end, that of the 'Gunner', Jack Rowley. United had two outstanding young left wingers in Yorkshireman, David Pegg and Manchester boy, Albert Scanlon. The 'Gunner' had a prolific career at Old Trafford, and it would have been even better had the war not claimed six years, as was the case for Chilton.

Both Chilton and Rowley had played such a huge pivotal part in the emergence of Busby's team of Babes. They were the experience, the tough, hard 'minders', and they kept the exuberant youngsters in check in the dressing room, never allowing their feet to get above ground. They had done their job and Matt Busby was thankful to them, allowing both to move on without a transfer fee being involved. Chilton left to be player-manager of Grimsby Town, and Rowley took up the same appointment at Home Park for Plymouth Argyle. They left the United fans with many memories, and as I myself have grown older, I consider it a great privilege to have watched these two old stalwarts play.

The movement of both Rowley and Chilton away from the club brought the average age of the United first team down to just below 22 years. For the more knowledgeable fan, the remainder of the 1954/55 season gave some insight into what was about to happen at Old Trafford. Of the 14 fixtures after the FA Cup tie, six were won, six were drawn, and only two games were lost. The team finished 5th in the table, five points behind the champions, Chelsea. It was ironic that Chelsea's last game of the season was at Old Trafford against this emerging United team. It was a game I attended, and I saw the young United side form a guard of honour in front of the tunnel to applaud the Chelsea players onto the field. The youthful Reds prevailed that afternoon by 2-1, and little were the Chelsea club to know that it would be 50 years before they tasted league success again.

There was a significant milestone in my own life in the spring months of 1955. I was desperate to play football for my school team. Goalkeeping seemed to come pretty naturally to me, and I knew no fear. On the gravel and concrete of the school playground I would throw myself around in attempts to stop any ball that came my way. There were so many times that my mother had to tend to my bruises and cuts once I got home from school. But they never deterred me, nor interfered with my passion for the job. St. Augustine's was not a big school and not too many of the kids who did play football relished playing in goal. It could be a daunting prospect to say the least. Every

Wednesday afternoon the specially-chartered buses would arrive at the school gates, and off we went to play football at Platt Fields Park. I just loved those afternoons. For a small boy like me those full-size goals – eight feet high by eight yards wide – were enormous, and I conceded so many goals, but I just loved the job and loved the game.

In April 1955, I learned that I had failed that 11 plus exam that I had taken in January. I wasn't too upset, though I shared a little of my mother's disappointment. However, that tinge of regret was more than compensated for when one afternoon I was called to my schoolmaster's office to be told by Mr. Avery that I had been selected for the school's third team, to play a match the following evening against a school named Bishop Billsborough, who hailed from Moss Side. I could not get home quickly enough to tell my parents. I felt so proud, and told everybody in the street and anybody else that would listen to me of my achievement. Sleep didn't come easily that evening, and I imagined every scenario possible, hoping that this would be the start of my road to playing one day for Manchester United.

The following morning I collected my old bulbous football boots (they were two sizes too big for me, but who cared?) and I made my way to school. The excitement and adrenalin coursed through my young body. As I always did when I was excited, I looked out of the classroom window every few minutes, watching the huge clock on the Refuge Assurance building tick the time away so slowly. I willed the hands to go round quicker! The boys who had been selected to play in the school's teams were always released from classes early so they could make their way to the parks or recreation grounds where they would be playing. The schoolmaster would distribute the Manchester Corporation red tokens that gave free passage on the buses, and off the team would go.

The game was being played on what we termed our home ground, Hough End Playing Fields in Withington. The team assembled, and there was plenty of enthusiasm, chatter and excitement as we set off. The boys who played in the team that evening included Eddie

McDonough, Barry Nixon, Brian Walsh, Joey Howard, Johnny Concar, David McGinty, Peter Cassin, Michael Carragher, Peter Hardiman and David Shea. Three of those players, McDonough, Howard and Concar, went on to have decent careers in non-league football years later. However, that evening we were a motley looking crew as we made our way to Hough End.

Back in those days there were no changing facilities at these parks, and we changed behind the goal. For me, the thrill of donning the school playing kit for the first time still gets to me even today. I will never forget it – I had arrived. The Bishop Billsborough boys were rather bigger than us, and we were steamrollered in that game by 8-2, but it didn't matter to me. The goal was huge, and I'd had a large number of goals struck past me, something that in the next year was to be a regular occurrence! However, I had played in the first competitive match of my life, and my appetite had been whetted for more. I was so proud to tell Dad and Mum all about the game when I got home, and even Dad's gentle ribbing about the number of goals I'd conceded went right over my head – I was on cloud nine.

The weekend after that game my mother walked me to her sister's home in Hulme to watch my first ever FA Cup final. Manchester City had reached Wembley to face Newcastle United, and a ding-dong battle for the famous old trophy was anticipated. Aunt Gertrude and Uncle John had a small 12 inch black and white television set in their ground floor flat, and we all gathered around it. The pre-match events really did fascinate me, as the community singing was conducted by a large man in a white suit, stood high on a rostrum in the centre of the pitch. I was to learn later that this man was Sir Arthur Cager. I recall the gusto with which the fans entered into the spirit of it all. The waving of their programmes and the resonance of their singing was so different to what we see at FA Cup finals today. I will never forget hearing the Cup final hymn *Abide With Me* for the first time. It sent a shiver down my spine, and it has never ceased to do that since.

I watched in awe as the teams appeared side by side from the famous old tunnel, City resplendent in their blue and white tracksuits, the Geordies in their famous black and white striped kit; the walk to the half-way line in front of the Royal Box; the teams being introduced to the Duke of Edinburgh. The whole pomp of the occasion made a lasting impression upon my young mind, and taught me how important Cup final day is. Within 45 seconds of the game starting, City found themselves 1-0 down to a wonderful headed goal from the legendary Newcastle centre forward, 'Wor Jackie' Milburn. It was the quickest goal ever scored in an FA Cup Final, and a record that stood until 1997, when Roberto de Matteo scored for Chelsea after just 43 seconds against Middlesborough. The record books show that Newcastle triumphed for the third time in five years that afternoon by 3-1. I'll never forget hearing *The Blaydon Races* roar out across Wembley Stadium, and then as the game ebbed into the dying minutes, the Geordie fans blasting out the old song *Now Is The Hour*. I watched as the Newcastle team led by skipper Jimmy Scoular climbed the steps to receive the FA Cup from the Queen and how, after they had come down from the Royal Box, the Newcastle players hoisted Scoular high onto their shoulders, and he raised the FA Cup in a victory salute to the Newcastle fans. For me it was all so exhilarating, and I can still see those scenes even today.

The day after the FA Cup final, the season was over, and all thoughts of football were put away. The cricket season was here, and in the space of 24 hours our boyhood dreams of becoming great footballers were replaced by thoughts of being England's next great batsman or fast bowler. That's the way it was back then – the FA Cup final marked the last day of the football season, and once the match was over, so was football for the next three months. There were a number of professional footballers who also excelled at cricket, and who made a living from both games. Freddie Goodwin, the tall United reserve wing half, played cricket for Lancashire; Ken Grieves, the Bolton Wanderers goalkeeper, was one of Lancashire's finest ever slip fielders; Derek Ufton, the Charlton centre half, played for Kent during the summer; and there were many more instances of other players doing the same thing.

Indeed, well into the 1970s there were men who were both professional footballers and cricketers, including the United centre half Arnie Sidebottom, who starred for Yorkshire, and who played test cricket for England.

The summer of 1955 was hot, and when the summer school holiday arrived in July one of the most popular places to spend an afternoon was the swimming baths. For the kids in my area the nearest pool was on High Street, Chorlton-upon-Medlock; it was known as High Street Baths, and was owned by Manchester Corporation. It is still there today, but High Street was renamed Hathersage Road some years ago. The building, which featured prominently in the television series *Cracker*, was a wonderful facility with three pools – one for males, one for females and one for mixed bathing. Most of the kids in my area didn't own swimming costumes, but you were allowed to swim in the buff in the male pool.

That summer we learned of an open air facility in Didsbury, called The Galleon Open Air Swimming Pool. The Galleon Hotel stands on the site today. Back then it had a wonderful Olympic size swimming pool and diving boards at different heights. It was a mixed facility so costumes were a must! It was idyllic to be there when the sun was beating down, but on my very first visit, in late July 1955, something else attracted me to the place. It was the middle of the afternoon, and two young men came into the pool with a football, and proceeded to play head tennis in the shallow end. I was mesmerized to watch the 17 year old Bobby Charlton, who at that time had just broken into United's reserve team, and 20 year old Billy Whelan, a young Irishman who had made his debut in the United first team just months earlier. Both were instantly recognisable to me, and after a while they had attracted a large crowd of children. To everybody's surprise, Charlton started throwing the ball to various children, who returned it to him, then Whelan joined in the fun. Soon both Whelan and Charlton were throwing the kids, me included, over their shoulders into the pool. I found it hard to understand both of them – Whelan spoke with a soft Irish brogue and Charlton had a pronounced Geordie accent.

When they'd had enough of the frolicking around with the kids, I watched them join a group of young men who were sat on the grass banking just above the shallow end of the pool with a number of young ladies. My heart raced – there was Tommy Taylor, David Pegg, Wilf McGuinness, and little Eddie Colman. I couldn't take my eyes off them. These were my heroes, players I watched week in and week out. Shyly, I edged closer and closer to where they were sitting. Big Tommy Taylor, such a good looking lad who would never have looked out of place on a movie set, never mind a football field, called out to me in his strong Yorkshire accent. Both he and David Pegg were laughing, and they asked me if I was one of the kids who hung about outside the main entrance of Old Trafford – they actually remembered me! Pegg took me to a small kiosk and bought me an ice cream, at the same time buying one for himself and his girlfriend. Later, they were all in the pool, frolicking about with the young kids, and there was much laughter and banter between them all. It was the start of weekly ritual for me until the new season began, and which continued over the next couple of summers.

Oh, what a happy set of young boys they were. Full of fun, living for the moment, and all friends together. Their numbers at the Galleon Pool would fluctuate each week but invariably it was the same routine. I smile today when I hear the accusations which are so often made about Bobby Charlton's personality, and the names that he is saddled with. Whenever I hear such things my mind always goes back to that young, happy, carefree 17 year old boy, and the way he played with the kids in that pool, and the way he and the other young players handed out the weekly ice cream cones. Some of those boys were already football stars, but there were no big egos, no pretentiousness, no bigging it up. Just a wonderful bunch of 'boy next door' characters enjoying their youth and their health.

Charcoal, Talacre and Wine!

If there had been a disappointment for the United board when reflecting on the 1954/55 season, it was in the attendance figures for home fixtures. Contrary to the myth that is spouted in the modern era, United haven't always had the support in the large numbers that we see today. Back in those days it seemed as though fans were very selective as to which games they wanted to attend. United's average home gate for that season for the 21 league games and one FA Cup tie played at Old Trafford was just 33,933. Gates fluctuated depending upon who the opposition was, or how the team was faring. To illustrate what I mean, immediately after the two derby defeats against Manchester City in February 1955, United played Wolves at home. Wolves were probably the glamour team in English football at the time, but even so, on the Saturday of the game only 15,679 turned up to watch United lose by 4-2.

Attendances didn't really improve at the beginning of the following season either. The first home game of 1955/56 was against Tottenham Hotspur on a Wednesday evening, drawing just over 25,000 fans. The United team had an average age of just 22 years, and the regular turnout consisted of Ray Wood in goal; Bill Foulkes and Roger Byrne at full back; Jeff Whitefoot, Mark Jones and Duncan Edwards as the half back trio; and Johnny Berry, Jackie Blanchflower, Tommy Taylor, Dennis Viollet and David Pegg making up the forward line. There had been signs towards the end of the previous season that this young team was beginning to gel. As they gained experience, so did they gain confidence, and they began to express themselves in the manner that the manager and his coaches had envisaged when they first implemented their youth policy some ten years before. What they were looking for now was consistency.

There was a conveyor belt of young players rolling steadily along below first team level, and these teams were virtually unassailable. The FA Youth Cup had become Manchester United's own property. The

Youth team had certainly captured the fans imagination, and during the previous three years some of the gates at their home ties exceeded some first team attendances. When the competition began in the 1952/53 season it was no surprise that for the first two seasons the final was contested between Manchester United and Wolverhampton Wanderers, and it is interesting to see the progression of players from the United teams which contested those two finals. Of the 19 United players who appeared in those games, 15 would play at First Division level.

Of the team that started the 1955/56 season, Foulkes, Byrne, Whitefoot, Jones, Edwards, Blanchflower, Viollet and Pegg all came through United's junior ranks. In reserve there were also players like Ian Greaves, Geoff Bent, Eddie Colman, Ronnie Cope, Wilf McGuinness, Billy Whelan, Eddie Lewis, Albert Scanlon, Shay Brennan, Gordon Clayton and Freddie Goodwin, most of whom, had already appeared in the first team sporadically. There was more talent developing in the 'A' and 'B' teams, and in the junior team. Busby's policy had at last borne fruit from the seeds that he had sown.

The 1955/56 season began in mid-August and I missed the first two home games because for the first time in my life, I was taken away on a family holiday. Not I might add, by my own parents, but by my dad's sister and her family. I idolized Aunt Mary and she took a great deal of interest in my well being. She and her husband, Jack, had a daughter the same age as me, named Myra, and also an adopted daughter, named Margaret, who was four years younger. We all got on so well. The holiday had come out of the blue because it wasn't until a week beforehand that I knew anything about it. Mum and Dad had kept it a secret from me, because after the way that I had reacted when going away to Dr. Garrett's in Wales they didn't want me throwing any tantrums, especially as the holiday would clash with the start of the 1955/56 football season!

The truth was that I was happy to go, especially as I would be with Aunt Mary and her family all the time that I would be away from home. Mum took me up to Blackley, where Aunt Mary lived, on the Friday evening and I stayed at her house on Benmore Road overnight. The following morning, suitcases and bags in hand, we all trooped down to Rochadale Road and caught the number 60 bus to Cannon Street in Manchester city centre. We walked down Cannon Street, crossed Corporation Street and then over Cateaton Street and then up the steep driveway to what was then Manchester's Exchange railway station.

I smile now when I recall that Saturday morning. Unlike today when families jet off to destinations all over Europe, and indeed even further afield, in those days going away on a two week holiday to the seaside resorts of north-west England or north Wales, was a hugely exciting experience. The station platforms that morning were absolutely packed with people, just ordinary working class families escaping from the drudgery of everyday life for just a week, or perhaps two weeks, each year. Late July and early August were the times when most of the cotton mills and industrial factories in the various Lancashire towns closed down for 'Wakes Week'.

'Wakes Week' originated before the industrial revolution. When agricultural workers worked a long six day week (animals and crops could not be just turned on and off like a factory switch), Sundays were a day of rest and for attending church. Each year, churches and parishes would hold a special day of celebration in honour of their patron saints. Parishioners would stay up all night, keeping vigil, and so these celebration days became known as 'wakes'. There were many of these wakes days throughout the year, but with the advent of the factory system, this tradition died. Factories enveloped more and more agricultural land, and people left the agricultural environment for industrial work where factory owners were less generous than landowners, and had little time for the old traditions.

In 1871 bank holidays were introduced, and inexpensive public transport systems (trains and horse drawn buses) enabled families, for the very first time, to spend days out in the local countryside, or at the beach. Day trips became very popular, and it was a relief for families to get away from the sooty, grime-ridden mill towns. By the middle of the

1870s 'Wakes Week' had become a term that signified the closing down of a town's factories and mills for one week, and it was obligatory for the workers to take holiday time during that week. The various small mill towns had their own particular weeks. From this time onwards, seaside holidays became very popular with families, who would save up throughout the year to could afford to travel to resort towns such as Blackpool and Southport. They would stay in the many boarding houses that had sprung up due to this 'Wakes' phenomenon. It was a tradition that would carry on well into the latter part of the 20th century.

On that Saturday morning in August 1955 we were headed for the north Wales coastal resort of Talacre. The rail journey would take us to Chester where we would have to change trains, and then on to Prestatyn where we would have to catch a bus to our final destination. Other families were going on further down the north Wales coast to the resort towns of Rhyl and Llandudno. The trains were full, and many people stood in the train corridors for the whole of the journey. It was a long trip, and like my journey to the north Wales two years previously, it took over four hours. Talacre is a small place, and at that time, apart from the village where the local people lived, holiday accommodation was in hundreds of little wooden chalets that littered the road along the sand dunes. Throughout the holiday season, and particularly in 'Wakes Weeks', these chalets were always fully booked.

There would be thousands of families from all over the North West of England staying in these seaside resorts, and Talacre was no different. On either side of our chalet were a large family from Liverpool and a family from Hindley near Wigan. It was an idyllic two weeks, with lots to occupy the children. We rose early and didn't go to bed until it was dark. We played football, cricket, rounders, and other games with all the other kids. Aunt Mary and Uncle Jack took us on excursions to Prestatyn and Rhyl, and it was such an adventure for us all.

Just before we left for that holiday, I had begun training to become an altar boy at St. Augustine's. Under the supervision and guidance of the young Father Doran, I had begun to learn all the Latin responses for the Mass, and was quite competent. However, for the actual serving of the Mass, I was still very much a novice. It wasn't anything spiritual that had taken me along the path to becoming an altar boy – it was the fact that the altar boys had a football team! They played against the altar boys from other parishes in the diocese, and also against the boys from the Cathedral, St. John's in Salford. For me, it was another chance to play 'proper football'. But being an altar boy, albeit a novice would get me into trouble at Talacre.

The altar boys at St. Augustine's were a motley crew – cherubic while carrying out their sacred duties in the main church, but rascally and mischievous in the vestry and surrounding areas. Their was a pecking order amongst them that went by age, and you walked in fear of the senior altar boy, a 15 year old lad named Tommy Hopkins. There were several 'initiation ceremonies' for a new kid to go through before he became an accepted member of the altar boy fraternity. One involved eating small charcoal blocks. These blocks were used for burning, inside what was called the sanctuary lamp; incense would be added to produce the sweet smoking smell that was emitted as the altar boy or priest swung the lamp.

My charcoal initiation came minutes before 11 o'clock Mass one Sunday morning, when I was held down by the other altar boys as charcoal was stuffed into my mouth. There was no time to clean my mouth out as the parish priest, Father MacLernon, entered the vestry, and we all had to line up and follow him out into the church and then on to the altar. I couldn't get rid of the horrible taste of the charcoal, and I had swallowed some of it. Every altar boy was expected to receive Holy Communion whenever they served at Mass. When the time came, we all knelt on the altar steps as Father McLernon began to give out the Blessed Sacrament. He stood before me holding the large golden ciborium, and took one of the wheat hosts in his fingers and as my cherubic face looked up towards him. I opened my mouth and stuck out my tongue, onto which he would place the host. What he saw must have shocked him, because his face changed instantly and he nearly dropped the ciborium. My tongue and mouth were pitch black from eating the charcoal. When Mass was over, and we got back into the sanctity of the vestry, he really gave me a dressing down; it was strange – there were only two of us stood there – the rest of the altar boys had scarpered very quickly.

My aunt and uncle were staunch Roman Catholics, and on the morning after our arrival in Talacre we all went down to the local Catholic church to attend Sunday Mass. We arrived in the little local church some 15 minutes before the Mass was due to start, and some five minutes later the local priest came onto the altar and announced to the congregation present that he was short of an altar boy to serve the Mass, and appealed for a volunteer. Of course my aunt shoved me forward, and I was pressed into service.

Upon entering the vestry I found another young boy dressed in the normal cassock and cotta. The priest, in his defined Welsh accent, introduced us and said that this young boy had never served Mass on his own before – what he didn't know was that neither had I. The priest and the other boy did something that I intensely disliked, a throwback to my days at Dr. Garrett's. They started talking to each other in Welsh – I hated it. It got my hackles up, and immediately I mistrusted and disliked the other boy. We went out onto the altar with the priest and began the Mass.

It was a bit of a comedy when I look back on the events that happened. As the Mass began I found it extremely hard to follow the priest's pronunciation of the Latin, and so my responses were slow and often labored. The priest looked around at me in annoyance on several occasions – the Welsh boy may well just have been dumb, as there were no responses from him. I hated being where I was. The priest read the epistle, and I had to move the large altar missal from the right hand side of the altar to the left hand side so that the priest could continue and read the gospel. The missal was a huge heavy book resting on a wooden plinth, and I collected it in both hands and started to move away from the altar, down two steps. Unfortunately for me I lost my footing, as I descended and went arse over tip down those two steps, losing my grip on the missal; the missal flew one way and me the other. I collected myself together, rescued the missal and plinth, and went around to the gospel side of the altar, placing them where they were meant to be. The glowering look that I received from the priest told the whole story – I was not a popular boy.

At St. Augustine's, one of the other initiations was during the offertory. When the altar boys collected the wine and water, you had to take a crafty swig from the wine without the priest or the congregation seeing it. Up and until that Sunday morning in Wales, I had never tried to do this, but I decided this would be my day. Both I and the Welsh boy went over to the table where the two silver cruets containing the water and wine sat on a silver platter. As the Welsh boy stood behind me obscuring my view from the congregation, I bent, lifted the cruet containing the wine, and took a mouthful. The congregation didn't see me and the priest didn't see me – but the Welsh boy did, and he let out a roar in Welsh that alerted everybody to what I had done. There was a murmur throughout the church, and at the same time I spun around and spat the wine into the Welsh boy's face. Pandemonium ensued and without further ado, and after a few choice words from the priest, I was banished from the altar in disgrace.

I returned to the vestry, removed the cassock and cotta, and made my way back into the church and out through the main doors, hastily followed by Aunt Mary, Uncle Jack, and cousins Myra and Margaret. To say they were embarrassed by what I had done, and were not pleased, is an obvious understatement. For the rest of that day I was in disgrace and made to stay inside the chalet. It hurt me that I had upset Aunt Mary, but they knew that I had not wanted to serve that Mass at all.

The following day all was forgiven, and it was then that holiday really began. Uncle Jack and I roamed the dunes and the beach at Talacre. Part of the sand dune area was a dis-used military rifle range and we spent many an hour locating spent brass cartridge shells which were buried in the sand. Uncle Jack explained to me the different calibre of ammunition that the shells had come from, and by the end of the holiday, I had more than 100 of these.

We went on day trips to Prestatyn, Rhyl and Llandudno, and it was all so different than the time that I had spent at Dr. Garrett's in Conway. We spent a lot of time socialising and playing games with the families who were holidaying in the adjoining chalets. It was all so much fun and the weather was glorious throughout those two weeks. The clean air of the seaside did wonders for me, and I had enjoyed every minute of the holiday – apart from the church incident.

All too soon it was time to repack our suitcases and head back home to Manchester. We left early on Saturday morning, 3 September 1955. Again, the railway stations were crammed with families returning to their homes in Lancashire. We arrived back in Manchester in the middle of the afternoon, and I stayed in Blackley with Aunt Mary and her family overnight. Of course my immediate thoughts upon being back in Manchester were of how Manchester United had fared that day. My feeling of happiness turned sour when I listened to Sports Report on the radio, and learned that once again United had lost to Manchester City in a derby game, this time by 1-0 at Maine Road earlier that afternoon. It didn't matter to me that this was United's first loss of the season: I had yet to see them take a single point off City in a game.

The following morning we all went to Mass, and afterwards Uncle Jack took me to watch his local club, Victoria Ex-Serviceman's, play against the Clough Hotel. The game was played at what used to be the ground of Miles Platting Swifts, which was situated at the top of Monsall Street in Miles Platting, Manchester. Like the ground of Newton Heath Loco,the site was often mistaken for the original site of Manchester United's (or rather Newton Heath's) first ever ground on North Road, just a few hundred yards further on from Monsall Street. The Miles Platting Swifts ground was situated in a natural bowl of an arena, and had grassy slopes all the way around. On this particular Sunday morning, there were several thousand people in the ground, on those slopes. Sunday amateur football was very popular back in those days, and the best pub or club teams attracted a good following. It is no exaggeration to say that on any given Sunday morning or afternoon during the football season, the top amateur teams in Manchester and the surrounding areas would have as many as two or three thousand people packed around the touchlines. There were many fierce rivalries between local amateur teams in those days, and those local leagues were a haven for Football League club scouts, particularly from the lower divisions.

After the game Uncle Jack and I returned back to Benmore Road, and all too soon I was making my way back home to Royle Street in Chorlton-upon-Medlock. There was a tear in my eye as we said our goodbyes, and I slowly walked, suitcase in hand, back down the hill, to the bus stop on Rochdale Road. I'd had two wonderful weeks away in the fresh air of north Wales, and even today I still have so many happy memories of my very first holiday. It had been over two weeks since I had seen my mum, dad, brother and sister. Of course, as soon as I arrived home they all wanted to know how much I had enjoyed myself. Not surprisingly, the story about Mass on the first Sunday was conveniently left out of my tales.

On the Brink of Success

The week following my return from Talacre, it was back to school after the summer break. I did look forward to it, as I hadn't seen some of my friends for several weeks, and it meant that I would be playing competitive football for my school again. On the Wednesday evening before the new school term, I made my first visit that season to Old Trafford, and saw United defeat Everton by 2-1. Everton were something of a bogey team for United in those days, and had won both league games between the clubs the season before. They were an ageing team, but experienced, so to see United's young team win with goals from Blanchflower and Edwards, who played at inside left. It was a happy young boy who left Old Trafford that evening.

The following Saturday it was back down to earth again, as United lost 1-0 to Sheffield United at Bramall Lane. In later years Bramall Lane was a ground I disliked visiting; it doubled as a Yorkshire county cricket ground, hosting a number of first class cricket fixtures each summer. There were only three spectator stands on the football side of the ground; one touchline adjoined the cricket pitch and no spectators were allowed on this side. It was always a place that I felt was devoid of any real football atmosphere. While United were losing in Sheffield, Manchester City beat Cardiff City by 3-1, which promised an interesting return to school on the following Monday morning.

At this stage of the 1955/56 season, United were lying in seventh position after an inconsistent start. Wolves were the form team – after just six games but they had scored an astonishing 21 goals, conceding only seven. But it was Blackpool, who had played one game more, who were early leaders at the top of the league. Already the pundits were speculating about who would lift the famous old First Division championship trophy – Hughie Kelly of Blackpool or Billy Wright of Wolves. Manchester United's youngsters were apparently out of the picture, and were not considered any real threat. But this ignored the fact that since the opening day of the season (a 2-2 draw with

Birmingham City at St. Andrews), United had been without their main centre forward, Tommy Taylor. The Taylor/Viollet duo was as deadly a goal scoring combination as you could ever wish to see.

School started, and I found myself back amongst familiar faces and the banter. I also found myself in Mr. Hardman's class – Standard 4. Mr. Hardman was a new teacher, and we were to find out that he was quite a character. He was from Australia, a tall, thin man, with a large, hooked nose. He spoke with a high-pitched, nasal twang, and for the first few days of the term the kids in the class found it difficult to understand him. After a few days we found out that the afternoon classes were what you could only call interesting – quite often, after resuming class after lunch, Mr. Hardman would give us work to do, then promptly fall asleep at his desk!

Later we discovered that his lunchtime routine consisted of a visit to the Clarendon Hotel on Oxford Road, just around the corner from the school. His lunch apparently consisted of three or four pints of Wilson's best bitter. For urchins from the inner city this was like manna from heaven, and we played some outrageous practical jokes upon him. There were times when someone would crawl up to his desk while he was sleeping, and tie his shoe laces together. Kids would write graffiti on the classroom blackboard. One day, one of the kids found a dead pigeon in the schoolyard, and this pigeon mysteriously found its way into Mr. Hardman's desk – it was there for two days before he realised. His first term was certainly something of a baptism of fire.

Mr. Danny Avery was in charge of the football teams at St. Augustine's, and our football season began almost as soon as the boys returned from the summer break. My whole life was consumed by football, either playing the game, or reading about it. In the autumn and late spring months, after school was over each day, we couldn't wait to get home, as after a hastily eaten evening meal there were always football games to play. Throughout most of areas of Manchester there were what were termed 'street leagues' – games of football played in the streets, and on the wasteland crofts, with teams competing from the different streets in the area. They were tough, hard fought, competitive affairs, and often disputes were settled by fisticuffs. The balls used could be anything from a tennis ball to a plastic 'Frido' football. But we honed and developed our skills in those games.

Looking back, I am amazed at some of the skills those young kids displayed. Dribbling was an art, and the use of walls was particularly useful for kids with quick feet and quick brains. It was from such games that we got the phrase 'wall pass': as a defender came in for the tackle, the attacking player would play the ball against the wall so that it rebounded behind the tackler, and he would go around him to collect it. The games used to finish with some astronomical score lines (20-19 was not uncommon), and if the scores were tied as dusk fell it would usually be agreed that "the next goal is the winner". Those games were certainly not for the faint-hearted.

'Gussies third team that season was easy picking for most of the school teams they played against. From Hulme there was St. Wilfred's (Albert Scanlon's old school), St. George's, and City Road. From Moss Side came St. Edwards and St. Kentigern's, and Bishop's Billsborough. From Chorlton-upon-Medlock came Mansfield Street, St. Aloysius's and the Holy Name. They were all tough schools, and most of the time 'Gussies were on the receiving end of a drubbing. But that never deterred our young spirits, or our enthusiasm for the game. All the games were played on full sized pitches with full sized goals. The teams from Hulme played on a ground named St. George's Rec, but it was commonly known as 'The Barracks' because at one time a military barracks had stood on the site. The football pitch was on red shale – it was like playing on a concrete surface littered with chippings. It was not uncommon for a player to feel the nails that held the studs in his boots protruding through the sole of the boot and into his foot. It explained why some players, particularly late on in a match, would be moving around like 'Bambi on ice', and were not their normal selves.

In the summer of 1955, the kids of Chorlton-upon-Medlock made a great find. Situated at the junction of Upper Brook Street and Rusholme

Road was a small plot of land, measuring approximately 60 yards long by 30 yards wide. It had once been the site of some shops but they had fallen victim to the German bombs during World War II. As it was in other parts of the inner city, and also in the city centre itself, such derelict buildings were still half-standing some ten years after the conflict ended. This particular group of buildings was finally demolished, and a company named Raven Limited proceeded to put up some large advertising hoardings on the site, surrounded by a nice flat grass lawn, with a raised flower bed just in front of the hoardings. It was probably the only grassy, lawned area in Chorlton-upon-Medlock. The whole area was bordered by a sturdy wire fence that stood about three feet high.

The local kids didn't need any encouragement to use the site for playing football, and it became our Wembley. Weekends would see many a game of football played there, occasionally interrupted by a passing visit from the local policeman who would give us a dressing down for what he termed as trespassing. But after a few weeks, even he turned a blind eye to us playing on that stretch of ground. I look back and remember those times with a lot of fondness because it certainly helped with my development as an aspiring young goalkeeper.

Night after night I would go there with one, or sometimes two, friends. We would set up a goal behind the flower bed by placing coats or jumpers down to mark our goal posts, and then I would have my friends fire the ball at the goal from the other side of the flower bed. They had to shoot the ball over the top of the flowers from a distance of between eight to 15 yards, and their shots came from all different angles. There is no doubt that all the practice certainly sharpened up my agility, reflexes and anticipation of where the ball was going to go. I became very good at reading what players were going to do when shaping to shoot, and this helped me enormously in later years. I became very good at stopping close range shots.

Saturdays would still find me making my journeys to Old Trafford for first team, reserve team, or even youth team games. It was like a magnet to me. The first team gradually progressed up the table and on 29 October, after defeating Cardiff City 1-0 at Ninian Park, United found themselves sitting at the top of the First Division table. The team was beginning to have a familiar look about it: Wood; Foulkes, Byrne; Whitefoot, Jones, Edwards; Berry, Blanchflower, Taylor, Viollet and Pegg. There were two players out injured for lengthy periods early on, Berry and Taylor, and other regulars missed the odd game as well. But their replacements, all youngsters, never let the team down: Freddie Goodwin, Walter Whitehurst, Wilf McGuinness, Colin Webster, Billy Whelan, John Doherty, Geoff Bent, Albert Scanlon, and Eddie Lewis. These nine players from the reserve team had an average age of just 19 years, while the first team itself had an average age of just 22 years. There was so much young talent within the club, and most of the young reserve team players would have been automatic first team choices at other First Division clubs.

It is interesting to note that United's reserve team at that time provoked a lot of interest among the fans. It was not uncommon for gates to exceed 10,000 at reserve team games. The young kids coming through found the Central League a good grounding, and a big step up from junior football. The Central league comprised 22 teams from the majority of First, Second, and some Third Division clubs, from the north of England and the Midlands. It was tough competition. Often there were first team players coming back after injury, or wizened old professionals seeing out their careers – some of them having been big names at the top level. It was very physical, and young players had to learn how to deal with it. United's youngsters relished the challenge, thanks in no small measure to the tuition of Jimmy Murphy.

One of the most significant first team debuts came on 12 November 1955, in an away fixture at Burnden Park, Bolton. That afternoon Busby pitched into the fray a 19 year old wing half, a local boy who hailed from the Ordsall district of Salford. He was brim full of confidence and, most of all, ability. It was to be another perfect blend within the team. At five feet, seven inches, and weighing just nine stones and two pounds, you would have feared for any young man's safety against such a physical team as Bolton back then. But not a bit of it – he was in amongst the 'Trotters' like a Jack Russell terrier hanging on to a trouser leg!

This was the first time that the young man's trade mark body swerve was ever seen at a top level game in England, and the opponent on the receiving end was none other than Nat Lofthouse, the 'Lion of Vienna'. Lofthouse was the typical old-fashioned centre forward, tough as teak and no-holds barred, and he was also a seasoned international player. Lofthouse was very physical in his game. In the opening minutes, the young man carried the ball away from danger, just beyond the 18 yard line in front of United's goal. Lofthouse made a bee-line for him. For the onlookers it was a David and Goliath situation – this young, blond, angel-faced kid making his debut was about to be introduced to the tough professional game of First Division football by the old master of his craft. But as Lofthouse moved in for the kill, the youngster made an exaggerated movement with his hips and backside, as though he was on the dance floor doing a rumba. It mesmerized Lofthouse into taking the movement, and with just another swift movement of those hips and his backside, this time in the opposite direction; the kid was gracefully off and away with the ball, leaving Lofthouse in no-man's land. Not only did that dummy confuse Lofthouse, but it also confused most of the people inside Burnden Park that afternoon, particularly those who were sitting in the Manchester Road Stand, for there was a murmur of appreciation that rippled along like you'd never heard before. Although United lost that game by 3-1, little Eddie Colman had arrived and was never to lose his place in the team – he was the perfect foil for the other super talented young giant of a wing half, Duncan Edwards.

By Christmas 1955, Manchester United still led the league, having beaten West Bromwich Albion by 4-1 at the Hawthorns on Christmas Eve. For the players, it was straight home to be with their families, but they had to take things easy because on Boxing Day there was a home fixture with Charlton Athletic at Old Trafford, and the following day, December 27, would see the reverse fixture down in London at The

Valley. Three games in four days, and Christmas Day in between – I wonder how modern players and managers would view that prospect.

The game against Charlton at Old Trafford saw United go nap and win by 5-1. The following day though, the Valiants gained their revenge, beating United by 3-0. This reversal of fortunes was not an uncommon thing back then, and was not surprising given the way the fixtures used to fall. Travel back was tedious, and was mostly by steam train; there were no motorways, so road travel was out of the question for long distances. In fact immediately after the game had finished at Old Trafford on Boxing Day, the players changed, and then travelled by coach to London Road station (now Piccadilly) for the trip down to the capital for the following day's game at The Valley.

Although United were beaten at Charlton, other results went their way that day, and their lead at the top, which was now 3 points, remained the same. It set things up nicely for the last game of the year, at Old Trafford on New Year's Eve against none other than our bitter rivals from across the town, Manchester City. Watching derby matches had been a sad experience for me as I had never seen United win one. However, my enthusiasm remained high, and I was convinced that United would at last be successful, and I couldn't get to Old Trafford quickly enough. Although very cold, the day was bright with winter sunshine, and I took my place behind the Scoreboard End goal. The crowd was swelled by a large contingent of City fans, and there was lots of banter between the rivals. It was a hard fought, end to end game, but goals from Tommy Taylor and Dennis Viollet secured United's victory, despite a late goal from City's young footballer/cricketer inside left, Jack Dyson (a man who, in later years, I would come to know extremely well). It was a happy and ecstatic young boy that waited with others outside the main entrance of the ground to see his heroes after the game. It was also the first time that I ever got really close up to Bert Trautmann, the City goalkeeper.

The Manchester City coach pulled up outside the main entrance of Old Trafford to collect their team, and a short time later the City players began to emerge from the ground. Even though they had lost the game they were good natured with all the kids, and they were happy to stand and sign autographs for everybody. Well, all except one, Don Revie, who disappeared inside the coach immediately. Eventually Trautmann appeared, and I was totally in awe of him. Standing so close to him, he seemed even bigger than when he was out on the pitch. His blond hair, piercing blue eyes, and wonderful physique made him a fine figure of a man. He too was so patient with the kids, and he signed everything that was thrust his way before boarding the bus. A lot of the City players seemed so big to me as they appeared – Ken Barnes, Jimmy Meadows, Dave Ewing and Roy Clarke. Little Joe Hayes seemed to be the most popular and sought after, though.

The United players also appeared, and I ran down to the ticket office to catch the big fella before he went home – I wanted to wish him Happy New Year! He eventually appeared and signed autographs for everybody. When he saw me he laughed and asked, "Don't you ever go home?" I wished him Happy New Year, and he once again signed my book, ruffled my hair, and set off on his bicycle for his short journey home. Again, the results in other matches that day favoured United, and the team went into the New Year with a four point lead. United fans were buoyant, and there was great optimism that this young team was going to bring home the First Division championship, becoming the youngest team ever to accomplish that feat. As the year 1955 drew to an end, little did we know that a brand new era, with such an effect on Manchester United's great history, was about to dawn.

My First Away Match

The first week of January 1956 was an exciting time for my older brother, Peter, as he was about to start his adult working life. He had left school in December 1955, aged 15, and had found employment with the National Coal Board – he was going to be a miner. His training was to take place at the Mosley Common Pit which was situated in the Worsley area. The Lancashire coalfield was a thriving industry during the 1950s, and it may surprise people to discover that in Manchester and the surrounding area there were more than 100 working pits. It was the most prolific coalfield in England, and was probably the county's largest employer. At the beginning of the 20th century, there were over 500 working pits in the Lancashire coalfield – today there are none.

Well known local collieries inlcuded Agecroft, Snipe, Bradford, Clifton Hall, Delph, Hurst, Mosley Common, New Town, Pendlebury and Worsley. Bradford pit was less than a mile and half from Manchester city centre, and it was here, after completing 18 weeks' training at Mosley Common, that Peter would be regularly employed. For our family, his employment by the NCB also brought an unexpected, but much appreciated, perk. He was entitled to a free monthly supply of coal. The amount depended on your employment status within the NCB, and the initial allocation to Peter was one ton of coal per month. Obviously for our family this was an enormous help, and the allocation began on the day that he started work. Thus began a regular monthly appearance of an NCB coal wagon in Royle Street, dropping twenty one hundred weight bags of coal down our coal shute and into the cellar. For me it was a relief, for no more would I have the task of walking around to Huskinson's coal yard in Temple Street, queuing up with our coal sack, watching while it was weighed, and then paying for the 56 pounds of coal it held, before carrying it back home.

For a 15 year old just starting work, Peter's wage was very generous. He earned four pounds and ten shillings (£4.50 today) per week whilst he was training, and this rose to over eight pounds, immediately training was finished. He was now able to help out Mum financially, and it did make a big difference with the family income. Living conditions at home, though, were still not ideal, and it was a situation that still caused friction between my mum and dad. My young sister and I shared a bedroom, and Mum had turned the downstairs parlour into a bedroom for Peter. The house was in a poor structural state, though very little could be done to it to improve it – and, as I have mentioned before, there was no way the landlord was going to spend money on doing so. Even decorating the walls was futile because within days the heavy dampness would cause the wallpaper to peel away.

Manchester United's first match of 1956 was on 7 January, an FA Cup 3rd round tie, away to Second Division Bristol Rovers at Eastville. For the fans this seemed an easy draw, and they were already looking beyond the 3rd round before a ball was kicked. United travelled down to Bristol the evening before the game, but left Duncan Edwards in Manchester because he had take a knock in the derby game on New Year's Eve. Apart from Duncan, United were at full strength, and Jeff Whitefoot (who had lots of first team experience) deputised for Edwards. The playing surface at Eastville was bereft of grass, and heavy rain turned it into a mud heap – commonly referred to in those days as a 'glue pot'.

That afternoon we waited for the results to come in. Sure enough, at 5 o'clock the rousing sound of the march *Out of the Blue* came blaring out of Dad's radio, introducing the weekly *Sports Report* on the BBC's Light Programme. Eamon Andrews read the headlines, and announced that there had been some shocks in the FA Cup, none more so than at Eastville in Bristol. Dad and I thought not too much of it, and I can recall him saying, "They must have drawn". The classified results sequence began, and you could tell by the intonation of the reader's voice which way a game had gone. My stomach turned over as he announced, "[upbeat] Bristol Rovers 4, [pause and downbeat], Manchester United 0". Both dad and I were dumbstruck! We sat there in silence as tears ran down my face. I just could not believe that my beloved Babes had been on the receiving end of a real pasting from a lowly Second Division team, and had been unceremoniously turfed out of the FA Cup. The newspaper and radio reports were to show that Bristol Rovers fully deserved their victory, and had outplayed United all over the park. They had adapted to the heavy pitch much better, and in Geoff Bradford, their big centre forward, had a player who led United's defence a merry old dance throughout that afternoon. Bradford, who was amongst the goal scorers, slotting home a penalty, spent his entire career at Bristol Rovers, playing some 626 games and scoring 355 goals. He had won his one and only England cap just three months earlier, against Denmark in Copenhagen, in a forward line that included Finney, Lofthouse and Milburn, and he scored the last goal in a 5-1 victory. The result of that 3rd round tie was the biggest upset in the FA Cup that season. Bristol Rovers went out in the next round, losing 1-0 at Doncaster. Meanwhile, Manchester City's 3rd round home tie with Blackpool had been postponed due to a waterlogged pitch, so school that next week was a trial. There was plenty of mickey-taking from the City fans, even more so after City beat Blackpool 2-1 when the game was played the following Wednesday.

Saturday 21 January 1956 was another milestone day in my life – the day that I attended my first away game that was out of town (I had already seen United play City at Maine Road, of course). I had been badgering my parents for some 12 months previously to allow me to travel to an away game. They had resisted my pleas, but finally, because of my persistence, they relented. Obviously, my parents could not afford to fund an away trip, but I saved every copper I could get my hands on. I ran errands for people and did odd jobs wherever I could, and whatever proceeds I received were secreted away. My brother, now that he had started work, had also started to give me one shilling a week pocket money – just five pence in today's currency, but a lot back then. It was a tremendous gesture on his part, and it helped fund my trips to United matches enormously.

United were to play Preston North End at Deepdale, and once the go ahead to attend was given, the excitement surged through me all week.

The idea to go was conceived in the classroom, with my young friends, Brian Walsh, Peter Cassin and Tommy Hibbs. It was to be the first time that I travelled on the famous 'football special' – a dedicated train service that was laid on by British Rail. For four youngsters this was to be a huge adventure.

We met on the Saturday morning at All Saints, and walked to Victoria Station. On arrival at what was then a dirty, sooty, grime-covered, dingy railway station, we joined a long queue of United fans at the ticket office. At the window a "half return to Preston, please" was our request, and the ticket man duly asked us for the princely sum of 1 shilling and nine pence (about ten pence today) before handing over our precious return rail tickets. We followed the crowd of supporters down to the platform, had our tickets checked at the barrier, and after passing through found a carriage and boarded. We were so excited and full of energy. Some adult fans joined us in our carriage, and finally the train pulled away.

There was a lot of banter on the way, and lots of talk about the forthcoming game. Much of the discussion centred on Preston's new centre forward, Eddie Lewis, who had joined North End from Manchester United just eight weeks previously. Eddie was one of the original youth team members, and had acquitted himself well at Old Trafford, playing 24 first team games and scoring a creditable 11 goals. Unfortunately for him, he was playing in the shadow of Tommy Taylor, and there was never a chance of him dislodging big Tom from the first team. Also coming through from the junior and reserve teams were players like Bobby Charlton, and a bullock of a young man named Alex Dawson. Busby allowed young Eddie to leave, and going to Preston should have kick-started his career.

By the time the steam train arrived in Preston, the weather had turned nasty, and as the hordes of fans left the station, it was raining heavily. Not one of the four of us had any idea where Deepdale was, and it was a case of following the crowd. Out we went into the pouring rain and we walked up through Fishergate in Preston town centre, then on to

Church Street, and finally onto Deepdale Road, passing HM Prison Preston on the right hand side. The trail of fans grew denser as we got closer to the Deepdale ground and finally we were there. We found the entrance for juniors at the Deepdale End and paid nine pence (less than five pence today) at the turnstile. On entering the ground we made our way past the goal and around to the half way line next to the players' tunnel. We actually stood on the cinder track next to one of the dug outs. There was a large contingent from Manchester, mainly congregated behind the goal at the Deepdale End. Deepdale was much smaller than Old Trafford, but it still fascinated me. There were four floodlights towering over the ground, and a large covered terracing at the Fulwood End. Along the touchlines there were covered stands, but they only covered the seating areas, with the paddocks in front being open to the elements. Little was I to know that in a few short years' time, those terraces, and Deepdale itself, would become so familiar to me.

The rain never ceased, and when the players emerged at five minutes to three we learned that United were without Johnny Berry and Tommy Taylor, with Johnny Scott and Colin Webster deputising. The Preston team was led out by a young fair-haired mascot, resplendent in full kit, and after the captains had tossed up, he took his place in the wooden dug-out, right next to where I was standing. I had seen this young boy's picture in a *Charles Buchan's Football Monthly* magazine some months previously, and as I stood by the dug-out, we were able to converse with each other as the game progressed.

United were top of the league and North End were down in 15th position, so it looked as though this game should not pose too many problems, especially as North End had only won four of their 13 home fixtures to date. However, the pitch was an absolute glue pot and turned out to be a great leveller. North End opened the scoring, and it was none other than Eddie Lewis who got the goal. Obviously, he had a point to prove, and he gave Mark Jones a torrid time that afternoon. Billy Whelan was able to level the scores before half-time, but there was never a doubt that Preston had been the better team up to that point.

Something happened midway through the first half that will stay in my memory forever. As the rain catapulted down, and we were getting saturated, I stood talking to the Preston mascot who sat inside the dugout. Seeing this bedraggled young boy soaked to the skin, the Preston trainer must have felt sympathy for me for he called out and beckoned to me to sit inside the dug-out. I needed no second invitation, much to the envy of my young friends from Manchester. As the players left the field at half-time, I will never forget David Pegg approaching the tunnel and then shaking his head and laughing when he saw where I was sitting.

The second half belonged once again to North End, and they scored twice more. Eddie Lewis again put the ball into the United net, as did their left winger, Angus Morrison. This was also a game where I saw Roger Byrne given the run around by Tom Finney. Byrne is probably the best left back I have ever seen, but on this occasion he had no answer to Finney. Finney absolutely mesmerized me that day with his skills and his pace. On that heavy pitch nobody could get near to him, and when the game ended he left the field with hardly a blemish of mud upon him. He also left the field arm in arm with Byrne, such was the respect they had for each other. It is interesting to note that after his two goals against United that afternoon, Eddie Lewis's career went into free fall. He only played 12 games for North End before being transferred to West Ham United in 1957, and from there he slipped into oblivion.

United lost 3-1 that afternoon, while a win for Blackpool cut United's lead at the top of the table to just two points – and Blackpool had a game in hand. We left Deepdale and followed the throng back to the town centre and the railway station. Once again we boarded the football special for the journey back to Manchester. We were saturated, but even though United had lost, we were not despondent. By the time the train pulled into Victoria Station it was just after seven o'clock in the evening, and we walked through the city centre to Piccadilly where I said "Cheerio" to my young friends, me setting off down London Road, and they walking across to Oxford Street. On arrival home, my mother was relieved to see me as she had become a little worried. I was thrilled to tell both Mum and Dad of the day's exploits, and to show them my match programme which had cost the princely sum of three pence. It had been a great adventure, and going to away matches would now feature prominently in my weekend activities.

The Babes Come of Age

As we left Deepdale that Saturday afternoon, little did we know it would be the last game United would lose that season. Going to school the following Monday my young pals and I were full of ourselves, and we told anybody that would listen about our adventures on the previous Saturday. It was as though we had become something special; we now looked upon ourselves as fully fledged Manchester United supporters, and we could brag that we attended away games!

February 1956 brought some tragic news to our family, and it was devastating, especially to my father. We learned that his sister, my Aunt Mary, who had taken me on holiday to Talacre the previous summer, was terminally ill with cancer. Aunt Mary was just a few months past her 43rd birthday. Initially this news was kept from me, and I could not understand why I wasn't allowed to go up to Blackley and visit her. Once again Dad was so despondent and he became very, very depressed. It put a lot of pressure upon my mother, especially as he began to lose interest in things. His absences from his work became more and more frequent, and it was noticeable that he began to drink more.

February also gave me a second attempt at the 11 plus examination, and this time I only had to take the short walk down through Ardwick Green to St. Gregory's Catholic High School to sit the papers. My mother dearly wanted me to pass the examination because she obviously wanted me to better myself. The examination was held over two days, but to be honest at that time I was rather ambivalent towards it. I was happy in my own world at St. Augustine's and I didn't really want to leave. I enjoyed the every day life at school with children that I had grown up alongside for years. We were all local kids, and all suffered the same hardships that inner city living brought. It was the world and life that we knew. Kids going to high school were looked upon as being posh, and snobs, and coming from upper class families. They were the 'haves' and we were the 'have nots'. They were 'mummy's boys' in our eyes, soft and molly-coddled. I spent the two days of the exam not really caring whether I passed or not. There was a large group from St. Augustine's sitting the exam, but expectation of passes wasn't too high. In previous years, very few pupils from our school had gone on to grammar school or high school.

Saturday was the day that we most looked forward to, the focal day of the week. School football had begun to play a hugely important part in my life, and I looked forward so much to our Saturday morning games. I would be up early, making sure that my football boots and school kit were clean. I would walk to the bus stop on Cambridge Street and catch any bus that was going to Wythenshawe. Normally, schools games kicked off at 10 o'clock, and were of 35 minutes each way. They were refereed by one of the team's schoolmasters. Hough End in Withington, my school's home ground, was a large area of land that housed some 25 football pitches. The pitches were owned and maintained by Manchester City Council – owned being the operative word. It was hard for them to be maintained because there was extensive use of the pitches, especially on Saturdays and Sundays. As well as schools games, local amateur teams also played there. During the winter months the pitches would become a mud bath, and pools of water would lie in the goal areas because the drainage was so poor. It was not uncommon during those months for me to find myself wading about in three to four inches of water during matches! There were no changing facilities for school games, and everybody got changed in the open behind one of the goals.

Although St. Augustine's didn't win many games, losing never seemed to get the boys down. We always wanted the next match to come around quickly. One game that I will always remember came in a junior Catholic Cup match, when 'Gussie's were drawn against the mighty St. Gregory's. The game was played on Greg's home turf at Greenbank Playing Fields in Levenshulme. For the boys from 'Gussie's, this was an adventure, because we were only used to playing against schools in our local area. Greenbank was like going to Wembley for us – it had dressing rooms, and the pitches were better maintained than we were used to. Greg's had a big reputation in Manchester school's football, and were well known for producing players who went on to play for Manchester Boys.

There was no way that 'Gussie's could win that game, and we didn't. But boy did we give them a fright. We lost by 2-1, but what a battling performance, and it was a game in which I played so well. It was a game that Greg's schoolmaster was not to forget, and would be recalled later that year.

Saturday afternoons were 'match day', and by now I had started attending United's home games with my young mates, particularly Brian Walsh. After the loss at Preston, United went on a five match winning run scoring 11 goals and conceding just two. Brian and I would also go and watch the reserve team when we were unable to follow the first team away from home. It was exciting to see the young players that were starting to appear at that level, many of them not too much older than ourselves. Bobby Charlton was fast becoming a real favourite with the fans, and already it was thought that he was knocking on the first team door. Ian Greaves had forced himself into the first team at Bill Foulkes's expense, as John Doherty did to Billy Whelan later on. Jeff Whitefoot, Albert Scanlon, and Jackie Blanchflower all figured prominently in the reserves, along with Wilf McGuinness, Freddie Goodwin and Geoff Bent. The reserves were prolific goalscorers, and fans used to pack behind their opponent's goal, marching round to the other end at half-time.

United fans were now beginning to scent that the league title was coming back to Old Trafford. After beating Chelsea 4-2 on 3 March, United had opened up a six point lead at the top of the table. It was evident at this time that Blackpool were the only team who could stay in contention because Newcastle United, in 3rd place, lay some 11 points distant. So it was a two horse race with just ten games left to play, and Blackpool still had to come to Old Trafford.

One day in March 1956, an envelope dropped through our letterbox, and I learned I had passed the 11 plus examination. My mother was ecstatic; my father much less so. Initially, I was down to start at St. Bede's Grammar School in Whalley Range in September that year, but personally I didn't want to go anywhere! I did not want to leave St. Augustine's. It was an unusual year for 'Gussie's because against all the odds, five boys passed the 11 plus – myself, Bernard Gilmartin, Patrick Cahill, Barry Cunningham and Wilfred Connors. I did not want to leave the boys that I had grown up with, and I made this known to my parents. Dad was happy for me to stay where I was, but mum was not having any of it. She was determined that I would take this opportunity to have a better education and therefore a better chance in life. St. Bede's was an unknown quantity for me, but what I did find out horrified me. It was a boarding school and run by monks. Although I would be a day pupil, I still didn't like the fact that it was considered to be an 'upper class' school. Dad was more concerned about what it was going to cost in uniform, school bag, gym shoes, etc. Mum dug her heels in, and I was going – that was that. She did spend time explaining to me that this was all for my own good, and eventually I did come to terms with the fact that my school life was going to change.

I put it to the back of my mind, as September was a long way away yet. The main thing was to see United win the First Division championship. On Good Friday, I was at Old Trafford to see United play the FA Cup holders, Newcastle United. Newcastle were a team packed with international players; they had a wealth of experience, and were driven by their captain, one of the game's all time hard men, Jimmy Scoular. The great Geordie centre forward Jackie Milburn was in their side, as were Ronnie Simpson, Bob Stokoe, Vic Keeble, Bobby Mitchell and George Hannah. The third biggest home crowd of the season, just under 59,000, saw United run the Geordies ragged, winning by 5-2. At the end of the match United had one hand on the championship trophy, maintaining their six point lead at the top with just five games left to play.

The following day, my friends and I made the short journey over the Penines to Huddersfield Town's Leeds Road ground. Huddersfield were languishing at the bottom of the division and were expected to pose no problems for a rampant United team. Again we joined the hordes leaving by the 'special' from Victoria Station. The journey took just one hour. Once again we followed the crowd on the walk from the station to the football ground. Leeds Road was a small ground, nestled against a Yorkshire hillside. The ground was dominated by the huge Popular Terrace at one side of the pitch. This terrace was covered, and extended around one corner of the ground towards the smaller open Dalton Bank Terrace. Opposite was the Cowshed, a covered terrace with an unusual looking roof, which was bevelled in shape. The Main Stand, on one side of the pitch, was a covered, all seated stand. Many United fans had travelled by coach and car, and there were almost 40,000 fans inside when the game kicked off.

United dominated from start to finish and the 2-0 defeat flattered Huddersfield Town – it could, and should, have been a cricket score. The local populous, with their strange accents, were resigned to relegation from the top flight. For me as a young boy they seemed to be a dour, miserable crowd, and I could not help recall the way that my father used to describe Yorkshire people: "Tight. The only things that they ever give away are boomerangs or homing pigeons!" In later years I learned that this was a totally unfounded description.

United fans were ecstatic once again as they left Leeds Road, for news filtered through that Blackpool had drawn their game. United's lead at the top had therefore stretched to an almost impregnable seven points, with just four league games left to play. On Easter Monday, United travelled to Newcastle where they battled out a 0-0 draw. Blackpool won their game, reducing the points deficit to six. The scene was now set for a mammoth showdown when Blackpool arrived at Old Trafford the following Saturday, 7 April.

The newspapers were all full of it throughout the rest of that week, and the game was built up to be the championship decider. Many pundits wanted United to lose the game to give Stanley Mathews the chance to win a First Division winner's medal. Unfortunately, it was a nigh on impossible task for Blackpool. They had to beat United to stay in the hunt, but they would still need United to lose their remaining games while they won theirs. Nonetheless, the reporters built the game up, and excitement grew in both towns as match day approached.

On the Saturday I made my way to Old Trafford on my own. I couldn't leave home until my Mum and Dad returned from visiting Aunt Mary that morning. As the morning dragged on into lunchtime, I had an uneasy feeling that I was not going to get to the match. Shortly before one o'clock my parents returned home. I knew by their expressions that all was not well. Unfortunately, I wasn't too interested, and my sole focus was to set off for the game. It saddens me today when I think of those particular minutes of that afternoon. Aunt Mary was someone who really did mean so much to me, yet I didn't even have the time to enquire as to her well-being. All that mattered to me was getting to Old Trafford, and as soon my parents returned I was off faster than the Road Runner! I dashed to All Saints, where there was a long queue at the bus stop. It seemed that every bus that came along was full, and my anxiety and impatience began to get the better of me. It seemed an eternity before I was able to catch a bus, and once it set off I willed it to pass every stop between All Saints and Warwick Road.

Arriving at Warwick Road, it didn't take much to realize there was something special about this match. There were huge queues at every turnstile, and it was no different at the juniors' entrance on United Road. I took my place in line but surreptitiously moved forward at every opportunity, until at last I was handing over my nine pence to the gateman, then pushing through the turnstile into the ground. I bought my match programme and was staggered to see that the ground was already quite full. Manoeuvering round to the back of the Scoreboard End, I could not find a vantage point that would allow me to view the game in comfort, so I made my way back towards the corner flag area on the Popular Side. I noticed a small area just behind the corner flag that was not too crowded, and muscled my way down there.

I found a spot behind a group of four boys who were standing against the picket fence. For some reason they seemed to find it funny blocking my view. One of them moved away for a split second and I was in like a rocket, up against the fence. The boy took exception to this and tried to pull me out of the way. Instinctively I threw a right hander and it landed flush on his nose causing it to bleed profusely. The other boys backed away. An adult called out to the St. John's Ambulance crew who were situated close by, and they lifted the boy over the fence and tended to his injury. My heart pounded, for I knew that I was in real trouble and was in danger of getting ejected from the ground. A policeman appeared and asked what had happened. Obviously I was wrong, but fortunately all I received was a telling off from the constable.

The ground was packed, and I focused on what was going on. A tall man wearing a tangerine and white striped top hat, a tangerine tail coat and white trousers was walking around the ground followed by a strutting duck! These were the Blackpool mascots, and were the source of much merriment directed at them by the United fans. The familiar figure of United's mascot Jack Irons, in his colourful bowler and tails, followed shortly after. Appearing on the touchline in front of the Popular Side stand was a man dressed in a red vest and white shorts. On closer scrutiny, he only had one leg, the other being a prosthesis. He set off, sprinting up the touchline towards the Stretford End, and was roared on by the crowd, receiving a huge ovation on completion of his sprint. Shortly after, the Beswick Prize Band began their customary march around the stadium, playing the Radetzky March – kick off time was imminent.

At five minutes to three, Roger Byrne led the United team out from the tunnel, and they trotted down to the Scoreboard End. Seconds later, Hughie Kelly led the Blackpool side out. Instead of their normal tangerine shirts and white shorts, they were in white shirts and black shorts. It was rumoured that the gates had been closed and that thousands of fans were locked outside. Blackpool had some famous players in their team that day, the obvious being Matthews. It wasn't often that he appeared at Old Trafford, and it was a well known fact that he didn't like facing Roger Byrne. Matthews was electric over the first few yards, but Byrne could match him for pace and had great recovery skills. Matt Busby had a theory about Matthews, which was "he loves to play the Palladium!" What he meant was that he saved his best performances for games that took place down in London.

By now Matthews was 42 years old, and it is a tribute to his fitness and dedication that he was still able to perform at the very top level of the game. He was still England's first choice at outside right in 1956. It is fair to say that by this stage he did pick and choose his games, and there was no chance that he would turn out against Bolton Wanderers and Tommy Banks! Alongside Matthews in the Blackpool team that day was goalkeeper George Farm, a seasoned Scotland International; Roy Gratrix, a towering beanpole of a centre half; the tough Kelly, Jim and Hughie, brothers at right and left half, respectively; little Ernie Taylor, who would do so much for United just a few years later, was at inside right; Jackie Mudie, another experienced Scotland international, was at centre forward; also present was Bill Perry, a South African who had scored the winning goal in the famous 'Matthews Final' of 1953.

As the referee blew his whistle to start the game, the crowd let out a deafening roar, and it began to rain very heavily. Within two minutes Blackpool stunned United's biggest crowd since the war by taking the lead. Mudie got away down the right hand side and put in a cross, which Durie got on to and headed firmly into the net. It was just the tonic the Seasiders needed, but the young United team was undeterred, and got a grip on the game. They absolutely battered the Blackpool defence, but without any luck. Tommy Taylor thumped a header against the bar, John Doherty had two efforts cleared off the line, and had another two that hit the woodwork; George Farm was playing a blinder, and saved a Duncan Edwards pile-driver that in reality he had no right to reach. When the half-time whistle blew, Blackpool were out on their feet, but still led by the only goal. United were like a boxer who had battered his opponent but couldn't find the clinical blow to finish off the job.

Was this to be one of those days? The pitch had cut up quite badly, and the goal areas were a quagmire. The second half began, and progressed much as the first half had done. Taylor, who was roaming around all over the place, saw another headed effort rebound from a post and into Farm's hands. Viollet missed a tremendous chance when he was through one on one with Farm, rolling his effort agonisingly past the upright. Things weren't going according to plan. The game was so one-sided, and little was seen of the Blackpool forwards as they tried to shore up their midfield and help stem the attacking red tide.

In most games there comes a turning point, and this was no different. Johnny Berry had begun to make inroads into the Blackpool defence, and had given Jackie Wright, the Blackpool full back, a roasting. Just on the hour mark, Berry had the ball wide on the right, and saw John Doherty begin to make a run behind the Blackpool rearguard. Berry slipped a perfectly weighted through ball between the Blackpool defenders, putting Doherty through on goal. George Farm advanced to meet him, and as Doherty went to go around him, he brought him crashing to the ground. The referee's shrill whistle marked the award of a penalty kick. The whole ground waited with baited breath as the smallest player in the United team placed the ball on the penalty spot at the Scoreboard End. There was silence as Berry ran up to the ball, and he struck it powerfully to Farm's right hand side. As the ball flew past the Scottish 'keeper's outstretched hand, Old Trafford erupted in a cacophony of noise.

A few minutes later United were down to ten men, as big Tommy Taylor had to leave the field after an aerial clash with Roy Gratrix. The big Yorkshireman had sustained a deep cut above his left eye, and it needed stitching. Still United dominated, and the woodwork again saved Blackpool when another Viollet effort was palmed onto the post. Taylor returned with his forehead swathed in a white bandage, having had three stitches inserted into the wound. Time was running out and the game was into its 81st minute when once again Johnny Berry got free of Wright on the right hand side, advancing to the bye-line just in front of the Old Trafford paddock. His cross was too close to Farm and should have caused the goalkeeper no problems, but Taylor was racing in before him. Perhaps Taylor's movement caused the big Scot to take his eye off the ball, but it suddenly rebounded from his chest and into Taylor's path. Big Tommy swept the ball into the net, and at last United were in front. It was the final nail in Blackpool's coffin, and their resistance had at last been drained.

Old Trafford was jubilant, and when the final whistle blew there were roars of appreciation. Our young team were finally champions of the First Division of the Football League, and with the youngest-ever average age – just 22 years. It is ironic that Matt Busby was not at Old Trafford that day to see his young Babes finally come of age. Because of a family bereavement, Busby had returned to Scotland the day before, leaving Jimmy Murphy in charge.

The players left the field to a rousing ovation, and the fans drifted off out of the stadium. They were deliriously happy, and could not wait for the last game of the season, at home to Portsmouth on 21 April.

The defeat at Old Trafford burst Blackpool's bubble, and they lost their remaining three games, eventually finishing 11 points behind United. I attended the Portsmouth game, and watched as Jimmy Dickinson, their England international wing half and captain, led his players out early to form a guard of honour for the new First Division champions. It says something about the game back then when you consider that on the day that the Babes received their first championship trophy, there were some 24,000 fewer fans inside the ground than had attended the Blackpool game, two weeks previously. The game against Pompey was drab and boring, and there were times when United's young players were slow handclapped for just knocking the ball around and playing keep-ball. Today's fans would have revelled in it, but back then fans didn't appreciate that kind of play. Dennis Viollet scored the only goal of the game, and as the final few minutes of the game ticked away, thousands of fans clambered over the picket fence, and stood just feet from the touchline. At the final whistle the fans raced onto the field, me among them. Players were hoisted shoulder high, and were carried over to the tunnel.

The presentation of the Football League championship trophy was made by Mr. Joe Richards, President of the Football League. A rostrum had been erected in the area of the tunnel, and Roger Byrne led his young colleagues up to the platform. There were thousands of fans congregated in front of the Main Stand, and across the pitch. As Roger lifted the trophy high, there was rapturous applause and cheers. One by one, the players descended from the rostrum and milled about in the tunnel area after they had received their medals. They were happy to sign autographs for the fans and show off their silverware, before disappearing back to the dressing room.

This wonderful drawing by artist Paul Windridge shows United captain Roger Byrne holding aloft the Football League First Division championship trophy, while on the left Dennis Viollet shows his medal to the fans.

Immediately after they had bathed and changed, they boarded a coach that took them to Manchester Town Hall for a civic reception. The coach had open widows on the roof, and the players were able to climb up and sit on the top of the bus. As they left Old Trafford, thousands lined the route down Chester Road, Stretford Road, into All Saints, then down Oxford Road and Oxford Street, past St. Peter's Square, and finally into Albert Square and the Town Hall, where they were greeted by the Lord Mayor, Alderman Harold Sharp, and other civic dignitaries. I walked alongside the coach from Old Trafford to All Saints. There were hordes of young kids doing the same thing. The young players were so happy as they showed the championship trophy off, and held up their medals for the crowds to see. I left the coach as it turned into Oxford Road and made my way home to Royle Street, a happy, happy young boy, having seen my heroes win their first league title.

The Babes had finally come of age – they were champions, and so much lay ahead in their young lives. The next two years were to be such a wonderful ride for the players, management, staff, and fans of Manchester United Football Club. There was something about this young team that had begun to stir the passions of football fans all over the country. The 1956/57 football season was to be such a wonderful time as the Babes were to enter unchartered waters – Europe!

Summer 1956

As well as winning the First Division championship in 1956, Manchester United also won the FA Youth Cup for the fourth year running. This time they met the unfashionable Third Division (North) club, Chesterfield, in the final. From the team that had beaten West Bromwich Albion in the previous year's final, gone were Eddie Colman, who had played in the competition's previous three finals; the mighty Duncan Edwards, who had also appeared in those previous three finals; Alan Rhodes, Shay Brennan, and Terry Beckett. The captaincy had been handed over to the barnstorming young wing-half, Wilf McGuinness. The other replacements were Joe Carolan, Reg Holland, Kenny Morgans, Mark Pearson and a young hulk of a 15 year old centre forward, named Alex Dawson.

The first leg of the final was played on a Wednesday evening, and over 25,000 turned up at Old Trafford to see it. The full United team was: Tony Hawksworth (who was also to play in three FA Youth Cup finals) in goal; John Queenan and Peter Jones at full back; a half back line of Joe Carolan, Reg Holland and Wilf McGuinness; and a forward line comprising Kenny Morgans, Mark Pearson, Alex Dawson, Bobby Charlton and Dennis Fidler. Only Queenan, Holland, and Fidler never appeared in the first team during their time at Old Trafford.

Little did we know it that sunny Wednesday evening, but just ten years later, two players who played in that game would help England win the World Cup. Bobby Charlton was always destined for greatness, and that was so obvious from the time he stepped foot inside Old Trafford. The other youngster destined for World Cup glory was Chesterfield's goalkeeper, who was the main reason his team did not get annihilated that night. He was just 18 years old at the time, and such was his wonderful performance at Old Trafford that his team were still in with a chance of winning the trophy when the final whistle sounded to end the first leg. He had been beaten three times, but his teammates, on the rare occasions they had troubled the United goal, had scored twice! Of course his name was Gordon Banks.

He was superlative in that final. The Old Trafford crowd knew that they had seen something really special, and showed their appreciation. However, he first had to fight his way off the ground, as straight after the final whistle the kids came over the picket fence in their hordes, pinned him in the back of the net at the Stretford End, and tried to get him to sign autographs. I was among them, and I will never forget his beaming smile as he tried to oblige. In the end he had to be rescued by a policeman so he could get back to the dressing room. As he got near the players' tunnel there was still a crowd in the Main Stand who had waited for him to leave the field, and he was given a huge standing ovation.

The return leg the following week, at the Recreation Ground in Chesterfield, was a real hard fought affair, and finished as a 1-1 draw. United therefore won the FA Youth Cup for the fourth successive year, and for the fourth year of the competition's existence. For Matt Busby and Jimmy Murphy, the FA Youth Cup was as important as the FA Cup itself. There was great importance and pride attached to the club's efforts to retain the trophy, which was fast becoming United's own property.

For me, the summer of 1956 brings back many memories, some of them a little bitter sweet. As I have described, in February that year I had managed to pass the 11 plus examination, and this meant that I would be leaving St. Augustine's school in July and heading for grammar school. It would be a huge culture shock for me. I would be leaving behind all the young kids I had grown up with, and also my partner-in-crime, Brian Walsh. I was crossing over the line and becoming one of 'them' – a 'high school wallah'. I certainly understood the implications of that, and did not look forward to it as some kids may have done.

As the season ended I still had May, June and July to look forward to, and I made the most of it. Manchester City returned to Wembley for the last game of the 19955/56 season – the FA Cup final, where they played Birmingham City. After being at my aunt's the previous year to watch City's Cup final defeat by Newcastle United, I was very happy when my Granddad invited me over to watch the 1956 final with him in the parlour of his little terraced house. City performed much better than the previous year and won the game 3-1. It was in this final that my goalkeeping idol, Bert Trautmann, suffered a serious neck injury. He was fearless, and with just 17 minutes of the match left, he dived at the feet of Peter Murphy, the big Birmingham inside left, to prevent him from scoring. In a complete accident, Murphy's knee connected with the back of Trautmann's neck and the big German 'keeper lay comatose on the Wembley pitch. It took some time for Laurie Barnett, the City trainer, to bring him round, and when he did get to his feet he was still very groggy.

When the game resumed, Dave Ewing, City's Scottish centre half, made sure that neither the ball nor any of the Birmingham City forwards went close to Trautmann again. Every time the ball went to Ewing inside the Manchester City area, he deliberately hoofed the ball way up into the Wembley stands. The final whistle sounded and Trautmann went up to the Royal Box to collect his winner's medal, holding the back of his neck. He did the same as he left the field. At first, he and the medical people at Manchester City thought that he was suffering from a 'stiff neck'. Three days later, because the pain persisted, he took himself off to the Manchester Royal Infirmary, where x-rays showed that he had in fact broken two bones in his neck.

At five o'clock in the morning on 6 June, just four weeks after that FA Cup final, the family was awakened by a loud knocking on the front door. Mum and Dad got up, and as Mum led Dad downstairs, I heard him say, "This is our Mary". When they opened the front door, Uncle Jack, her husband, was standing there. He came into the house and told my parents of Aunt Mary's passing at just after one o'clock that morning. Dad was devastated, and it was another huge blow to him. My sister and I were told when we got up, and even though I went to school that morning, I cried so much that before lunchtime I was sent home. Aunt Mary was somebody I loved so much. She was such a wonderful woman, and at that young age her loss was incomprehensible to me.

The morning after any FA Cup final, people always put football aside, and cricket became the game of interest. I played in the school cricket team, and was also able to watch Lancashire at Old Trafford on several weekends. The Australians were touring England that season, and playing in an 'Ashes' series. Australia had some truly great players: the magnificent fast bowler, Ray Lindwall; the charismatic all rounder, Keith Miller; Neil Harvey, as fine a batsman as you would ever see; Ritchie Benaud, another terrific all rounder; Gil Langley the wicketkeeper; Peter Burge, Colin McDonald, Alan Davidson and Ian Johnson, the captain. England, too, were so strong with tremendous players like Peter May, Peter Richardson, Colin Cowdrey, Tom Graveney, Trevor Bailey and the character behind the stumps, Godfrey Evans. England also had a fine bowling quartet of Brian Statham, Freddie Trueman, Tony Lock and Jim Laker.

It is strange to recall that football played no part in our lives during those summer months. Yes, there was anticipation and optimism for the season to come, but it was as though immediately after the Wembley final somebody had drawn a curtain over football. You didn't see kids playing football in the streets or in the parks – it was cricket instead. During the early evenings, especially during Test matches, you would see men sitting on their front doorsteps in the street, listening to the last hour's play on their old radios, and the commentary of the late John Arlott.

In late July 1956, with the series tied at one game apiece, I was at the Test match at Old Trafford in which Jim Laker, the England off-spinner took 19 wickets. He dismissed nine Australian batsmen in the first innings, and all ten in the second. It is ironic that while I can always say I was present at that Test, the reality is that I only saw one Australian wicket fall! I went to Old Trafford on the Saturday, and already the

Australians were following on in their second innings – they had been bowled out for just 84 runs in their first innings, in response to England's first innings total of 459. Armed with my lunchbox, I went to Old Trafford on the Saturday morning looking forward to a full day's play. Although play started on time, and I saw Burke caught by Lock off Laker's bowling, after about half an hour the heaven's opened, and the rain came pouring down. And it stayed like that for the rest of the day!

Just before I was due to leave St. Augustine's in July 1956, we had a wonderful occasion when our headmaster, a Mr. Hammond, brought the late, great Frank Swift to the school to talk to the boys who had played in the school's football teams. Even now, I can see the giant of the man that was 'Swiftie' as he was introduced to us in the main school hall. He looked enormous to us young waifs, and standing at six feet four inches, he was. What I do remember is that he was so softly spoken. We were all introduced to him individually, and his enormous hands engulfed mine when we shook hands.

I had become somewhat resigned to leaving 'Gussie's, though as I have explained I did not want to leave the friends with whom I had grown up. Then, just before the end of term, a letter from the Manchester Education Committee informed my parents that I would not be attending St. Bede's school the following September after all. The letter said my admission had been deferred for one year, and that I would start at St, Bede's in September 1957. Of course I wasn't too disappointed by the news, but my Mum was. Upon contacting the education authority she was given the run-around, and never found out the reason for the deferment. For me, it was like another birthday. My schoolteachers were also a little disappointed, but they too were unable to discover the reason.

And so we passed through those holiday months, carefree, happy and completely oblivious as to what was going on around us. The big political story was that on 26 July, just a few days after the end of the school term, the Suez Canal Crisis occurred. Because Britain refused to

169

fund the building of the Aswan Dam, Egypt's President, Gammal Abdul Nasser, decided that he was going to nationalise the Suez Canal. There was a short-lived military conflict between Britain and Egypt, which people feared would break out into war.

As kids, and in the holidays, such matters were never in our minds, and we were unable to grasp the potentially serious implications. We spent the summer months doing what kids do – being outside all the time, we went off to places like Altrincham where we swam in the buff in the River Bollin – girls and boys! Boggart Hole Clough, a big public park on the north side of Manchester was another popular place, as were Fog Lane, Birch Park, Platt Fields and Barney's Croft. We would go fishing for 'tidlers'; swim in the rivers and canals; and explore areas that we had never been to.

If the weather was bad we would go to one of the local cinemas along Oxford Street and 'sneak in'. The most popular cinemas for sneaking in were the Tatler and the News Theatre, as they only showed cartoons, and the duration of the programme was only 90 minutes. As people filed out after watching the show, we would one by one slip into the cinema without alerting the cashier or usherettes. The foyer of the cinema would be packed with people leaving so we would slip in through the crowd, but if we did get rumbled we would tell the usherette that we had just been to the toilet. The Regal Cinema was another favourite to sneak into. It was in the building that now faces the BBC studios on Oxford Road, and it showed full length feature films. However, there were times when we did get rumbled in the Regal – mainly because we hadn't checked which film was showing. Quite often films had an 'A' or 'X' certification from the British Board of Film Censors, and children under the age of 15 were not allowed to view them.

On Sunday afternoons I always made a bee-line for the Galleon open air swimming pool. After the previous summer's fun with the United players, I just wanted to be around them. Sure enough, once they had returned from their international tours and summer holidays, they were back in pre-season training. If the weather was good, the single guys would relax down at the Galleon pool. It had become something of a ritual. Despite their status in the sporting world, they were just ordinary 'boy next door' types, enjoying their weekend break. There was so much laughter from them. They always seemed to have smiles upon their faces, and they never seemed to have troubles of any kind. They had become even more high profile in the city than in previous years, but you could find yourself sitting next to them in the cinema or on the bus. But now they were champions, were looking forward to the 1956/57 season, and the new European adventure.

United Into Europe

But for the vision of Matt Busby, English football would have been on the outside of the European game, looking in, for many years. While clubs from other countries competed for the glittering prize of the first European Cup in 1955/56, English football's governing bodies wanted nothing to do with this pesky new competition, and they didn't want their clubs to have anything to do with it either.

The first invitation to an English club to enter the European Cup was received by Chelsea after they had won the First Division championship in 1954/55. The competition had been the brainwave of the editor of the French sports magazine *L'Equipe*, and the idea was to bring together 32 European champion teams to contest for the trophy on a knock-out basis, with home and away legs in each round. The ties would be played during mid-week and would not affect the clubs' domestic league commitments.

Chelsea declined that first invitation, not that they had any objections to entering this new exciting competition. They were simply forbidden to do so, and they feared reprisals from the insulated and isolated mandarins of the Football league, who quite clearly believed that there was nothing those foreigners could teach the nation that had invented the game of football.

Undaunted by that snub, the organisers of the European cup sent out a second invitation to the English champions of 1955/56, who just happened to be Manchester United. Fortunately for them, they addressed the letter to Matt Busby personally. It was read by a manager with the courage to defy the Football League, and who had the vision to realise that English football, indeed British football, had to become part of a European and global game.

In 1957 Matt Busby explained why he had taken the decision to defy the Football league and blaze a trail for English football in Europe:

"It is apparently fashionable to brand the League Management Committee as a collection of not-very-progressive old men, but it should be made quite clear that, when Manchester United ignored suggestions about by-passing the European Cup, we did so in no spirit of open defiance. This was not a revolt against authority, in fact I believe there was an amount of sound common sense in the League contention that a full League programme of forty-two matches, plus ties in the FA Cup, added up to a vey busy season for any normal club.

"Any normal club, yes, but I have never regarded Manchester United in that light. United, even though perhaps the manager should not say so, are an exceptional club ... and that is why my directors and I felt we were doing the right thing to pursue our international ambitions, even if by doing so we might antagonise certain legislators back home." [1]

Busby argued that United's wealth of talent made the club exceptional. He was confident that the club's reserve strength would allow him to contemplate a season of up to sixty matches, and in favour of participation in Europe he cited the benefits of experience against the finest players in Europe, the financial benefits to United and the importance of English representation in a prestigious event, following two World Cup failures by the national side.

What a momentous decision that proved to be – not just for Manchester United, but for every other English football club that subsequently followed the path United had trodden to the great football stadia of Europe. For Manchester United and Matt Busby it was to be a European adventure sprinkled with triumph and, eventually, great tragedy.

We all know what happened on that dark, dark day in February 1958, and it will forever be remembered as the blackest day in Manchester United's long and illustrious history. But like the phoenix, United

---

[1] Taken from My Story by Matt Busby, Souvenir Press, London, 1957.

somehow managed to rise from the ashes of that sad inferno to build a new team which would give Matt the chance to hold aloft his Holy Grail. On a never to be forgotten night at Wembley, not even the mighty Benfica could deny the lovable United manager the achievement of an ambition which many believe had helped him survive the aftermath of the Munich disaster.

However, the tears of Munich and the ecstasy of Wembley were events still waiting to unfold when Matt Busby and his directors sat around that boardroom table in June 1956 to take a decision which would affect the whole destiny of Manchester United, and English football. It was Europe here we come!

Anderlecht, September 1956

History was made on the evening of 12 September 1956 when, thanks to the vision of Manchester United manager, Matt Busby, the club became the first English team to compete in European competition. United were drawn away in the Preliminary Round first leg against the Belgian champions RSC Anderlecht, which meant that a real test for United would have to wait.

The Preliminary Round first leg was played in the Park Astrid Stadium, Brussels, and a capacity crowd of some 35,000 turned up to watch the game. United lined up that evening: Wood; Foulkes, Byrne (capt); Colman, Jones, Blanchflower; Berry, Whelan, Taylor, Viollet and Pegg.

To say that the match turned out to be an evening's stroll for Busby's Babes would be rather unkind to the Anderlecht team, which contained a number of Belgium internationals, including the national team captain, Jeff Mermans. However, it is true to say that United dominated for most of the game. Dennis Viollet opened the scoring after 20 minutes with a blistering 20 yard drive. In the early part of the second half United did ride their luck a little, and were rather fortunate when Anderlecht's inside forward, Lippens, struck a penalty kick against the foot of the post, the ball rebounding to safety. From then on, United re-established their dominance, and it was no surprise when centre forward Tommy Taylor scored with one of his trademark headers. David Pegg had switched wings and moved over to the right hand side of the pitch, and after rounding the full back his cross was superbly delivered for Taylor to imperiously rise above his marker, and then thump home a bullet of a header. This sealed the game for United, who took a comfortable 2-0 lead back to Manchester.

Fans at home in Manchester had to wait for the ten o'clock news on the radio to find out the result. There was, of course, no live European football on the television, so we would wait, crouched around the old steam radio, listening to the news and then the shipping forecast, before the short sports buletin. It was a happy family that went to bed that night, and I was up early the following morning to run to the paper shop for Dad's Daily Herald, with the match report by George Follows.

United fans were still high on the euphoria of our young Babes winning the First Division championship by a margin of 11 points the previous season. It was an unheard of winning margin in those days. As with Alan Hansen's remarks in the mid-1990s about not being able to win anything with kids, the sportswriters of that day had similar thoughts. It was so unusual in those dark days for players under the age of 21 to be playing first team football, but the average age of the United team was just 22 years, and 1955/56 had been the real breakthrough for Busby's youth policy. The team had played with fluency and audacity, but also a ruthless streak, throughout that season, especially in their home games. They were so entertaining to watch, and they proved those sportswriters quite wrong in the predictions and assumptions that they had spouted before the 1955/56 season had even begun.

The challenge of European football was new to both the players and fans alike. European football was not well reported. The names of the clubs, and where they came from, were quite alien to us all. I'll be honest: I didn't have a clue at that time where Anderlecht played their football. Brussels seemed a million miles away from Manchester. The European players were also unfamiliar to us, but entry into this competition had fired our imaginations, and we all looked forward to the second leg of the tie, on 26 September 1956.

There was great excitement leading up to the second leg of the Anderlecht tie. However, the Saturday before that match, United had a little matter of a derby game against Manchester City at Old Trafford. City certainly had the edge on United in the preceding years, with 1954/55 being particularly painful to witness. In that season United were knocked out of the FA Cup at Maine Road, by 2-0; were beaten 3-2 there in the league; and then suffering a real mauling at Old Trafford in the return league game, losing 5-0. In 1955/56 the first game at

Maine Road game was drawn, but on New Year's Eve, I finally watched United beat the old enemy at Old Trafford, 2-1.

For the derby game on 22 September 1956, I stood behind the goal at the Stretford End. I was awestruck at the size of the City goalkeeper, John Savage, as he first trotted towards the net for the kick about before the start of the match. He stood some six feet eight inches tall, and had huge hands. He was in the City team because of Bert Trautmann's neck injury, sustained in the previous season's FA Cup final. Savage was so big that I didn't think anything could possible get past him. Fortunately I was wrong, and United won that game 2-0, thanks to goals from Billy Whelan and Dennis Viollet. For us, the bus journey home was a celebration, like going to a wedding feast, but the City fans looked like they were going to a funeral – the bus was the hearse, and the evening's 'Pink' and 'Green' were the papers that carried their obituary!

Wednesday night's European game could not come quickly enough for me. Unfortunately, at that time, Old Trafford had no floodlights, so Manchester City had kindly agreed to allow United to play their home games at Maine Road. My Granddad grumbled that the game should have been played in the afternoon – he hated going to Maine Road, and used to tell me that the only time that he would go there was if the place was on fire! Well, little was he to know that Maine Road would be on fire that night, although it was fire of a completely different kind!

The day of the match was a normal school day at St. Augustine's, though my parents knew I would not be home till late that evening. I left home that morning with my pockets stuffed with pennies from the jar I still kept secreted away behind a couple of bricks in our backyard wall.

I could never concentrate in my classes on match days, and this was no exception. From the classroom window I could see the big clock on the Refuge Assurance building tower, and I willed its hands to move around quicker. The schoolmaster, Mr. Gibbons, knew it was useless talking to me on days like this, and quite often would throw me a question like, "What's the score now then?" as I fantasised about the forthcoming game. Lunchtime came, and it was off to the 'dinners' on Upper Brook Street, where we would hastily gobble up our meals, then rush back to the schoolyard to play football on 'the big pitch', which was our Wembley. We would play the parts of our heroes, and I was always Bert Trautmann, in the goal, throwing my young body all over the concrete floor. I idolised 'Big Dunc', but whenever I played, Trautmann was the player whom I wanted to be.

The afternoon dragged on slowly. Finally, at four o'clock, with my great friend Brian Walsh (who now lives in San Francisco) I was off out through the classroom door, into the schoolyard, then out through the gates. Brian's parents owned an off-licence in Clarendon Street, Chorlton-upon-Medlock, and we went there first so that he could have his tea. I had to wait around outside, but sure enough some half hour later Brian was at my side as we began the great adventure of watching our first match at night time, under floodlights, and the very first European Cup tie played on English soil. We obviously didn't know it then, but we were playing our part in United's great history.

We walked from Clarendon Street, then up into Cambridge Street. As we got into Lloyd Street, the first sprinklings of rain started. From Brian's home to Maine Road was little more than half an hour's walk for two young whippersnappers, and we must have arrived at the ground before six o'clock. Maine Road was then a huge stadium, with covering only on the Main Stand and at the Platt Lane End. Only the Main Stand had seating, opposite which was a huge Spion Kop that arced like a quarter moon – later in years it became known as 'The Kippax'. The ground's capacity was 75,000 with ease. We spent some time just walking around the ground in the steadily increasing rain. My curiosity was always heightened just by being at a football ground, wherever it happened to be, and I would be fascinated by every little thing I saw. The gates opened around quarter past six. We paid at the turnstile, and made our way down to claim our places on the concrete wall at the front of what became known as the North Stand, but back then was the Scoreboard End. The rain became a steady stream, and even before the game started we were soaked through. Some 40,000 passed through the turnstile that night, all, I am sure, quite unprepared for what they were about to witness.

At quarter past seven the players appeared from the tunnel over to our right. The teams walked out side by side, something we had never ever seen before except for FA Cup finals. United wore their red shirts and Anderlecht were in blue and white halves. The players were presented to various dignitaries, and gifts and pennants were exchanged. Then, at last, we were ready for the kick off. United lined up at full strength: Wood; Foulkes, Byrne (capt); Colman, Jones, Edwards; Berry, Whelan, Taylor, Viollet and Pegg. I am certain that the vast majority in attendance that night expected a United victory, but no one could have predicted the earth tremor that the Babes were about to send out across Europe that evening.

Immediately the game started United were at the Belgians like tigers, and by half-time had steamed into a 5-0 lead. The lethal spearhead of Tommy Taylor and Dennis Viollet had shared the goals between them, Viollet having a hat-trick to his name. Unfortunately for Brian and me, all five goals had been scored at the Platt Lane End, and we had to be content watching Ray Wood unemployed at the Scoreboard End. What I can remember most vividly from that wet September evening was David Pegg's performance. He tormented the Anderlecht defence, switching from wing to wing, and putting over quality crosses for the other forwards to get on to. The power of United's half back line and the interplay of the forwards completely dominated the Belgian champions, and they had no answer. Going off at half-time they looked demoralized, and rightly so. They were champions of their country and were going in 5-0 in arrears, something they had probably never experienced before. They were being hammered by a team of very young men.

United began the second half as they finished the first. Nine minutes after the restart, big Tommy Taylor completed his own hat-trick, and Billy Whelan made it 7-0 just seven minutes later. With 15 minutes of the game remaining, and the Belgians completely demoralised in the Manchester rain, Dennis Viollet scored his fourth goal; and three minutes later little Johnny Berry stole in to meet one of Pegg's crosses, firing home to make it 9-0. The crowd bayed for the tenth goal, and United duly obliged with almost the last kick of the game when Billy Whelan tapped in from another Pegg cross. All the forwards had scored, apart from David Pegg, despite his dazzling and blistering performance. The Belgians had no answer to his speed, his dribbling skills and his unselfishness in releasing the ball at the right time. United's power and movement completely overwhelmed them. For the last ten minutes or so, United's players tried to set up a goal for David Pegg, but despite their efforts, and his own, the ball just would not go into the net for him, and unfortunately the final whistle sounded to leave him without the goal that his play so richly deserved.

What a sensational start to their first ever European campaign - United were trooping off that sodden Maine Road pitch, victors by 10-0 on the night, and by 12-0 on aggregate. It had been a wonderful evening. Despite the rain, and being wet through, Brian and I were delirious as we trudged home along Lloyd Street. There was certainly a buzz in the air that night, and we couldn't wait for the draw to see who United's next opponents would be. Brian and I parted company at All Saints, and I made my way home past the old Grosvenor cinema, and into Grosvenor Street. An old friend of my father's, Chris Dunn, was standing outside the snooker hall adjoining the cinema. "How've they done young Tom?" he asked me.

"Won 10-0," was my reply.

"You little bugger, don't tell bloody lies," he fired back at me, but I didn't care, and I was off home, down the street, across Brook Street and finally into the house in Royle Street. Mum and Dad, my sister and brother were all there waiting for me, and Dad said that he could not believe the score when it had come through on the radio. He actually told my Mum that it must have been a misprint on the newsreaders script and that the score must have been 1-0. I was so happy to confirm to Dad that it was indeed 10-0.

I went to bed so happy that evening after Mum had got me out of my wet clothes, made me bathe in the old tin tub, and fed me. As I lay there I relived what I had seen, and even today, after all these many years, I can still see the ghost of David Pegg tormenting that poor Belgian defence, time after time after time. The excitement of European football really did begin to grip the city of Manchester after this result, and indeed the whole of the country. By the end of the week we knew who the next European opponents would be – Borussia Dortmund, some mugs from some place in Germany.

Borussia Dortmund, October 1956

Manchester United's 10-0 defeat of Anderlecht inspired a 'European fever', as the display of pure football by such a young team became the talk of the country: in offices, on shop floors, in the pubs, the schools, and out on the streets. The news media were beginning to appreciate just what a special young team Matt Busby had put together now that his youth policy had begun to bear fruit.

As I have mentioned, Alf Clarke, the sports reporter for the Manchester Evening Chronicle, had affectionately dubbed the Manchester United team 'Busby's Babes' some two years earlier when Busby introduced several teenage players into the team for a First Division game against Huddersfield Town at Leeds Road. From that moment on, Manchester United entered a glorious period in their history, and really did make the English football community sit up and take notice when they romped away with the First Division championship in 1955/56 by the stunning margin of 11 points. That championship win inspired the Edmundo Ross Band to record a Caribbean calypso record entitled *The Manchester United Calypso*. Wherever you went in Manchester, the tune seemed to be on everybody's lips.

Now football is a pleasant game
Played in the sun and in the rain
And the team that gets me excited
Is Manchester United.

Oh Manchester, Manchester United
A bunch of bouncing Busby Babes
They deserve to be knighted.
If ever they're playing in your town
You must get to that football ground
Take a lesson come and see
Football taught by Matt Busby.

It was no coincidence that other clubs attempted to copy Busby's policy of recruiting the best young schoolboy players, but unfortunately for them, Busby had stolen the march. Wolverhampton Wanderers, managed by the autocratic Stan Cullis, and Chelsea, under the affable Ted Drake, were the closest adversaries at that time, but although they unearthed some fine young players, they were no real match for the quality that Busby had on the Old Trafford conveyor belt.

The atmosphere in Manchester was a joy to be part of. Manchester City had been top dogs in the city for a number of years, and had been to two successive FA Cup finals, losing to Newcastle United 3-1 in 1955, and beating Birmingham City by the same score in that famous 1956 final when Bert Trautmann played on for the last 17 minutes with a broken neck. But City's win against Birmingham was overshadowed by United's title success, and there was a healthy banter between the two sets of fans. City's was an ageing team, whereas at Old Trafford we really were seeing the birth of a new team, and the rejuvenation of the whole of the Manchester United Football Club. Old Trafford was a wonderful place to be around. With smiles upon everybody's faces, match days were a wonderfully happy experience. We knew we were going to see total football by a team that was allowed to express itself, both individually and collectively. And now we had this new European Cup competition firing the imagination of the nation.

After the demolition of RSC Anderlecht, United were drawn against the German champions, Borussia Dortmund. As far as the fans were concerned, it was a case of, "Bring them on!" As stated earlier, not too much was known about continental teams because foreign football was very rarely reported on in the newspapers, or on the radio. I was clueless as to where Dortmund even was, and it was my father who explained that it was in a place called the Ruhr Valley in Germany. This got me hastily looking through my school geography book, and from what I read it was a city that shared many similarities with our own Manchester. It was characterised by heavy industry, particularly steel mills and engineering factories. I also learned that just to the north and north east of the city were the Mohne and Eder dams, which had been so successfully breached in the air raids by the famous 'Dambusters' led by Wing Commander Guy Gibson VC, some 14 years earlier, using Professor Barnes Wallis's famous 'bouncing bomb'. Little was I to know that years later I would actually become very familiar with the city of Dortmund, and would actually stand upon the ramparts of those two dams.

Between the game against Anderlecht on 26 September and the first leg against Borussia Dortmund on 17 October, the atmosphere in Manchester was something we hadn't experienced before. These European games were breeding a different kind of expectancy. The match was again played at Maine Road because work on United's own floodlight system at Old Trafford was still in its early stages. The board at Old Trafford sensed the interest in the fixture with their German counterparts, and they decided that the game would be 'all ticket'. The tickets were to go on open sale on Sunday, 14 October. Because of the goal feast that had occurred in the previous game, fans were expecting a repeat, and everybody wanted to be there to witness another drubbing of foreign opponents. You also have to take into account that World War Two had only ceased 11 years earlier, and there was still a lot of anti-German feeling. Some of the older generation expressed their hope that United would 'rub the Jerries' noses into the Maine Road mud'.

The only previous time that I had queued for match tickets, was in April of that year, for the FA Cup semi-final between City and Sunderland. One of my aunts was getting married the week before that semi-final, and her husband to be was taking her to the game, which was to be played at Villa Park. So it was that I was given the task of going standing in line at Maine Road for the tickets. I was an altar boy in 1956 at The Holy Family Church, which is still there today, nestled in the square at All Saints, just off Oxford Road. A fellow altar boy was my partner-in-crime, Brian Walsh. We were both down to serve the seven o'clock and eight o'clock Masses that Sunday morning, but we went missing because were at Maine Road queuing for the semi-final tickets, earning the reward of half a crown each from a very happy, and generous, groom to be. What it didn't protect us from though was the wrath of one Father (later Monsignor) Bernard McClernon who really laid into Brian and me when we turned up for Benediction later that Sunday evening! I have had some bollockings in my time, but Father McClernon's remains the one that I will always remember.

On the Sunday morning that tickets for the United v Dortmund game went on sale, Brian and I were again due to serve at the early Masses. We were in a quandary, as neither of us wanted to endure Father McClernon's wrath once again. But we were also desperate to be in the queue for tickets the game. Imagine, then, our surprise when on the Friday morning Father McClernon visited St. Augustine's school, and asked Mr. Gibbons, our teacher, if he could speak to Brian and me outside. We both had wobbly knees as we made our way out of the classroom to face our venerable cleric. Looking at each other, we wondered what transgressions we had committed this time. I can recall the conversation clearly, even to this day.

"Well boys, how are you both today?"

"Fine, Father," we replied.

"Will you be going to the United match at Maine Road next Wednesday?" he asked.

Brian and I did not know what to say to be honest. I piped up, "Well if there are any tickets left on Monday, Father, we'll try and get some because we both want to go and watch the match."

Looking down on us both, Father McClernon's face went quite red as he exploded, "Monday? Monday? Why are you waiting until Monday?"

Brian quickly interjected, "Because you have us both serving the early Masses on Sunday, Father, and we don't want to get in trouble again by queuing for tickets and missing the Mass."

"Ah! Now! Well there has been a little change of plan. You two have been changed for some of the boys who are City supporters. They will serve the early Sunday Masses, and you two will do the early Masses during the week. What do you think of that?"

Brian and I were speechless. He'd never, ever done anything like this before, and we were both elated, to say the least. Unfortunately, we couldn't see what was coming next.

"Oh! Father that's smashing, thank you! "

"But there is a condition, you both understand," he said, and Brian and I looked at each other not really understanding what he was about to say.

"You are going to queue for the tickets on Sunday now aren't you?"

"Yes, Father," was our cherubic reply.

"Well then, I want you to also get four tickets for the priests as well as your own."

"But Father, you are only allowed to buy one ticket each, it would mean us having to queue twice more, and that would take ages."

"I don't care how many times you have to queue, don't come back without those tickets! Now here's a pound to pay for the tickets. Put that in a safe place and be off with you both."

Brian had been doing some reckoning. "Father, there are five priests, but you only want four tickets?"

"Father O'Hara likes City too much, so he'll be the one on duty on Wednesday evening – he doesn't need to be going to watch United!" And with that, there was a swirl of his long black coat, and he was gone just as quickly as he had arrived.

I was left holding a green pound note in my hand. I honestly don't think that at that time of my life I had ever held so much money in my hands. One pound could get you an awful lot of things in those days. Walshie looked at me and said, "Tommy, do you think you should go home with that money in your pocket?"

I knew exactly what he meant. If my father knew I possessed a pound note, it would have disappeared faster than anything David Copperfield has ever made disappear in his career! No doubt about it, he would have treated himself and his buddies to eleventeen pints each of Annie White's best mild beer, and Mum would not have seen him for days! So being prudent, I handed the pound note to Walshie for safekeeping in their off-licence.

Walshie and I made plans to meet at the early time of half past four on the said Sunday morning at All Saints. It seems incredible, when I think of it now, that we could do this quite safely, with the agreement of our parents, and that there would be no worries for anybody. We were able to catch the 'all night' 49 bus from All Saints to Warwick Road, and we were surprised at just how full the bus was. It must have been some time after five o'clock that we arrived at Old Trafford. It was still very dark, but when everybody alighted from the bus it was just like match day, with thousands of people making their way down the Warwick Road. The tickets for the game were not going on sale until ten o'clock, so we still had some four and a half hours to wait. We followed the throng and could not believe our eyes as we walked along the road, past the Scoreboard End of the ground on our left hand side. The turnstiles that would be open for the sale of the tickets were to be on the Glover's side of the ground (the North Stand today), and a line of people, four or five deep, snaked out of United Road, back over the canal bridge, down into Trafford Park Road, then bent left past the Glover's cables works. As we walked down and over the canal bridge and into Trafford Park Road, the queue stretched forever backwards, and by the time we found the end we were winding into Ashburton Road!

We were horrified when we remembered that we probably had to do this three times each. Taking our place in the line, we began our wait. Two little street urchins surrounded by crowds of adults at half past five on a cold mid-October morning. The mood was expectant and good natured. People of that era were used to queuing for everything. Rationing had not long ceased, and people accepted standing in line as being a part of the normal everyday life. There was no aggression from anybody, just good natured banter. There were plenty of women standing in the queue, and they were quite happy to share their flasks of tea and sandwiches with these two scruffy little imps as dawn and daylight came. When I think back to those days now, it's incredible to remember how orderly people were.

At ten o'clock, the line started to shuffle along as the gates opened for the sale of the tickets. We inched along, and Walshie and I racked our brains as to how we were going to get the priests' tickets. Obviously, we didn't fancy having to go back and join the end of the queue again, so we formulated a plan. On Trafford Park Road, the United secretary, Walter Crickmer, walked along the queue, shaking hands with the fans and telling them that they would all get a ticket. By half past eleven we were up on the canal bridge, and there, standing on the corner of United Road, were God and St. Peter – Matt and Jimmy! They passed time of day with the fans, and had a word for all who were fortunate enough to be in their earshot.

At last the turnstiles were in sight and it wasn't long before we heard their steady click, click, click. For Walter Crikmer, those turnstiles were playing a beautiful new tune, as it was all money in the bank for the club. At last, Brian and I were at the turnstile, and just as quickly we were inside purchasing our junior tickets for nine pence each. We then had to walk around the ground to the Scoreboard End, and out through the huge wooden double doors.

Once outside we put our plan into action for the purchase of the priests' tickets. As the queue approached the turnstiles on United Road, it fragmented into four different lines for four different turnstiles. Instead of joining the back of the queue again, Brian and I made our way back onto United Road, very unobtrusively – two young kids larking about, watching the grown ups queue for match tickets. We inched up to the point where the queue fragmented, then joined the end of a line outside a turnstile. Once again we purchased tickets, only this time adult tickets for one shilling and threepence. It worked like a dream, and by midday we managed to get all our tickets with no problems.

Like the two young bucks we were, we were delighted, and took off for home on the 49 bus to All Saints. Brian and I parted there, and I continued down Grosvenor Street, and across Brook Street, until I reached the presbytery on the corner of Greek Street and Grosvenor Street. The front door of the presbytery was a big, black, wooden, imposing thing, with a huge brass knocker in the shape of a lion's head. It was all I could do to reach it and make the necessary knock. After what seemed an age, the door opened and there stood the youngest priest, Father Doran. His eyes lit up when I handed him the match tickets and the change from the pound note. He expressed his thanks, and said that Father McClernon would be more than delighted with our efforts. It was a very happy little bunny that made the short trip down Grosvenor Street until I reached the sanctuary of our home in Royle Street. I was tired, but very, very happy in the knowledge that once again I would be seeing United against another continental team on the following Wednesday evening.

The atmosphere really did build up prior to the Wednesday, and on that cold October evening, Walshie and I once more made our way to Maine Road. Compared with our previous visit this was sublime, as there was no rain, just a hint of frost. We were into Maine Road fairly early, and this time we took our place on what became known as the Kippax, down at the front on the half way line. That night Maine Road was filled with some 75,598 souls (don't ask me where the extra 598 people came from!), all baying for the destruction of the German champions. As kick off approached we eagerly awaited the arrival of the teams from the tunnel directly opposite. United were to line up that night as: Wood; Foulkes, Byrne; Colman, Jones, Edwards; Berry, Whelan, Taylor, Viollet and Pegg.

The roar that greeted the teams was like nothing I had ever heard before, and it must have frightened the life out of the Germans, because inside the first thirty minutes they were 3-0 down. Busby's Babes looked to be heading for another demolition after Dennis Viollet had scored two terrific goals and David Pegg had at last opened his European account by scoring the third on the half hour mark. At half-time and the mood among the fans was ecstatic, delirious, and we waited for another goal glut in the second half. Talk of another 10-0 was rife.

The Germans tightened up considerably in the second half, and began to take the game to United, pinning them back in their own half for long periods. The penny began to drop with the fans – these Jerries were not a bad team. Three-nil seemed an unassailable lead, though, and that would be more than enough to take to Dortmund for the second leg. No team could give United a three goal lead and expect to win. Unfortunately, the situation changed dramatically in the last ten minutes of the game. First, Duncan Edwards made an uncharacteristic mistake when he allowed himself to be dispossessed on the edge of his own area, and the German inside forward Kapituluski fired the ball past Ray Wood to make the score 3-1. Just two minutes from time, Priessler, the other German inside forward, latched on to a loose ball following a scramble in the goal area, and knocked the ball over the line to make it 3-2. All of a sudden, the whole complexion of the tie had altered, and the mood of the fans changed dramatically. As people trudged home in the black night it was a very muted atmosphere.

The return leg was played on 21 November at the Rota Erde Stadion in Dortmund. It was a bitterly cold and frosty evening as 44,450 fans packed into the compact ground in the heart of the city, including a few thousand British soldiers and airmen who were doing their National Service. United lined up as: Wood; Foulkes, Byrne; Colman, Jones, McGuinness; Berry, Whelan, Taylor, Edwards and Pegg.

United had been forced to move Duncan Edwards to inside left in place of Dennis Viollet, who had been injured some weeks earlier. Bobby Charlton would have played but was required to play for the army instead – he was also doing his National Service and the army had first call on his services. Could you imagine a situation like that today? The pitch was like a skating rink – bone hard and very icy. To compound United's problems, a box containing the rubber studs that would have replaced the normal studs on the players' boots mysteriously went missing on the day of the match. Tom Curry, the United trainer, was unable to find replacements in any sports outlet in the Rhur area! United took to the field wearing the normal leather stud in their boots, ostensibly going out to commit football suicide. But this was Manchester United, and they showed another side to their make up. We all knew how skilful they were, but their guts, determination and sheer doggedness shone through in a defensive performance that probably has never been bettered since. There was a world class goalkeeping performance from Ray Wood, a wonderful captain's performance from Roger Byrne as he marshalled his ice skaters around the penalty area, and a superhuman performance from Duncan Edwards. The big fellow was magnificent in this game, breaking up the German attacks and finding the strength and energy to support Tommy Taylor whenever he could. He tackled everything in sight that night, and Dortmund understood why he had been christened 'Boom Boom' the previous year in Berlin. Even the German fans took him to their hearts that night as he strove to keep his team afloat.

Nearing the end of the game, he brushed off a German forward who was holding the ball inside the centre circle. He took off with the ball at his feet and made a bee-line for goal, shrugging off defenders as they came to tackle him. Just outside the area he let fly with his left foot and the ball hurtled along the ground like a bullet shot from a gun. Unfortunately for United it struck the upright, and the whole goal shuddered as the ball rebounded to safety out by the touchline. Soon after, the final whistle was blown and the match ended 0-0. It was a tremendous performance by United's young team. The morning after the game the British hacks could not praise Busby and his young team enough for the bulldog spirit that they had shown in getting the result required to progress into the next round.

Once again, the mood in Manchester was buoyant to say the least. European fever was becoming the 'in thing'. Everybody waited for the draw to see who United would face in the quarter-final of the competition, and the following week we learned that United faced a trip to Spain to play Atlético Bilbao. Again, I had no clue where Bilbao was, so it was back to the geography book again. Spain, land of sunshine, at least United wouldn't have to put up with bad weather over there. Little was I to know that this draw would bring what I consider to be the finest game of football I have ever seen, and that the tie would see one of the greatest goals ever scored in Manchester United's proud history.

Snow in Bilbao

After the hard fought battle with Borussia Dortmund in November 1956, Manchester United had to wait another eight weeks to face European opposition again, having been paired with Atlético Bilbao in the quarter-final. The matches were to be played in Bilbao on 16 January 1957 and in Manchester on 6 February 1957.

Atlético Bilbao had been founded in the early 20th century, partly by English steel and shipbuilding workers with connections to the towns of Sunderland and Southampton. The club thus had the English name of *Athletic Bilbao*, but in 1941 was forced to change its name to *Atlético Bilbao*, following a decree issued by Franco, banning the use of non-Spanish language names and outlawing the club's the policy of signing only Basque players. The club reverted to its proper name of Athletic Bilbao after Franco's death in the 1970s.

As European fever really began to take hold within the city of Manchester, the magic word 'treble' was first heard. I think it was Tom Jackson of the Manchester Evening News who first wrote about the possibility of United achieving the unprecedented. It was hard enough to do the double, since that had not been achieved since before the turn of the 20th century, so the treble was seemingly impossible. But this did not faze Busby's young Babes, and after the Dortmund tie they went about the bread and butter business of retaining their league title. Between the second game with Dortmund, and the first leg of the quarter-final in Bilbao, United only dropped three points in the league – a 2-2 draw with Tottenham Hotspur at White Hart Lane, and a 1-3 reversal at St. Andrews to Birmingham City. The team was in great shape, and firing on all cylinders with the trio of Whelan, Taylor and Viollet hitting the back of the net with regularity.

The draw for the 3rd round of the FA Cup had been made in mid-December, with United given an away fixture at 3rd Division, Hartlepool United. The game was to be played on 5 January 1957, and come the day of the game the Victoria Ground was bursting at the seams, as 17,882 people crammed inside. There were people sitting in trees overlooking the ground, and others on the roof of the stand. They found any vantage point they could to catch a glimpse of the Busby Babes.

The pitch was very heavy as I recall, but it made no difference to United, who by half-time were strolling in with a 3-0 lead, courtesy of goals from Taylor, Berry and Whelan. Whatever was put in the Hartlepool players' tea during that interval we shall never know, but after 75 minutes, Hartlepool had shown the audacity to have drawn level with United at 3-3, and a tremendous upset seemed to be on the cards. But cometh the hour, cometh the man, and the quicksilver Billy Whelan wheedled his way through the Hartlepool defence to score his second goal of the match to make the score 4-3 in United's favour. United used their experience and ability to hang on to their lead, and they travelled back to Manchester that evening a very relieved team.

The FA Cup 4th round draw was made on the following Monday lunchtime, and United once again came out of the hat second to 3rd Division opposition – this time we would play Wrexham at their Racecourse Ground.

Meanwhile, Manchester was buzzing with excitement as the game in Bilbao approached. My school geography book told me Bilbao was in the Basque Country of Spain, and so I naturally assumed United were off to a land of sunshine.

On the Saturday before the European tie, United had a home league game against Newcastle United which they duly won by 6-1 with Pegg, Viollet and Whelan each scoring a brace. I attended that game, and my memory of it was that Newcastle's goal was the best of the seven scored in the game. It came from a free kick routine that they worked so well in front of United's wall, and involved four or five quick, short passes, before Jackie Milburn ran on to the ball and thundered it through the defenders who had broken, and past the unsighted Ray Wood.

United left Manchester Airport for Bilbao on a bitterly cold Monday morning, 14 January 1957. The trip was rough, and the aeroplane was tossed about in the turbulent air for most of the way. It was a journey of over three hours, and for most it certainly was not a pleasant one. Duncan Edwards, who was not the best of travellers at any time, was violently sick throughout the journey. Shortly after leaving Manchester, Bill Foulkes had put his feet up against a bulkhead which was in front of him. In doing so, he inadvertently knocked the lever that controlled the cabin heating out of position. As they progressed into the journey, the cabin got colder and colder. The aeroplane approached Spain, and the weather turned really nasty. There were heavy snowstorms around Bilbao, and the pilot had trouble finding the airport, but finally got the break that allowed him to land safely on Spanish soil. The passengers could not disembark quickly enough, and as the doors of the plane opened they were met by an icy blast blowing right through the already freezing cabin. Outside, it was snowing heavily. The players had expected sunshine, so this was a big disappointment to them. Little Eddie Colman stepped through the aircraft door and took one look around, then he turned back inside and with that impish, boyish grin upon his face, exclaimed, "Caramba! Just like Salford!" He had such a mischievous personality.

Duncan Edwards was still feeling unwell late on the Tuesday evening, and Busby delayed his team selection until the following morning to allow the big fellow every chance to recover. Fortunately, on the Wednesday morning, Duncan declared himself fit and ready to go – did we ever expect anything else from him! The weather was awful that day, still heavy snow, and there was some debate between the two clubs as to whether the game should go ahead. The pitch was an absolute mud heap, and in many areas it was so soft that the boot would sink so far into the surface and the mud would ooze inside. United wanted to play because they could not afford a postponement due to the autocratic restrictions placed upon the club by the Football League –

they just could not be late back to Manchester and not fulfill their league fixture the following Saturday.

The clubs agreed to play, and United lined up as follows: Wood; Foulkes, Byrne; Colman, Jones, Edwards; Berry, Whelan, Taylor, Viollet, and Pegg. Sixty-thousand Basques crammed into the Estadio San Mames that afternoon and braved the heavy snow that fell throughout the game. United just couldn't cope – not only with the conditions, but with the Bilbao team as well, as the home side adapted much better to the awful conditions. After just three minutes the Babes found themselves behind when Uribe scored, and it was no surprise when, on 28 minutes, the same player scored again. The body blow came just two minutes before the break when Marcaida scored a third for the Basque side, and their crowd was delirious as the players trooped off for the half-time break. Busby never flapped at half-time, but went about his business quietly, cajoling, encouraging and telling the players that they were not out of the game, especially if they could pull a goal back early in the second half. Roger Byrne, the captain, was the one who got stuck into the team, and they went back out in a much more determined mood.

United began the second half brightly and started to gain the upper hand. A goal came early from Tommy Taylor, just three minutes into the second half – just the fillip they needed. They pressed the Bilbao team back in to their own half, and six minutes later Dennis Viollet managed to get the ball over the line for United's second goal. At 3-2 it was now game on! However, the exertions of their efforts began to tell, and in those horrible conditions the United players began to tire. Bilbao took full advantage of the situation and scored twice more in the 73rd and 78th minutes to make the score 5-2. The game, and more than likely the whole tie, looked to be ebbing away from United; to all intents and purposes, they were down and out. Nobody could envisage them pulling back a three goal deficit against this very good Bilbao team.

But, as in the FA Cup tie at Hartlepool, cometh the hour, cometh the man, and it was that same man again – Billy Whelan. With the time ticking away, and just five minutes left, this long-legged, lean, young Irishman picked up a loose ball just a little over the half way line out on the left hand side. What he was doing there we will never know, because Billy was the inside right, but he brought the ball under control and set off on a run towards the Bilbao goal. Where he got his strength from at that point in the match is a mystery, but he dragged that heavy cannonball of a football along with him. He beat one defender and then started to veer towards the inside left position; he beat another and advanced diagonally towards the goal. As he approached the penalty area he beat another, then Jesus Garay, the big Bilbao centre half, alert to the threat, came thundering along the 18 yard line to make a tackle. Billy had just shoved the ball slightly in front of himself, and Garay, sensing that he had the opportunity to win the ball, lunged into a sliding tackle. Billy was too quick for him, dragging the ball backwards with the sole of his right boot, as Garay went hurtling past him along the ground, tackling thin air. Billy moved forward a yard or two more, inside the penalty area, and then cracked a curling thunderbolt of a shot away from the goalkeeper Carmello. The ball entered the net just beneath the angle of the right hand post and the crossbar. At 5-3 United had a lifeline, and it was little wonder Billy Whelan was mobbed by his young team mates.

I have a video of this goal, and even today I never get tired of watching it. For me, it is one of the greatest goals scored in United's great history. Where that dear boy drew his energy, spirit, and resolve from at that stage of the game was beyond comprehension. The players were very upbeat at the reception that their Spanish hosts had organised on the evening after the game. A deficit of 5-3 was a lot better than going back to Manchester at 5-2, and they now fancied their chances in the return leg.

The following morning, Thursday 17 January, the United party and the English press corps arrived at the little Bilbao airport, which was covered in snow. The aircrew were already there, but there was a problem with the aircraft. The captain announced that unless he could get all the ice and snow off the fuselage and wings, it would be impossible to take off. The airport had few facilities, and once again the worry about missing the league game the following Saturday hovered over the United officials. The captain asked for volunteers to help sweep the ice and snow off the aeroplane, and some ten minutes later there was the extraordinary sight of the Manchester United players and the men of the press, brooms and scrapers in hand, working on the aircraft to get rid of the ice and snow. There is a famous picture that shows Bill Foulkes and David Pegg posing on a wing with the brooms held on their shoulders. The operation took over four hours to complete, and once the captain was satisfied the party embarked, and finally took off for Manchester.

Manchester was abuzz with excitement. The team was into the 4th round of the FA Cup, they were leading the league, and now they had a chance of progressing into the semi-finals of the European Cup. The Treble now seemed a possibility, and the expectation and excitement started to crank up again during the next few weeks. Everybody was talking about the second leg of the quarter-final tie with Bilbao and asking the question if United were good enough to turn around a two goal deficit against a very, very good Spanish team. The odds were heavily stacked against United in reality, and for most pundits the best United could hope for was a two goal win to force a replay in Paris.

Little did I know at that time, but having just read about one of the greatest goals ever scored in United's history, I was about to witness what I still consider to be the greatest game of football that I have ever seen in my life.

The Greatest Game I Have Ever Seen

It was quite late on Thursday 17 January, 1957, when the silver Elizabethan aircraft took off from Bilbao's small municipal airport, and into the wet and dim Spanish sky. The United players now just wanted to get back to Manchester for some rest before their First Division fixture against Sheffield Wednesday at Hillsborough the following Saturday afternoon. Once again, the ride home was bumpy and several in the party, including poor Duncan once more, were violently airsick.

On the Saturday United made the short trip across the Pennines to face the Owls of Sheffield Wednesday. It was a bad afternoon for United and a very lethargic performance saw them lose 2-1, Tommy Taylor scoring for the Reds. In retrospect, a defeat was always on the cards given the tough match and harsh conditions the players had endured in Bilbao on the Wednesday, and the exertions at the airport the following day.

United's next match was a 4th round FA Cup tie, away to Third Division Wrexham. Given the experience in the 3rd round at Hartlepool, this was a potential banana skin. Incredibly, 61,803 spectators packed into the Racecourse Ground that afternoon, and they were not to be disappointed. United were at full strength and ran the Welsh team ragged, winning 5-0, with Tommy Taylor and Billy Whelan bagging a brace apiece, and Roger Byrne scoring the other.

As fate would have it, the league game before the return leg with Bilbao saw United face Manchester City at Maine Road, on Saturday 2 February 1957. It was a cold and frosty day as I took my place behind the goal at the Platt Lane End. With the Bilbao game to come, this derby match couldn't have come at a worse time. City were well and truly up for it, especially as they had been turned over 2-0 at Old Trafford in September. But United were again at full strength, and they turned on the style once more as they steamrollered City from the off. Edwards was first on the scoresheet with a typical blockbuster from

199

outside of the area which the giant John Savage never got anywhere near. Tommy Taylor soared like an eagle above Dave Ewing to get onto a cross from Johnny Berry and bullet the ball into the back of the net. Joe Hayes pulled one back for City just before half-time, but almost immediately after the restart Billy Whelan went on one of his mazy runs before squaring the ball to Dennis Viollet who walked around Savage to make it 3-1. Billy Whelan completed United's scoring towards the end of the game, but United did allow Don Revie to score a second for City just before the final whistle. At 4-2 for United, the red half of Manchester was ecstatic, and as we trudged home through the darkness of a bitterly cold evening most of the talk was about what time to get to Old Trafford the following morning to queue for tickets for Bilbao match. Brian and I decided on a 4am start once more, and again we were under orders to bring back tickets for the parish priest.

United had been drawn at home to Everton in the 5th round of the FA Cup, the team was top of the First Division, and now had an outside chance of progressing to the semi-finals of this wonderful new European competition. Everybody wanted to see this game against Bilbao. The newspapers were full of it, the radio was full of it, the pub talk was full of it – "Can they do it?" After the derby game Busby took the team away from Manchester and up to Blackpool where he had them ensconced at The Norbreck Hydro Hotel, a familiar place to the players as it was Busby's preferred retreat when he wanted them out of the limelight.

When Brian and I arrived at Old Trafford around four o'clock on the Sunday morning, the queue stretched down Warwick Road and then down Ashburton Road towards the Trafford Hotel and the western part of Trafford Park. I can honestly say that I have never, ever, seen a queue such as this. Even at that hour, on a bitterly cold frosty February morning, there was an anticipatory buzz amongst the fans. People had come prepared for a long stay, and those that had flasks of hot, or even cold beverages, were only too willing to share them with other fans. It was all part of belonging to the 'United Family'. You felt that you belonged, that you were wanted, and that the players were 'our boys'. The club was part of the community, and they embraced it totally.

There was a constant hum of chatter as we queued, and most of the chatter was about the coming Wednesday evening. Daylight broke after what seemed an age, and come ten o'clock there were the first signs that the lines were starting to move. By now the queue up Ashburton Road was out of sight, going out towards Taylor's steelworks and Turner's asbestos cement factory. Slowly, inch by inch, yard by yard, the queue moved like a snake slithering on its belly towards its prey. Walter Crickmer was again out on the bridge, puffing on his pipe. I can recall Jimmy Murphy walking down the lines passing time with the fans. There was no aloofness, no prima donna outlook, just a football man spending time amongst football people.

As I look back on those days, it always fascinates me just how controlled people were. I cannot imagine fans today queuing like that, standing in line for over 12 hours for a match ticket. Maybe back then people were conditioned to it. Rationing had not long ceased, and the war just 11 years in the past; it was an everyday occurrence to see queues outside the grocer's, the butcher's or the bakery. However, there was never any whining, just a lot of good natured banter among working class folk. Brian and I obtained our tickets and also once more worked our dodge of getting back into the queue at the top of the line, and even though we were rumbled by a policeman, he turned a blind eye as nobody complained.

Over the next few days, tickets were changing hands at ridiculous prices. It is interesting to recall that Bobby Charlton was doing national service in the RAOC and was not expecting to get to the game. But when his company sergeant major told him he would love to go to Manchester for the match, Bobby told him he could get them both tickets if the sergeant major could get him the leave – the deal was done right away! They travelled together, and they stood alongside the dug-out at Maine Road for the duration of the game. What a memory for that sergeant major.

That Wednesday night is imprinted in my memory forever. There are certain days, moments in your life, that you never forget, and that you recall with great clarity. This was one of those days for me. Brian and I took our places on the Kippax side, on the small white wall that ran all around the ground. We were at the half-way line, facing the players' tunnel. The ground filled rapidly once the gates had been opened, and although there was no singing and chanting back then, there was an expectant drone, a murmur, a buzz – call it what you will – all around the ground. For 45 minutes before kick-off the Beswick Prize Band marched around the pitch as they played.

As the clock ticked towards 7.20 there was movement in the tunnel, and we saw the teams lining up to make their entrance onto the pitch. They would emerge side by side, with the Bilbao skipper, Garay, carrying a huge bouquet of flowers. The referee and linesmen took their places in front of the teams, then slowly they walked onto the pitch. Roger Byrne led out United, of course, carrying the pennant that would be exchanged for the Bilbao skipper's flowers. The roar which greeted the teams as they marched out of the tunnel and into view of everybody inside Maine Road was like nothing that I have ever heard, before or since. It must have sent a shudder right through the Spaniard side. It's often been said that fans don't score goals, but I believe on that night they were close to doing just that.

The Beswick Prize Band played the two anthems as the teams stood side by side on the far touchline in front of the Main Stand. The wordless Spanish anthem was first, followed by the British anthem, which was belted out by the fans with enormous gusto. Then, as the band marched off beneath the streaming floodlights, the crowd erupted once more. It was an experience that I will never forget, and recalling it today makes the hairs rise on the back of my neck. It is difficult to describe, but the roars that evening were incredible, and could be heard from miles around. My dad told me he stood on our front doorstep in Chorlton-upon-Medlock, worried to bits that I was in such a huge crowd. He need have had no concerns. Again, the fans were controlled and disciplined.

United lined up at full strength: Wood; Foulkes, Byrne; Colman, Jones, Edwards; Berry, Whelan, Taylor, Viollet and Pegg. A crowd of 70,000 was crammed into Maine Road, and, as Tommy Taylor started the game by rolling the ball to Bill Whelan, their voices reached incredible proportions, roaring United on.

Urged on, United attacked the Platt Lane End in the first half, and went at the Spaniards from the kick off, but in all their excitement and exuberance, left themselves open to the counter attack. After ten minutes a thunderous roar rent the heavens apart as Dennis Viollet latched on to a knock down from Tommy Taylor, and he slid the ball home – but all to no avail as the linesman on the Kippax side had his flag in the air for offside. United were too frenetic in their attacks, and as one such advance broke down, the Spaniards countered. As the Bilbao inside left broke free, Bill Foulkes was alert to the danger and came inside to cover. He won the ball and sent a back pass to Ray Wood – unfortunately 'Cowboy', as he known then, under-hit the back pass and it slowed in the Maine Road mud. Deathly silence. The Bilbao attacker was after it like a flash and looked certain to win the race for the ball as Ray Wood catapulted through the area. Whether or not it was the sight of the big Geordie keeper racing to meet him that put him off, or whether it was the crowd's momentary deafening silence that distracted him as 70,000 people held their breath, I don't know – but he suddenly bottled it, and pulled out of the race for the ball, leaving big Ray to gather safely, as another huge roar reached the skies.

Big Duncan was all over the place, working in tandem with Eddie Colman, and as the first half progressed they started to command the midfield. A clever ball from little Eddie down the right, inside the full back, saw Johnny Berry go whizzing round the defender. Looking up, Berry spotted big Taylor drifting towards the penalty spot, dragging Garay along with him. Instead of aiming for big Tommy, Berry drove the ball low and across the six yard line to find Viollet ghosting in from the left, and Dennis made no mistake planting the ball beyond the outstretched hands of Carmello, the Bilbao keeper. But once again, despite the deafening roars of the partisan crowd, United were denied by a linesman's flag – and nobody could understand why. Was it going to be one of those nights when United did everything right, but where that little rub of the green was not going to go their way? The linesman's parentage was certainly questioned by more than just a few fans!

There was now a great fluidity in United's play, but the minutes were ticking away towards half-time. Time was of the essence as Bill Foulkes put in a thundering tackle on the Bilbao left winger over on the far side towards United's goal line. He won the ball and, quickly pulling himself up, he cleared into space down the right touchline into the Bilbao half of the field. Tommy Taylor began a diagonal run from the centre of the field and once again his shadow was Garay. Tommy was a big lad, with Adonis-like looks, but he was also very quick. As they both chased the ball, Tommy feinted as though he was going to stop and hold the ball up, and this movement completely fooled the big Spanish centre half. He too slowed, but in that split second Taylor was away from him, gathering the ball and looking up. Berry had come in from his right wing and was haring down the inside right channel. Tommy drove forward towards the Bilbao goal, and as the Spanish defenders raced across to cover he pulled the ball back and Berry made for the cross. At the last moment Berry allowed the ball to run through his legs and there ghosting in behind him was Dennis Viollet. Without checking his run he hit the ball first time, right footed, and crashed it past Carmello into the back of the net. No mistakes this time and no linesman's flag to rule the goal out. The roar that went up split the heavens and Viollet was totally engulfed by his ecstatic young United team mates – something that didn't often happen in those days, when a quick handshake or a pat on the backside sufficed! The goal had come at the right moment, just a few minutes before half-time, and it took some of the steam out of the Spaniards. The whistle sounded for the break, and as the players trudged off the field the applause continued until all the players and officials were out of sight down the tunnel.

On came the Beswick Prize Band to entertain the fans during the interval, and they marched around the Maine Road pitch under the pitch black night sky playing tunes like 'The Radetzsky March', 'Blaze Away', 'British Grenadiers', 'Soldiers of the Queen' and 'Rule Britannia', as the crowd joined in, and whistling the tunes as the band marched past. The smell of Oxo permeated the air around Brian and I as people opened their flasks and got to work on their butties – many people had come to the game straight from work. The half-time break now brought an air of expectancy – one goal had been scored, and one more was needed to take the tie to a replay in Paris; two more goals would win the tie outright. United were playing really well, but let's not forget Bilbao, who had also played well, even though they had been given the benefit of the doubt on two occasions by a shortsighted linesman! Defensively they were quite tight, but as in today's game they had the ability to break from defence very quickly, and on a number of occasions during that first half they had threatened United's goal. A goal conceded would be a disaster for United, and while we were in a rather euphoric state at half-time, there was always that nagging fear that the Spaniards were good enough to score a goal.

The break in those days lasted only ten minutes, and the players filed out from the tunnel once again. United now defended the Platt Lane End, and were attacking Maine Road's old Scoreboard End. Little Johnny Berry came over to take his position at outside right, and as he waited for the second half to get under way, there was much vocal encouragement directed towards him. I can recall quite clearly that he turned towards us and gave the widest smile and a wink, and as the whistle went for the restart he was back concentrating on the game.

From the off, the roars were again unbelievable as the fans got right behind United, then calamity. In the first few seconds of the second half, Eddie Colman was caught in possession, and Bilbao played a ball inside Bill Foulkes for their right winger. But he pushed the ball too far forward, and once again Ray Wood was off his line like a rocket. Unfortunately this time the winger was a little too quick and he managed to knock the ball past Wood. Agonisingly the ball rolled towards the empty net and we all held our breath. Suddenly there was a blur of arms and legs, and a red flash, as Roger Byrne appeared from nowhere to hack the ball away to safety just as it was about to cross the line. He got up, and I can recall him berating poor Eddie.

United once again dominated, but wave after wave of attacks floundered on the rock that was the Bilbao defence. To say the fans were getting anxious was an understatement. The roars, however, never ceased, and as the hour mark passed United were still battering away. Taylor hit the bar with a glorious header, Berry hit the outside of an upright, Carmello made some stunning saves – once again it seemed as though the ball just wasn't going to go into the Bilbao net. Then, on 65 minutes, a ball was fed out to David Pegg over on the far left touchline. He began one of his mazy runs, checked and turned, then checked and turned again. It looked as though he was going to get hemmed in by defenders, but dragging the ball inside with his left foot, he managed to make half a yard of space, before sending a cross whizzing into the penalty area around knee height. Taylor was moving like an express train, and though Garay watched the ball coming towards him, big Tom was in quickly across him to steer the ball home with his right boot. Maine Road erupted in a cacophony of noise. Once again the scorer was engulfed by joyous team mates, but most importantly the tie was now level. Complete strangers were hugging each other – caps and hats were flung skyward into the cold dark night, and the euphoria that abounded throughout that stadium was just an incredible experience to behold.

With 25 minutes left, could United get that elusive third goal? One thing was for sure, it would not be without the encouragement of the fans. The ball was played around by United sublimely; Edwards was all over, urging, prompting, watching, and defending. Little Eddie was spreading the ball about like a maestro. The forwards were interchanging telepathically, trying to drag defenders out of position. But the minutes kept ticking away until we were down to the last five. It looked as though the Spaniards were going to hold on and take the tie into a third game. They had come more and more into the game during the last 15 minutes as the United players' exertions began to take their toll and tiredness became a factor. United were defending their 18 yard area when a cross from the left was aimed in, and Mark Jones towered above all to thunder a headed clearance away, out to the right hand side. For the umpteenth time that night, big Tommy was after it, followed by his shadow, Garay. Taylor collected the ball just in front of Brian and me, on the half way line. He turned, and there was Garay shadowing him, showing him the touchline. Tommy held the ball, inviting the tackle, but Garay was having none of it. They jockeyed each other down that right hand touchline, and Garay looked quite comfortable. Tom started to take the ball towards the big Spanish centre half, level with the 18 yard line. He showed Garay the ball, and as he made a quick dip of his left shoulder and a movement towards the left, Garay pounced. Alas for him, the ball wasn't there! Tommy had pulled the ball back onto his right foot and was away a yard. Looking up he released a cross of stunning quality, landing the ball around the penalty spot – normally the area where he himself would be. But none of United's big lads were there, instead the smallest guy in United's team, little Johnny Berry, was haring in at full speed. He met the ball full on the volley with his right foot, crashing it into the back of the net. Maine Road really did erupt, as did all the United players. I'd never seen the big fellow jump and cavort like he did at that moment, nor had I ever seen Roger Byrne so emotional. Again caps and hats went up into the night sky, and I remember adults around me with tears streaming down their faces – tears of great happiness – a far cry from what just one more year would bring to us all. Busby and Murphy danced a jig along the far touchline. For the next five minutes United played keep-ball, and really did frustrate the Spaniards. And then, at last, as thousands of whistles echoed around the ground, the game was over. People hugged and kissed each other, and cried with joy. Our Babes had met the challenge once again, and they were now into the semi-final of this wonderful new competition.

The Spaniards took their defeat with great dignity. Handshakes and hugs for their conquerors – no laps of honour like there would be in today's game – respect for the defeated. There was a banquet for both teams at the Midland Hotel in Manchester later that evening, and the respect both clubs showed for each other was reflected in the after dinner speeches. The Bilbao president and manager said the crowd had certainly played a significant part in their defeat. Jesus Garay the Spanish captain said that on the night this young United team was just too good for his seasoned team of internationals. He too said the crowd had played a huge part in their defeat, that in all their years of playing football they had never encountered noise like it, and that it took them a long time to settle into the game. He paid a great tribute to Tommy Taylor, saying that he was the finest centre forward that he had ever played against – and that was some compliment, believe me.

In my opinion, this game was Tommy Taylor's finest ever performance for Manchester United. As I said earlier, he was a big lad – some six feet, two inches tall – but he had great skills. So comfortable on the ball with either foot, probably the best header of a football that I have ever seen – and I have never, ever, seen anybody head a ball so powerfully. He was exceptionally quick, and had terrific temperament. He took some fearful stick but just got up and got on with it. He had a smile as big as a barn door – especially when he scored a goal – hence his nickname, 'The Smiling Executioner'. But that night against Bilbao at Maine Road he led the line so ferociously, he pulled Garay all over the place, and whenever the defence was under pressure he was there to receive the ball from them and hold it up. He scored a terrific goal, and he laid two others on for his team mates. Even now, all these years later, I can still see him, standing there smiling, the dazzler that he was. Oh! That he was playing today, he would be bigger in marketing terms than anything that we have ever seen.

The fans danced their way home that evening. We were all so delirious with happiness. The excitement of reaching a European Cup semi-final at the first attempt had already started to consume us all. Brian and I walked home along Lloyd Street towards Cambridge Street, trying to imagine who would be United's next opponents. The chatter around us as we walked that dimly lit street was all so happy. The pubs along the route were overflowing with customers trying to get their 'last hour' in before closing time, which in those days was 10.30pm. We parted as usual at All Saints and I walked once again down Grosvenor Street to my home in Royle Street, to find many of the neighbours sat on their front steps out in the street. As I got half way up the street they all began cheering – it was as though I had won something personally. Dad was on the steps of our terraced home, and he got up and gave me a great big hug. He had been so apprehensive about me being in that crowd – so much so that he had stayed out of the pub that night! He'd sat there listening to the roars emanating from Maine Road, worrying that I'd get crushed in such a huge mass. Mum was her usual calm self, feeding me and making sure that I bathed before I went to bed – tired, but very, very, happy.

The sixth of February, 1957 is there in my heart and mind forever. One of those occasions that can never be expunged. I have never experienced a match with such intensity or atmosphere since. Time certainly does not dim my memory of that night, nor of the characters who played leading roles in it. I look back with so much fondness on those days, which were part of my growing up into the 'United Family'. It is so different for the kids today, as the club has lost that community spirit. The players were so accessible, they had no airs and graces, and you felt that you were part of something very special – indeed, we were! I'm so glad that I was around at that time and that I can relate those times to you now. Sadly, in my opinion, and it hurts me to say this, times like that are now dim and distant – in fact, gone forever.

Treble Chasers

Between that glorious night against Bilbao at Maine Road in February, and the first leg of the semi-final in Madrid in April, so much happened, both on and off the pitch. On the Saturday immediately after the Bilbao victory, United entertained Arsenal at Old Trafford. The Babes carried over their scintillating form from the previous Wednesday evening and demolished a good Arsenal team by 6-2. Billy Whelan and little Johnny Berry each scored twice, and Big Dunc and Tommy Taylor scored a goal apiece. I attended this game, and it was the first time I recall seeing David Herd (who scored both Arsenal goals). David later joined United and played such a big part in our success during the 1960s. He was brought up in the Manchester area (his father Alec having played for City and Stockport County), and father and son actually turned out together for Stockport County in a league game – a unique event in English football history.

The following Saturday, 16 February, saw United entertain Everton at Old Trafford in a 5th round FA Cup tie. I can recall this game with great clarity, notably for one of the best goalkeeping performances that I have ever witnessed. Everton had emphatically ended United's run of 27 league games without defeat in October 1956, defying the odds to win 5-2 at Old Trafford – a huge upset at the time. For the FA Cup clash it was a bright sunny February day, and Everton really did frustrate United for the majority of the match. The Everton goalkeeper was an Irishman named Albert Dunlop (who was later to be charged by the police in the match fixing trials in the early 1960s that saw Peter Swan, David Layne and Tony Kay, all Sheffield Wednesday players, sent to prison). Dunlop was not a big man for a goalkeeper, but that afternoon, his agility was something that had to be seen. United threw everything at Everton, bombarding Dunlop's goal throughout the first half, and well into the second period. Dunlop just seemed unbeatable – the range of saves he made that day bordered on the breathtaking. One particular effort was a twenty-five yard pile driver, hit with venom by Edwards. The Everton keeper flew through the air and to his right, and managed to get a hand on the ball, pushing it onto and over the crossbar. The force of the shot took the ball right over the top of the banks of spectators at the Stretford End! Another save was from a full blooded Tommy Taylor header, which Dunlop again turned over the bar, stretched high and to his left. Whelan hit the woodwork, as did Berry, and it just seemed it was going to be one of those days. Just on the hour mark, however, Edwards took a short pass from Colman inside the centre circle in his own half. Duncan looked up and then drove forward, towards the Scoreboard End goal. There were a couple of half hearted challenges from Everton defenders, which were brushed off contemptuously then, again looking up, just outside the penalty area, he let fly with a left footed shot of tremendous power which never left the ground – Dunlop didn't see it until the ball was bulging in the back of the net. It was going to take a special effort to beat the Toffeeman that afternoon, and this was it, but it came from a very special player. The goal proved to be the match winner, and United advanced into the 6th round draw on the following Monday lunchtime. They drew an away tie against Bournemouth and Boscombe Athletic, who were doing some unusual things that year!

United had to play a Division One fixture on the following Monday afternoon against Charlton Athletic at The Valley in London. There was a few knocks from the previous Saturday's Cup tie, and a few changes were made. Geoff Bent came in for Bill Foulkes, with Roger Byrne moving to right back; Wilf McGuinnes replaced Edwards, and Bobby Charlton came in for Dennis Viollet. Again, the Babes were magnificent, and went 'nap', winning 5-1. Bobby Charlton scored his first league hat-trick and Tommy Taylor weighed in with a brace. Bobby had made his league debut against Charlton earlier in the season and had scored twice, so he must have been more than happy with his second performance against the Addicks. Poor old Sam Bartram, the Charlton goalkeeper, had to watch a couple of thunderbolts from 'Wor Bobby' (as he was known back then) fly past him in both games. A big, bright, ginger haired man, and one of football's great characters, Sam was probably the best uncapped goalkeeper in the game during that era.

Sam Bartram was really famous for an incident in a game at The Valley a few years earlier. The fog had come down during the game, and grew so thick that Sam couldn't see too much. He was patrolling around his goal area for a long while, and finally found his way back to his goal line, where he was surprised to find a policeman standing there. He informed Sam that the referee had abandoned the game some 15 minutes earlier, but big Sam had no idea, as he couldn't see too far nor hear too much. To say that he was red faced when he returned to the dressing room is an understatement!

On the last Saturday in February, United were at home to Blackpool. They were back to full strength again, but unfortunately suffered a home defeat, losing 2-0 with little Ernie Taylor scoring one of the goals for the Seasiders. It is funny to recall some of these games, especially when I remember the visiting club mascots who paraded around Old Trafford. Just a week earlier I had watched Everton's 'Toffee Lady', dressed in a blue and white Victorian lace costume, complete with Easter Bonnet, walk around the perimeter track handing out toffees to the kids down at the front. Blackpool's mascot was a guy dressed as a magician – all in tangerine and white, but he used to have a duck that would waddle around the ground after him! Chelsea would bring along one of the old Chelsea Pensioners; Portsmouth had a sailor, dressed in the old 'Jack Tar' uniform; and of course United had their own mascot too, the ebullient Jack Irons, complete with 'Billy Pot' hat, frock coat and tails. And to add to this, the dear old Beswick Prize Band would regally entertain us pre-match and at half-time. There used to be an old catch question which went, 'Who played for United one week, City the next, and never a penny changed hands in transfer money?' Of course the answer was, the Beswick Prize Band!

On Saturday 2 March 1957, United travelled to Dean Court to take on Bournemouth and Boscombe Athletic. They were residing in the old Third Division, and had caused something of a sensation that season by knocking a number of First Division clubs out of the FA Cup, notably the mighty Wolves and Tottenham Hotspur. These were really great victories and this tie was a potential banana skin for Manchester

United. Bournemouth's team contained a certain Mr. Oliver Norris, an eccentric individual if ever there was one. He was tall for an inside forward, and what he lacked in skill, he tried to make up for in physical aggression – sometimes such that it bordered on the boundaries of legality. In those two previous rounds he had done enough to unsettle both Billy Wright and the Spurs captain, Danny Blanchflower. He made himself a real nuisance – he would stand in front of players at throw-ins, jumping up and down like a jack-in-the-box. The same ritual followed at goal kicks and free kicks; wherever you were, Norris was 'in your face'.

The match was a sell out. Tommy Taylor was out of the United team through injury, so Busby reshuffled, playing Edwards at centre forward with Wilf McGuinnes coming in at left half. The Dean Court pitch was small, and the ground was very hard. After just a quarter of an hour, United were a goal down and also down to ten men. Mark Jones went up for a ball with Norris and attempted to head clear, but he fell awkwardly and twisted his knee badly, and injury that ruled him out for the next few weeks. As Jones lay writhing on the ground the ball broke loose and Lewin hit the ball into the back of the United net. It was a setback, but big Duncan settled into a defensive role, and although Norris was up to all his tricks, United concentrated on their football. At half-time it was still 1-0, but upon the restart United controlled the game, passing the ball fluently, and moving their Third Division opponents around. Just on the hour mark, Johnny Berry received a ball out on the right hand side, moved inside the full back leaving him floundering, and cut across the 18 yard line. He checked back again, turned, and hit a left foot shot that flew into the top of the Bornemouth net – from that moment on, there was only ever going to be one winner. Fifteen minutes from time, Billy Whelan was hauled down in the penalty area and again it was Johnny Berry who duly obliged, smacking the penalty kick high and to the right of the goalkeeper. Norris had by this time run out of steam through all of his eccentric motions, and Bournemouth were happy to hear the final whistle go at just 2-1. United were now top of the league, into the semi-finals of both the FA Cup and the European Cup, and the treble was now on! Given that the elusive double of league and FA Cup had never been accomplished in the 20th century, it is easy to see why the thought of winning a treble was stimulating not only Manchester United's own supporters, but fans of football throughout Great Britain.

I spoke a little earlier about the strength in depth that United had at this time. The Wednesday night following the Bournemouth fixture, United played a First Division fixture against Everton at Goodison Park. The previous Saturday's Cup tie had taken its toll on the United team, and they had to make several changes to the side that had triumphed at Dean Court. Out went Jones, Foulkes, Colman, Edwards, Berry and Viollet, and Taylor was also still missing. In their places were Bent, Goodwin, Blanchflower, McGuinness, Webster, and Doherty. Although Goodison was never an easy place to go, even with a full strength side, United won by 2-1, with Colin Webster scoring both goals.

We were now into the middle of March and football fever really was gripping the city. For the fans it was a wonderful time – this young team was such a joy to watch, and showed very little inhibition in its play. The young players also learned very quickly that Manchester United really was a 'family' – both inside the club and out in the community. The players were a credit to the club, to the countries they represented, but more importantly they were a credit to themselves. No prima donnas, just a bunch of guys who happened to play football, and loved the club that they played for very deeply. If it had come to the crunch they would have turned out for nothing. They were all so in love with the game, and so in love with life. It is hard to put into words, but they were such an exceptional team of young men, both as skilled footballers and as human beings.

In mid-March they met Aston Villa at Old Trafford in a league game. Over 55,000 turned up to watch a 1-1 draw, with Bobby Charlton scoring a blockbuster that Nigel Sims the Villa keeper never saw. Again, five 'reserve' players turned out in this fixture. Looming up was the FA Cup semi-final against Birmingham City at Hillsborough.

United had a number of injuries, notably to Taylor and Viollet, and the backroom staff were frantically trying to get these players fit for this tie.

On 16 March 1957, United travelled to Molyneux to take on their nearest challengers in the title race, Wolverhampton Wanderers, and again were not at full strength. However, they did come away with a very creditable 1-1 draw, and Bobby Charlton continued his scoring run.

The following week, United faced Birmingham City at Hillsborough, with Taylor unfit to play. Once again Busby played a master stroke. Although Viollet was less than match fit, he sent him out to play in the centre forward's shirt and left Bobby Charlton at inside left, Viollet's normal position. His instructions to Viollet were simple: "Dennis, if you can move big Smithy [Trevor Smith the Birmingham centre half] around, and drag him out of position, the other forwards will get into the gaps he leaves, and they will do the damage." It worked like a charm. After 13 minutes, United were 2-0 up thanks to goals from Johnny Berry and Bobby Charlton. True to Busby's instructions, Viollet, although he saw little of the ball, pulled Smith out of position so many times it became embarrassing for the big man. The game, in reality, was over, and the final 2-0 scoreline really did flatter Birmingham City. United had reached the FA Cup final, and would play Aston Villa on the first Saturday in May at Wembley. On paper and form, Villa would be no match for a rampant young United team and to the fans, it certainly did look as though the first piece of the treble was in the bag.

Manchester City had been to Wembley for the past two seasons and were the current FA Cup holders, so the red half of Manchester had a real ball that weekend. However, there was no rest for the players. As soon as United had entered the new European competition, the board had authorised the installation of floodlighting at Old Trafford ground. Over the past six months fans arriving at the famous old stadium had witnessed the building of four floodlight pylons, which grew in size with each passing week. With the floodlights complete, United scheduled a First Division match against Bolton Wanderers, to be played just two days after the FA Cup semi-final. And so Monday, 25 March 1957 saw the first ever floodlit game to be played on Manchester United's home turf. I remember this match so well. With the away game against Real Madrid imminent, Busby had asked Bill Ridding, the Bolton manager, if his team would wear an all white strip for the game against United. This they agreed to do, and United wore all red, the strip that they would wear in a little over two weeks time in the Bernabeu.

I travelled to the Bolton match by car in the company of the man who owned the local chip shop on the corner of Royle Street and Rusholme Road. His name was Mr. Taylor, and we were also accompanied by his son Fred. Normally, I would have left for a game much earlier, but as I was going by car, I had to wait. Traffic was much heavier than usual and in those days, there were few car parking facilities in the vicinity of Old Trafford. We had a problem finding a place to park, and eventually finished up on what is now Elsinore Road at the back of Old Trafford Station. Once the car was parked I was away, running like mad towards the stadium. It was a much larger crowd than normal and the huge towering floodlight pylons shone like four great beacons in the sky. There were long queues at the turnstiles, but eventually I got through the juniors' entrance. By now it was well past 7pm, and it was a job trying to get through the packed crowd and down to the front of the Popular Stand. As I came to an abrupt halt, an adult, a complete stranger, saw my situation and hoisted me up and over one of the crash barriers. I was able to stand on the concrete foundation, and was afforded a great view of the whole pitch. The sight of Old Trafford under floodlights for the first time ever is something that I will always remember.

Over 60,000 fans crammed into Old Trafford that evening, but it was to have no happy ending for the Babes. United lost 2-0, and I can quite clearly recall Bill Foulkes scoring a classic own goal. Bolton had been attacking, and Foulkes had been drawn into the middle of the park, when Dennis Stevens whipped in a hard cross at waist height. Foulkes flung himself in front of Nat Lofthouse near the penalty spot, but the ball whipped off his forehead and flew past a bewildered Ray Wood in to the top left hand corner of the goal. Dennis Stevens added a second late in the second half, and as usual Bolton Wanderers had proved a real thorn in United's side.

United's floodlights were a huge big hit with the fans, and they were far and away better than any other floodlights in Britain at that time. After the game I made my way back to Elsinore Road to meet Mr. Taylor and his son, but they were not there, and neither was the car. I had to walk back home, and it was almost 11 o'clock when I reached the house. Mum was frantic, and none too happy with Mr. Taylor. It did transpire though that by the time he and his son had reached the ground, the turnstiles were being closed and thousands were locked outside – Mr. Taylor and his son included!

The following Saturday, 30 March, United played Leeds United at Elland Road – John Charles as well. United came away with the two points. They won 2-1 with goals from Colin Webster and Bobby Charlton. Jack Charlton was in the Leeds team that day, the second time that season that the soon-to-be famous Charlton brothers had faced each other in a competitive league game.

The game with Real Madrid was drawing near, and it was with relief that United fans heard that Tommy Taylor was almost back to full fitness after being out for six weeks with a groin injury. Busby brought him back for the First Division game against Tottenham Hotspur at Old Trafford. United were without Roger Byrne and Duncan Edwards that day, as they were away on international duty with England, playing against Scotland at Wembley. Big Dunc scored the winner with a blockbuster from outside of the penalty area to make the score 2-1 in England's favour. Meanwhile the game at Old Trafford finished in a 0-0 draw.

217

Real Madrid, the First Leg

After the euphoria of the victory against Atlético Bilbao on that never to be forgotten evening of 6th February 1957, United fans had to wait until 11 April for the 1st leg of the European Cup semi-final. United also had to wait to find out who they would be playing, as the semi-final draw pitted Red Star Belgrade against Fiorentina, and United against either Real Madrid or the French club, Nice. The quarter-final second leg between Real Madrid and Nice had been subject to a postponement, but Madrid carried a 3-0 lead from the 1st leg. Matt Busby and Jimmy Murphy decided to go over to France for the 2nd leg in Nice. Madrid eventually won that game by 3-2, but what the United managerial duo saw that night, opened their eyes wide to the task that would confront United in April.

It was a happy Manchester United party that left Ringway Airport that Tuesday morning. They posed for the press photographers, all smiles, resplendent in their club blazers, and wearing small trilby hats that they'd had made for the occasion. The flight over to Madrid was smooth and uneventful, and the players were in a happy and confident mood. They arrived in Madrid to find the city bathed in glorious sunshine, and they were whisked away to their hotel just outside the city. On the Tuesday, they trained for the first time inside the fabulous Bernabeu Stadium, probably the best stadium in the world at that particular time. They couldn't wait for Thursday's match to begin. Back in Manchester the atmosphere was building up, and most fans thought that Real Madrid would pose no significant problems for the Babes. The second half of the match was to be relayed on the radio from Madrid, courtesy of the BBC Light Programme.

Thursday came, and it was an excited crowd that gathered around the radio in the Clare household that afternoon. United's team that day was: Wood; Foulkes, Byrne; Colman, Blanchflower, Edwards; Berry, Whelan, Taylor, Viollet and Pegg. Busby had pulled off a magical tactical plan on the Spaniards – everybody thought that it would be

Edwards who would be given the task of marking the great Alfredo Di Stefano. Instead, the job was given to the diminutive Eddie Colman. Eddie was a terrific tackler as well as a good distributor of the ball, and he latched on to di Stefano like a Jack Russell terrier to a postman's leg! So much so, that he unsettled the great man and disrupted the normal flowing elegant style of this wonderful player. It also disrupted the service to Gento, 'the flying bicycle' as the speedy left winger was known, and it enabled Duncan to play his normal game. During that first half Edwards had caused Madrid several problems with his strong surges forward from midfield. United were on the wrong end of some bad refereeing decisions in that first half, having the ball in the net twice, only for the 'goals' to be ruled out for dubious offside decisions. Then with half-time approaching, di Stefano received the ball just inside United's half of the field in a central position. Little Eddie was on him in a flash, and quite cleanly took the ball away from him. Alfredo's temper snapped, and he blatantly kicked Eddie to the ground – an offence for which he should have been sent off. Amazingly, only a free kick was given, and there was no admonishment from the referee. Big Bill Foulkes took matters into his own hands and grabbed the Argentinian-Spaniard by the shirt, leaving him in no doubt what would happen should anything like that occur again. So the teams went to the dressing rooms on level terms, 0-0 at the break, and for United the job was half done.

The second half was a different kettle of fish – Madrid showed just why they were such a great team. David Pegg had given Becerril, their right back, a real old roasting in the first half, so they made sure that he saw as little of the ball as possible. United competed with them until the hour mark and then some quick interpassing and movement opened up United's defence, allowing Hector Rial to glide in unnoticed to fire home past Ray Wood. The goal seemed to unnerve the Babes, and five minutes later they found themselves two down. Gento got free of Bill Foulkes on the right, and from his cross, di Stefano appeared from nowhere, thumping a majestic header firmly into the United net. United had 25 minutes to try and salvage something from the tie, and they began to find their rhythm once again. Edwards surged forward, drawing defenders towards him, before releasing Berry on the right. Little Johnny skipped around the full back and drove for the bye-line. As another defender came to close him down he played the ball into the six yard area where Tommy Taylor used his strength against Santamaria to force the ball over the line. The Spaniards contested the goal as the goalkeeper dragged the ball back from over the goal line, but the linesman was perfectly placed to see that the ball had crossed the line. United were back in the game and they went forward searching for the equaliser. Viollet hit the post and Tommy Taylor had a legitimate call for a penalty kick denied after he had been upended in the area by Santamaria. Just before the end of the game, as they searched for that elusive second goal, Madrid caught them on the counter attack. Hector Rial was again in acres of space, and had the simple job of slipping the ball past Wood and into the net. The final whistle sounded shortly afterwards, and once again, United were returning home from Spain with a two goal deficit to claw back.

The game had been a strange affair as far as United's lads were concerned. Two goals disallowed, a strong penalty claim turned down – even today Bill Foulkes reckons that there was some suspicion of the referee having been bought! They returned home in an optimistic mood on the Friday morning. In Manchester, the fans were more than optimistic – if we could see off Bilbao then there was no doubt in our minds that we could see off Real Madrid as well!

The Babes' Last Title

United arrived home from Madrid on Friday, 12 April, and the following day they played Luton Town at Kenilworth Road. United had sustained some injuries from the game in Madrid – notably Eddie Colman, Billy Whelan and David Pegg. Into the team for the Luton game came Freddie Goodwin, Bobby Charlton and Albert Scanlon. Although United won comfortably with a brace from Tommy Taylor, Busby was a little worried as the team left Luton and returned to Manchester.

The following week brought Easter weekend, and United's programme was probably the most punishing schedule I have ever seen in professional football. They had to play six games in ten days, and in the middle was the return fixture against Real Madrid! The fixture list looked like this:

> Good Friday, 19 April – Burnley away
> Saturday, 20 April – Sunderland at home
> Easter Monday, 22 April – Burnley at home
> Thursday, 25 April – Real Madrid at home
> Saturday, 27 April – Cardiff City away
> Monday, 29 April – West Bromwich Albion at home

It is impossible to overstate what a punishing schedule that was, especially given the importance of the Real Madrid game.

Good Friday fell on 19 April in 1957. I have some very vivid and fond memories of that day, and of the weekend that followed. Being brought up in a strong Catholic environment, Good Friday was a 'Holy Day', and in our family it was normally observed in just such a way. Good Friday began very early for me because I was an altar boy at the Holy Family church in All Saints, Manchester. My roster showed that I was down to serve the 7am Mass, and so I had risen at six, completed my ablutions in the cold water sink in the downstairs living room of our old terraced house, dressed, and then quietly slipped out the front door into Royle Street.

It was just beginning to get light as I made my way to All Saints, where the church still faces All Saints Park. Every step of my journey from my home could be heard as I clattered along the streets because I was wearing clogs! My parents had become so fed up with me kicking the toes out of my shoes playing football, that they had realised a threat, made several months earlier, to put me in clogs.

It is strange how I remember those clogs with such reverence because it turned out that I loved them, and nurtured and cared for them, just as I did for any pair of football boots, despite having to endure a lot of piss-taking from my young friends of that time! As I walked along those quiet streets that morning, my mind wasn't on the task that lay ahead of me at church. As usual it was solely focused on my one and only true love – Manchester United. My head was racing ahead because I would be travelling to Turf Moor, Burnley for a First Division match later that day. The mystique of away travel was wonderment to me back in those days. Today, for most kids, I suppose travelling to a place like Burnley would not seem to be too much of an adventure, but back then it was like going to a foreign country. It was the start of a tremendous few days: Turf Moor on the Friday, Old Trafford on the Saturday, Old Trafford again on the Monday, and then the big one against Real Madrid at Old Trafford the following Thursday. For a starry eyed kid it was the 'Roy of the Rovers' stuff that I read about every week in the Tiger comic.

As my young imagination ran wild, it was me that would lead the United team out at Turf Moor that afternoon; and as I skipped along I became Raymond Glendenning (the radio commentator on the BBC's Light Programme), talking to myself – anyone passing me in the street that morning must have thought that there was something wrong with me as I commentated out loud. But it didn't matter to me – I didn't see or hear anything – I was oblivious to it all and in a little world of my own.

At Holy Family, my entry into the Church couldn't have been more spectacular. As I went through the doorway, and across the carpeted entrance, I stepped into the church with its highly polished wooden floors. The minute my wooden clogs met the shiny floor my legs went from beneath me, and I slid feet first into the marble baptismal font that had a large vase of flowers standing above it. Both the font and flowers came crashing down around me, causing a real old crescendo in the quietness of such a holy place. The parishioners who were waiting for Mass to begin came to my aid, and almost immediately there was an appearance from the parish priest, Father McClernon. The result was that after the mess was cleaned up, I actually served the Mass in my stockinged feet!

But even as I knelt on the altar, supposedly following the Mass, my mind was wandering away towards Turf Moor. What would it be like? What were their supporters like? And (most important of all) would United win? As United approached that Easter, they needed just four points to retain the First Division title. Several times throughout that Mass Father McClernon had to turn around and politely cough to bring my attention back to what I was supposed to be doing.

Time could not pass quickly enough for me, and after what seemed like an age, Father McClernon finally turned around and faced the congregation, saying, "Ite Missa Est". The Mass was over and I responded with, "Deo Gratias" (Thanks be to God). Then I waited for him to descend the altar steps, and followed him into the sanctuary, where I received my usual bollocking from him for being inattentive. Of course, I also got a warning from him not to forget his tickets for the Real Madrid game the following Thursday. It had become a ritual that as well as queuing at ungodly hours for my own tickets for matches, I had to bring his back as well! Discarding my black cassock and white cotta, and donning my clogs once more, I left the church via the housekeeper's entrance, and down the side alleyway besides the church. I was off back home as quickly as my legs could take me. My parents were off to Mass themselves just after I arrived home, accompanied by my younger sister, but before leaving, my Mum asked me whether I was doing the Stations of the Cross later that afternoon. My face reddened as I told her a white lie, saying that I had to go to St. Joseph's at Victoria Park to do a retreat there and that I wouldn't be home until seven o'clock. I'd certainly be gone by the time they returned home later that morning from church.

Whit Friday, 1957: St. Augustine's girls' school on the steps of the Albert Memorial in Albert Square, Manchester. I am the lower altar boy in the centre of the picture. My partner-in-crime, Brian Walsh, is the altar boy on the extreme right at the top. The black clad figure in the centre of the picture is parish priest Father Bernard McLernon.

In the previous year or so, I'd been to a few away games at Preston, Huddersfield, and Maine Road, but Burnley was a new experience for me. I'd arranged to meet my partner-in-crime, Brian Walsh, in Piccadilly. We wandered around Piccadilly for a while, but being Good Friday nothing was open, and next to nobody was about. We meandered our way down Market Street, and Corporation Street, and then finally into Victoria Station. It was a beautiful sunny day, and after we had bought our tickets for the football special to Burnley we sat around and waited. Back in 1957, the Victoria Station buildings were blackened with grime and soot, but it was still a fascinating place. The trains were the old steam type, and there was lots of activity in the as people caught their trains for the Lancashire coast, and a long weekend away. Families with pasty faced kids, dads carrying the suitcases, sweethearts getting away from the prying eyes of vigilant parents – remember, this was 1957! As time passed by, more and more United fans began to arrive in the old station, and before too long, there was a long, chattering line by the platform gate, and when finally the old steam train pulled in alongside the platform, there was a huge cheer from the waiting throng. The gate opened, the ticket collector clipped our tickets, and we were allowed onto the platform to board the train. It was the usual motley band of supporters that made the journey to Burnley, and the banter and camaraderie was terrific. Ladies with flasks of oxo and packets of sandwiches, fellows smoking Capstan Full Strength cigarettes, others drinking bottles of Jubilee Stout, but it was most of all a feeling of excitement, expectation, and togetherness – we all belonged to Manchester United.

The urban Manchester scenery began to disappear as the train steamed its way north, and into the pleasant East Lancashire countryside. It was hilly and green, and we passed through Bury, Ramsbottom and Haslingden, and then into Burnley, the journey taking just over an hour and twenty minutes. As the train doors opened, the supporters flooded out onto the platform, and then just like a snake sliding through the undergrowth, began to move slowly out of the station and into the streets. Brian and I had no idea where Turf Moor was, so as usual we just followed the crowd.

It was a happy throng that made its way through the cobbled and hilly Burnley streets towards the ground. Burnley was still very much a mill town back then, and the huge mill chimneys towered ahead as we walked along. We passed by lots of little corner shops, all closed because it was Good Friday – a far cry from today's world. The crowd became denser as we neared the stadium, Burnley and United fans exchanging banter, but for Brian and me, the Burnley people seemed to speak a foreign language.

It took no more than 15 minutes to reach Turf Moor, where we paid our ninepence entrance and took our places behind the goal at the open end, where the majority of United supporters had congregated. People chatted amiably, even with the Burnley fans – there was no pre-match chanting back in those days. The normal brass band paraded around the pitch for the pre-match entertainment, and the crowd whistled along in the April sunshine to the various marches that the band played. The excitement increased as kick off drew near, and then the Burnley team appeared from the tunnel in their claret and blue shirts. They had some big name players: Colin McDonald, Jimmy Adamson, Tommy Cummings, Brian Miller, John Connelly, Jimmy McIlroy, Ray Pointer, Brian Pilkington – all internationals – and they had a very canny manager in the Geordie, Harry Potts. United came out in blue shirts, and made their way to the open end United lined up: Wood; Foulkes, Byrne; Goodwin, Blanchflower, Edwards; Berry, Whelan, Taylor, Charlton and Pegg. United won comfortably that afternoon. They put on a terrific display of attacking football which really entertained a crowd of over 40,000. Billy Whelan was at his best and scored all three United goals, but it was a display of team power and flowing, attacking football. When the final whistle went, United were just two points away from retaining their title, with Sunderland to play at home the following day. (Some 40 years later an archived reel of colour film was found which showed clips of this match. It provoked considerable interest, as it was thought to be the only colour movie film in existence of the famous Babes – though more recently at least one other short film clip has come to light.)

It was a happy band of United fans that left Turf Moor after the final whistle. The talk on the journey back to Manchester was all about the forthcoming tie with Real Madrid, and whether United could repeat the comeback against Bilbao. I crept back into our house around half past seven that evening. Nobody, I suspected, was wise as to where I'd been, and I was full of myself because "I'd heard that United won 3-1". Dad then filled me in with details about Billy Whelan's hat-trick, with no inkling that I'd witnessed it all personally! Later that evening as I got ready for bed, Mum took me to one side in the bedroom and asked me, "Did you go to Burnley today?" I dropped my head and could not lie to her, very sheepishly saying, "Yes." She had talked to somebody at Mass that morning who had told her that there was no retreat at St. Joseph's that day, and so I had been rumbled. Fortunately for me, she never let on to my Dad.

Saturday, 20 April 1957 saw Sunderland arrive in Manchester, and there was tremendous excitement and expectancy within the city that United would clinch their second title in successive seasons. The city was also abuzz with the imminent arrival of Real Madrid for the second leg of the European Cup semi-final, in which United were trailing by 3-1. Having to play three games in four days, just three days prior to this semi-final, seemed no kind of preparation for a game of such importance. The Football League however, would never countenance a postponement of a league fixture to help the cause, so United just had to get on with it.

Saturday was again a nice sunny day, and as usual I made my way to Old Trafford early. It was a typical match day, but it did seem that this was larger than normal crowd. I performed all my pre-match rituals – walking around the ground; reading the posters on the walls; watching as the players began to arrive; chasing the big fella down to the ticket office. I saw the Sunderland team arrive in their 'charra', a team with many experienced internationals: Len Shackleton, Ray Daniel, Charlie Fleming, Billy Elliott, Billy Bingham, Stan Anderson and Colin Grainger, to name just a few. United made just one change from the team that had played Burnley the day before, Eddie Colman returning at right half in place of Freddie Goodwin.

Almost 59,000 fans packed into a sunny Old Trafford that afternoon, and Sunderland were no real match for a rampant United. Whelan quickly added to his three goals from the day before, opening the scoring very early on. Sunderland's cause wasn't helped by an injury to their goalkeeper, Johnny Bollands, in a collision with Tommy Taylor as he dived at the big centre forward's feet. The injury sadly meant that he took no further part in the game, and Sunderland were down to 10 men for the duration. Big Charlie 'Legs' Fleming, their Scottish centre forward, took over in goal.

Charlie was a real football character, and the old traditional centre forward. Arms and legs everywhere, which propelled him like a windmill, and he had courage that would take him through a barn door if necessary. He was a handful for any centre half, and he'd bagged lots of goals for Sunderland since he'd travelled south from Scotland some two seasons before. I was standing behind the goal at the Stretford End, where the injury to Bollands had occurred, and the game became pretty one sided from then on. It came as no surprise that United increased their lead with a goal from Tommy Taylor.

Then just before half-time, I witnessed one of those defining moments in football, something that stays with you, immersed in your memory bank forever. The big fella won the ball in midfield just inside the Sunderland half, and in his customary fashion he began to drive forward. From fully thirty yards out he hit a tremendous, venomous thunderbolt with his left foot. Charlie Fleming seemed to duck beneath the flight of the ball, and it hit the back of the net with a wallop. Nothing will ever convince me that Charlie did not fear for his safety when that shot came at him, and that he took the safe way out by getting out of the way of it.

It was game over, and the second half was a stroll for United. A fourth goal from Billy Whelan gave the likeable Dubliner a tally of five goals from two games, and when the final whistle went it was smiles and cheers all around as United retained their First Division title. Thousands of fans jumped over the picket fence surrounding the stands, and ran onto the pitch to congratulate their heroes once more – the championship flag would be flying again at Old Trafford the following season.

There was real anticipation and excitement fermenting in Manchester that Sunday. The championship secured, Real Madrid was now the big target. The tickets for the Real Madrid game went on sale on Easter Sunday morning and thousands of people queued throughout the night. Brian and I got to Old Trafford around 5am, and already the line was way down Trafford Road going down towards Ashburton Road. We eventually got our tickets later that morning, plus those for the priests, and we looked forward to the coming week immensely.

Busby now had the luxury of being able to maybe rest a few players for the Easter Monday game against Burnley at Old Trafford. However, nobody could have anticipated the extent of the changes. When the team was actually announced that morning, there was uproar. He had made nine changes, with only Wood and Foulkes remaining from the team that had beaten Sunderland two days previously. Bob Lord the autocratic Burnley Chairman, made scathing comments about United, and considered it an insult to Burnley that United could put out a 'Boy's Own' team (as he put it) against them. The Football League was also incensed, and there was immediate talk of punishing United for fielding a weakened team in a Football League game.

Busby was unperturbed and undaunted, and went ahead as planned. Just over 41,000 fans turned out that day to watch Dennis Viollet lead out the champions, with United lining up: Wood; Foulkes, Greaves; Goodwin, Cope, McGuinness; Webster, Doherty, Dawson, Viollett, and Scanlon. Most Manchester folk at that time knew just how good United's strength in depth was. The reserve team was strong, the junior teams were strong, and the youth team was unbeatable. But it remained to be seen just how good the youngsters would be against top notch opposition – and make no mistake about it, Burnley were a very good team. Roared on by a very partisan crowd, United's 'reserves' took the game to Burnley, displaying the attacking ethos of their first team mentors. That they scored first through young Alex Dawson came as no surprise, and the scoreline stayed the same until midway through the second half, when Welshman, Colin Webster, steamed in to power home a second goal. The game ended 2-0 to United, and the happiness in the young United players' faces as they left the field told the story.

Bob Lord went back to Burnley with his tail between his legs, as his Burnley team had been demolished by the young United reserves. It was a result that made him bitter towards United forever after, and he was never slow in showing that bitterness in later years. The Football League could hardly charge United with 'fielding a weakened team' after that result, and so the matter died a death and wasn't spoken of again. For United fans, it had been a tremendous weekend. Champions again, already through to the FA Cup final, and with Real Madrid to come just three days later – what a wonderful time to be around in the history of our great club.

End of the Dream: Real Madrid, the Second Leg

And so, once again, European fever gripped Manchester, and indeed the whole country. Such was the interest in this game that ITV decided to show the match live – the first time a European game had been screened in this way in Britain. Could we do it? There was so much optimism, and United would be back on home turf as Old Trafford was ready with terrific floodlighting. We all thought that this would be such an advantage to United.

Real Madrid pulled off a stunt before even a ball was kicked. Remembering the chasing that David Pegg had given Becerril, Madrid had brought in on loan a full back named Torres from Zaragoza, to counter David's strong running game – in effect, this guy was a hatchet man. They had this player on 14 days loan, and specifically for just this game. Matt wasn't at all happy, and countered by asking if Real would consider it was fair if he brought in Matthews and Finney. The outcome was that he accepted things and said he had faith in his youngsters to do the job. Old Trafford was full of expectancy and optimism, and millions more tuned in to ITV to watch on the little screen. The commentary was done by a journalist from the old Reynolds News, Gerry Loftus, and from what I am told the broadcast was a very amateurish affair.

I stood against the fence, on the half way line on the Popular Side, with a good view as the teams emerged from the tunnel, United in all red and Real Madrid in all white. Again the crowd tried to lift the team with their cheers and roars. The line-up that famous evening was: Wood; Foulkes, Byrne; Colman, Blanchflower, Edwards; Berry, Whelan, Taylor, Charlton and Pegg. Real Madrid were certainly a far different proposition than Bilbao, and in the early stages United just couldn't get control of the ball. The guy who was orchestrating everything was di Stefano – he was (I say grudgingly) magnificent that night. After twenty minutes' play the tie was all over, and the crowd had been silenced – United had conceded two goals, and in effect were

5-1 down. Their gung-ho attitude, and search for that early goal, left them vulnerable at the back, while Madrid were sufficiently classy, and experienced enough, to take advantage of this. First Raymond Kopa darted in and scored, then Hector Rial added a second to make the task insurmountable.

The Babes came out for the second half in a battling mood. They battered the Madrid defence, but I have to say Santamaria was outstanding for them that evening. He broke up or cleared so many United thrusts. However, Tommy Taylor scored on the hour mark, and the fans sniffed something – the atmosphere heightened, and it seemed to affect Madrid. They started to resort to gamesmanship, something we hadn't really seen back then. Their players began feigning injury, they wasted as much time as they could, and they contested every decision of the referee. It frustrated United, breaking up the flow of the play. With just eight minutes left Bobby Charlton equalised on the night, and the crowd were right back behind the team again. An abiding memory is of Miguel Munoz going down with nobody around him, and rolling over as though he had been shot. From out of a bunch of players strode Duncan Edwards, who literally took hold of Munoz by the back of his shirt, and pulled him along the ground, over the touchline onto the cinder track. In those days, there was no time added on for injuries and stoppages, and the final whistle blew to end our European dream for that season, and along with it our hopes of winning the treble. The United players were so disappointed as they trooped off the field, but they did so to the acclaim of the United fans. The following morning there was a picture of Edwards in one of the newspapers, which caught Duncan's expression just as the final whistle sounded. Disappointment was etched all over his face, and it's a picture that I can still see clearly even today.

So the dream was over, but as we reflected on that defeat to Madrid, we also looked back on the season's European campaign, and the thrills it had brought to us all. The club had made so many new friends and Europe now knew about the wonderful young team that was growing in Manchester. They had been terrific ambassadors, not only for

Manchester United, but for Britain as well. They now had a campaign under their belts, and like the fans the players could not wait to try again the following season.

Schoolboy Memories

I am sure that most football fans, at some time in their lives, have aspired to play the game at the highest level. Becoming a professional player is never easy, and very few reach such a pinnacle, but many achieve an acceptable standard, depending on their ability. At the end of the day, we look back on our playing days with great fondness and pleasure. Nothing compares with the joy of actually playing the game of football, enjoying the successes that playing in a good team brings, and, most of all, being young, fit, and healthy.

Today, most kids' skills are honed initially on the school playing fields or in junior football clubs. Promising young players may go on develop in representative schoolboy football, or in the academies and centres of excellence of professional clubs. Although there is no doubt that facilities today are so much better than they were in my younger days, I believe there is still a massive neglect, and underfunding, in the provision of facilities. Britain is light years behind its European neighbours in this field.

In the immediate aftermath of the Second World War, playing facilities were virtually non-existent in most localities. A trip to the park invariably meant either a very long walk, or a bus fare that parents could ill afford. We didn't have the distractions that the kids have today. Television was very much in its infancy, and computers were unheard of. The height of the week's entertainment was a trip to the ABC Minors Saturday morning matinee at the Apollo Cinema on Ardwick Green, or the old H.D. Moorehouse, Grosvenor picture house on the corner of All Saints. Otherwise, our leisure time was spent outdoors playing football, or cricket in the summer.

During the 1950s, and well into the 1960s, there were still many areas in the city of Manchester suffering the legacy of wartime from bomb damage. On open bomb-sites, which we called 'crofts', you would see games of football played by adults as well as youngsters. In front of the

Dunlop's and John Noble's factories, on Brook Street in Chorlton-upon-Medlock, there was a large expanse of waste ground, where every working day the lunchtime siren would see the workers emerge, put coats down on the ground to mark the goal, and play football. Those games were as competitive as you could get, and many a time arguments would break out, to be settled with bare fists there and then! It was the same all over the city, and in almost every large town throughout Britain.

As kids, we would play every waking hour. Even during the cold winter nights, in darkness and fog we played until the witching hour, when the call came from our parents that it was time to come in. In darkness we would move the game from the 'croft' to the gas-lit streets. The lamp posts were fifty yards apart, and the area between them became our pitch. The goal was the space between the lamp-post and the wall – normally a gap about six feet wide. Most of the time we used a tennis ball, and you had to be able to look after yourself in possession! Time on the ball was precious, because everybody was competitive; they wanted that ball off you, and it was always very physical.

You learned to control the ball with both feet, dribble, twist and turn, shield the ball, dummy, tackle, play wall-passes, and time your leaps to head the ball. At the end of the day, knee and elbow scrapes were commonplace, as were cut lips and bloodied noses, but there was sheer enjoyment in playing in those games. It was nearly always City against United – depending which club you supported. Your kit was your everyday clothing, and your footwear, your everyday shoes. Some kids had the luxury of owning gym shoes, or 'galoshes' as we called them, but for most of us it was a rare luxury.

At the end of each day it was a hot bath in the old tin tub in front of the living room fire. Most houses in my area had no electricity, and were lit by gaslight, so good old Mum would have prepared the bath. She would also be the first aider, tending to all the cuts, scrapes and bruises. After bathtime, and a light supper, it was off to bed to dream of your footballing heroes, and it was never very long before you were off into the world of your dreams.

To play in a competitive match, wearing football kit and football boots, was a thing not many kids got to enjoy back then. Most of us played in the old type of boot which had the leather bar across the instep, and six leather studs nailed into each sole. They were heavy and cumbersome, and the mud used to cling on the sole of the boot in between the studs, so if it was wet it was like playing on an ice rink. My Granddad solved the problem by showing me that if you coated each sole in shoe polish the mud wouldn't stick. We didn't win many games when I first started playing, but none of us lost our enthusiasm, and even if we were beaten 10-0 we would eagerly anticipate the next match. It was just such a great feeling to be able to tell your mates, "I play for our school!"

In 1956, because of my progress I was moved up into what was called the 'Shield' team, which meant I would be playing against boys a year or two older than myself. My father and mother were delighted, and gave me the biggest incentive to do well. They promised me a new pair of football boots! The first game was against St. Malachy's of Collyhurst in the 'Catholic Cup', a knock-out competition for all the Catholic schools which was administered by the Manchester Education Committee. The game was to be played at Monsall Rec, a brute of a ground, just like the Barracks in Hulme – all red shale and stones. It was, and still is, situated on Monsall Street in Miles Platting, just a stone's throw from Manchester United's first ever ground on North Road.

The day before the game I arrived home from school to be told by my mother that I could not go out until my father arrived home from work. Naturally, I was peeved to say the least. However, at six o'clock on the dot in he came, and without saying a word he handed me a brown paper parcel. Imagine my joy when, on tearing the wrapping paper off so excitedly, there in my hands was the first pair of Adidas football boots that I ever possessed! They were actually light tan in colour and had three dark brown stripes running down the inside and outside of each boot. Compared with the old boots they were like carpet slippers – they were so light. I knew the sacrifices my parents had made to purchase those boots for me, and believe me I treasured them from that moment on. The following day we surprised everybody and beat St. Malachy's by 5-2, an entirely new experience for me to play in a winning team! But as the season progressed, we got stronger, and we swept all before us in our age group.

In March 1957, it wasn't only Manchester United going in search of an unheard of treble – so was my school under-13s team. We'd won our evening and Saturday leagues with ease, but you never received individual medals for such feats back then. The school received a framed certificate from the Manchester Schools Football Association, but as players we got nothing. In March we were drawn to play St. Patrick's (the famous old school that produced Nobby Stiles and Brian Kidd) at Newton Heath Loco in the semi-finals of our knock-out competition. And as I stated earlier, to appear at 'The Loco' was akin to the professional playing at Wembley.

St. Pat's had a great football reputation, and their football master was a certain Laurie Cassidy, who had combined a school teaching career with playing for Manchester United. There was no quarter asked or given in this game, as both teams went at each other with a vengeance. Early on I made a terrible mistake which cost us a goal. The ball was crossed from way out on the right hand side, more in hope than anything else, and I got too far underneath it, allowing it to pass over my head and into the net. We equalised just before half-time and went in all square. Immediately after the restart, St. Pat's got a penalty for a silly handball by our full back Barry Nixon. My grandfather had taught me a theory about facing penalty kicks, and it was one I used quite successfully throughout my playing days. It involved observing how the penalty taker addressed his run-up to the ball. In this important game I guessed right and saved the kick, atoning for my earlier, costly mistake. As the second half ebbed away our superiority began to show, and we scored twice to win through to the final by 3-1. When I arrived home and told my parents they were delighted, especially at the

237

prospect of their young son winning his first competitive football medal.

The final was again played at Newton Heath Loco, against a school called St. Columbus from the Wythenshawe area, another side with a big reputation in Manchester schools football. There was a larger than normal crowd on the evening of the final, as immediately after our game Manchester Boys were playing Salford Boys. We had to change in an adjoining room off from the main dressing rooms. Again there was the huge thrill of running out in front of so many spectators, but my biggest thrill was yet to come. We didn't play as well as we could do that evening, and we lost the final by 4-2. Although I had played well enough myself, the disappointment inside me was immense.

The winners collected their trophy and medals first, and the presentation was made by none other than Mark Jones, the Manchester United centre-half, who was so tragically to lose his life just ten months later at Munich. As losers, we were presented with our medals after the winners. It was some consolation as I was handed my medal – a silver shield in a blue case – when Mark Jones ruffled my hair, saying in that deep Yorkshire voice, "Well done young 'un." My biggest thrill though came seconds later, as I stood among my team mates. A voice from behind whispered in my ear, "Let's feel your medal son." I spun around, and there stood my father and his dog, a black Labrador named Buffer. Because of the problems with his sight, Dad had never been able to watch me play school football. However, he had wanted to be present as his son played in his first cup final, and Mum had made sure he was there. They hadn't told me that they would be watching, so the thrill of having my Dad there completely removed the disappointment of losing that final. He kept that medal until the day he died in 1984, and although I was to go on and win many more medals during my playing days, that little piece of silver still holds pride of place in the cabinet today. It is my most treasured possession.

FA Cup Final 1957

Although elimination from the European Cup at the hands of Real Madrid left United smarting, the team was still in with the chance of the league and FA Cup double – something that had not been achieved in the 20th century. United already had the First Division championship wrapped up, and were through to the FA Cup final – so the Double really was 'on'.

On the Saturday immediately after the Real Madrid game at Old Trafford, United beat Cardiff City 3-2 at Ninian Park, with two goals from Albert Scanlon and one from Alex Dawson. The Madrid game had taken it out of the team and several changes were made – Greaves, McGuinness, Webster, Dawson, Viollet and Scanlon replaced Byrne, Edwards, Berry, Taylor, Charlton and Pegg. The important thing was though that they came away with the two points.

United's last league game of the season was at home to West Bromwich Albion on Monday, 29 April. Only 20,357 fans turned up to see a weakened United team draw 1-1, with Alex Dawson scoring United's goal. Gordon Clayton made one of his rare appearances in goal in place of Ray Wood; Ian Greaves continued to deputise for Roger Byrne; Freddie Goodwin, Mark Jones, and Wilf McGuinness were in for Colman Blanchflower and Edwards; Doherty, Dawson, Viollet and Scanlon were in for Whelan, Taylor, Charlton and Pegg.

With the championship won, the Babes only had to wait until the following Saturday, 4 May 1957, to face Aston Villa in the FA Cup final at Wembley. Surely Villa would be no match for this wonderful young team.

Busby took the players away again to Blackpool for a few days, before moving down to London on the Thursday before the final. The manager was wrestling with a couple of selection dilemmas ahead of the final: should the fit-again Mark Jones replace Blanchflower, and would

Dennis Viollet be fit to play in place of Bobby Charlton? Viollet had been carrying a long term groin problem, and had turned out in games when he was not fully fit. If he was not 100% fit then Wembley was certainly not the place to find out. Selection issues were probably responsible for the most unusual pre-Cup final story.

On the Wednesday evening before the Cup final, a photographer was passing Old Trafford, and noticed that the floodlights at the stadium were beaming down. Intrigued, because it was after 10.30 at night, he decided to find out what was going on. When he arrived on Warwick Road, behind the Scoreboard End of the ground, he could hear shouting from inside. His curiosity got the better of him, so he climbed up the floodlight pylon closest to United Road. He was staggered to see a full scale first team versus reserves practice game in progress – the shouts he had heard were from the players taking part. Being an opportunist, he took a quick picture and got in touch with the Daily Mirror. Sure enough, the picture appeared in later editions of the paper the following morning. In the event, Busby delayed announcing his team until the latest opportunity on the morning of the final.

Granddad travelled down to the game on the 'Wembley Special' train from London Road station with his good friend Tommy Coates. Mum had arranged for me to watch the final at Aunt Pat's house in Ardwick. They lived in an imposing terraced house just across Hyde Road from Nicholl's Grammar School. I got there early, and passed the time with her son, Peter Ingham. Mum and Pat had been friends for years, and Peter and I were good friends. We didn't see a lot of each other, but whenever we did we enjoyed each other's company. This Saturday was no different, but once the coverage of the Cup final started we were riveted in front of the small black and white television.

Having seen the previous two Cup finals, the pomp and ceremony of the occasion always got to me. Back in those days, there was a great mystique about Wembley. It was every player's dream to play there, a place every football fan wanted visit. It really did have an aura all of its own. In more recent years I feel that the intrusiveness of television has taken away much of that mystique, and for me has spoiled what used to be such a great occasion. Also there were relatively few games played each season on that hallowed turf – a few international matches plus the FA Cup final. Unfortunately, over the years (and especially since the 1990s) the FA's commercial greed surfaced, and more and more matches were played there, including FA Cup semi-finals. It spoiled it all, and Wembley lost all of its old charm and mystique.

But I was open mouthed that afternoon in 1957 as I watched the band of the Guards in tunics and bearskin hats, marching round the stadium. I sang along with the thousands at the game when the community singing began, conducted by Sir Arthur Cager high on his rostrum in the centre of the lush pitch, resplendent in his white suit. Since 1927, the hymn *Abide with Me* has always been sung prior to the players leaving the dressing rooms. Back then it was sung impeccably by the fans, and was a very emotional few minutes. Even today, I shed a tear when I watch this part of the FA Cup final pomp. Once finished, the 100,000 fans waved their Daily Express song sheets, and it made for a wonderful sight. I just wish that today's youngsters could experience the kind of atmosphere that Cup finals in the old days used to generate.

After *Abide with Me* it was so beautiful and sunny as Eric Houghton and Matt Busby led their teams from the famous old tunnel. Villa were in claret and blue striped shirts; United's shirts were all white with red piping. The teams lined up in front of the Royal Box, and were introduced to HRH the Duke of Edinburgh. After the introductions, the National Anthem was sung with great gusto by all the fans. The formalities over, the teams broke away and began their short warm up. As we sat waiting for the kick off, I just knew this was going to be our day. Villa were just not good enough to beat United, and once the final whistle blew, I was convinced that Manchester United would have achieved the famous Double.

Busby had decided to leave Jackie Blanchflower in his line-up, which was a great disappointment to Mark Jones. Sadly, Dennis Viollet didn't make the starting lineup either, so the team that marched out into that famous old stadium was: Wood; Foulkes, Byrne; Colman, Blanchflower, Edwards; Berry, Whelan, Taylor, Charlton and Pegg. On paper, this game was a foregone conclusion – Villa, man for man, were no match for this classy United team. Unfortunately we hadn't legislated for what was to happen very early in the game.

With the game just six minutes old United, in my honest opinion, were on the receiving end of the worst piece of skullduggery that I have ever witnessed on a football field. A harmless looking header had found its way into the arms of United's goalkeeper, Ray Wood. He had gathered the ball safely and was about to move out of his six yard area. To all intents and purposes the ball was 'dead' – it was safely in his hands – there was no danger. However, Peter McParland the Villa left winger, even though he saw that Wood had gathered the ball, came hurtling in at pace, and launched himself at Wood. The inevitable collision was horrendous. Wood was certainly not expecting a challenge like this and was caught as McParland's head impacted upon his face, shattering his cheekbone.

This incident was the only time that I ever saw Duncan Edwards come close to losing his temper. Duncan sprinted across to McParland, then stopped and turned away, probably counting to ten before the red mist descended. He stood above McParland, who had gone to ground and was lying on the turf holding his face. As Wood was treated by Tom Curry, McParland got to his feet, ready to play on. Wood left the field on a stretcher, and was taken on the long walk to the dressing rooms. There were no substitutes allowed in those days, and so United had to reorganise. On a hot day, and down to ten men having lost a crucial member of the team, it was going to be an uphill task. Jackie Blanchflower, who was more than a competent goalkeeper, moved into goal, and Duncan Edwards dropped back to centre half. United fought valiantly throughout that first half and went into the half-time break at 0-0.

During the break, Ted Dalton, the United physiotherapist, at Busby's request took Wood outside of the stadium and onto a grass verge, where he started to throw a ball to him. Poor Ray! He was so dazed and befuddled that he didn't see any of the balls properly at all, and he failed to collect cleanly any of those thrown up to him. Nearby was a group of young schoolboys playing football themselves on the grass. On seeing what had been going on, one of the kids approached Dalton and Wood and informed them, "Mister, he can come and play with us if he wants to!" Oh, the Irony. Inside the great stadium, less than 50 yards away, 100,000 fans were waiting to see if Ray Wood would return to take part in the season's showpiece finale – little did they know that just outside, Ray Wood was being offered a place in a game of street football.

Wood did return to the field, but unable to resume in goal he went to the outside left position, purely for nuisance value because he certainly could not play any meaningful part in the match. United held their own for the first 15 minutes of that half, but Villa eventually got the breakthrough, and of all people McParland was the scorer. Then, 15 minutes from time, he was to score again, although there was more than a hint of offside about the goal. United's dream of the Double was fast disappearing. With just 10 minutes to go, Busby gambled and sent out instructions for Wood to go back into goal. Obviously dazed and in pain, Ray made the short journey to the goal at the tunnel end of the ground. United now had to go on the offensive, keeping the ball away from their stricken goalkeeper. This they did, and they started to besiege the Villa goal. Just five minutes of the game remained when Tommy Taylor forced a corner kick. Sprinting from midfield came Duncan Edwards to take it. He floated the ball towards the penalty spot, where Taylor seemed to have got too far in front of the ball, but he arched backwards as he jumped, and with tremendous power met the ball with his forehead, sending it soaring in a high arc beyond Nigel Sims and into the net. United were 2-1 down with five minutes to go. United pressed, oh, how they pressed. Billy Whelan got the ball into the net two minutes from time, but it was ruled fractionally offside, and then all too soon time ran out and the final whistle sounded. Disappointment was etched all over the United boy's faces. A season that had promised so much had been cruelly thwarted by McParland's act of violence.

True to the spirit of that team, and the wonderful sportsmen that they were, as Johnny Dixon led his players up the famous 39 steps to collect the old trophy from Her Majesty the Queen, Roger Byrne led the United players in the applause for their conquerors. It must have hurt them, but they were so sporting in the way they accepted their defeat. The biggest cheers of that day were for the losers as they collected their medals. Villa had won the Cup, but the glory belonged to the Babes. Immediately they got back to the dressing room, Wood was whisked off to hospital where he was operated on for a broken cheekbone and other facial injuries.

I was heartbroken after the game and it was a tearful young boy that made his way home to Royle Street. I felt United had been cheated, and I still do so today. In the modern game McParland would have received a straight red card for his actions, and United would have been able to replace Ray Wood with a substitute. There had been some cries for substitutes to be allowed in the FA Cup final because there had been bad injuries in previous finals in the 1950s. Wally Barnes was carried off playing for Arsenal against Newcastle in 1952, while Eric Bell, the Bolton wing half, was nothing more than a passenger against Blackpool in 1953 after injuring his leg. In 1955, Manchester City had lost full back Jimmy Meadows after just a quarter of an hour, and played the remainder of their final against Newcastle with ten men. The request for substitutes did have some credence, but as far as the FA were concerned, it feel upon deaf ears.

Although the season ended in disappointment, it could not be called unsuccessful. The young United side had embarked on a journey that, especially in Europe, was uncharted. They had brilliantly retained their league title, and had come so close to achieving the Double; they had reached the European Cup semi-final at their first attempt, losing to a great team who were the eventual winners. All this was more experience for them, and as they departed for their summer break, each and every one of the Babes was eager for the start of the following season. They had an inherent belief in themselves, and feared nobody – they wanted to put the record straight, and they promised the fans that their goal for the 1957/58 season was nothing more than that so called treble.

Summer 1957

A few weeks after the FA Cup final, a letter from the Manchester Education Committee informed my parents that in September 1957, I would attend St. Gregory's High School in Ardwick, and not St. Bede's Grammar School. To this day I do not know what influenced that decision, and I can remember that my Mum was very disappointed. However, she thought that half a loaf was better than none, and at least I would be attending a high school, one that had a very good reputation in the Manchester area. I was more than happy with the situation. For one thing, I would not have to trek all the way to Whalley Range – Greg's was just a short walk away, at the top end of Ardwick Green, close enough for me to go home for lunch if I so desired.

However, I still had almost three months left at 'Gussie's and I decided to make the most of them. Once the FA Cup final was over, cricket again became the order of the day. Wickets were chalked onto the school yard wall, and bats were made from any old piece of wood that could be found. We invariably played cricket with a tennis ball, but the bowlers could still do some strange things with it. I used to read The Eagle comic each week, which had a sports section in the centre pages. One issue had diagrams on how to hold a cricket ball to bowl leg-breaks and googlies. It fascinated me so much, and in my leisure time I would spend hours bowling the ball at stumps chalked on the wall, trying to perfect the technique. That summer was the first time that I ever made it into the school cricket team and I really did enjoy every game that we played.

But knowing I was leaving 'Gussie's made me sad, and I tried to put the thought out of my mind. Dad was still unhappy about me going to high school, as he thought the cost of a buying uniform, schoolbag and gym shoes was too much to pay. However, one way or another, my mother determined that I was going to attend St. Gregory's. I also had a summer trip to Ireland to look forward to, as the school was taking a party to Skerries, just north of Dublin. I desperately wanted to go and

Mum came up with an idea to raise the money, and maybe also help with purchasing my new school uniform. The hobby shops had introduced a new kit for making plaster casts, and Mum bought one of these kits, which had two rubber moulds in the shape of garden gnomes, and one mould in the shape of a Victorian female flower seller. We made figurines from a mixture that turned into a kind of plaster of Paris. Once the plaster was dry, the moulds were peeled off and we painted and glazed them. Mum and Dad would sell them for sixpence each! We must have made hundreds of the things, and it is probably a reason why I don't like seeing garden gnomes anywhere near my home to this day! I have no doubt that as Dad sold them in the pubs, and at his work, a fair bit of the income he received found its way into his pocket to supplement his drinking money. Mum sold them wherever she could, and the sum required to send me on the school holiday, and also provide me with a small amount of pocket money, was finally achieved.

In the early summer months I would try and go to Old Trafford cricket ground to watch Lancashire. In early June, on a glorious Saturday, I attended my first ever 'Roses' match. The Lancashire and Yorkshire teams were filled with star players. Lancashire boasted Alan Wharton, Geoff Edrich, Jack Ikin, Ken Grieves (who also played in goal for Bolton Wanderers during the soccer season), Geoff Pullar, Cyril Washbrook, Roy Tattersall and the mercurial Brian Statham. Yorkshire had a formidable line-up, which included Frank Lowson, Brian Close, Ray Illingworth, Billy Sutcliffe, Johnny Wardle, Jimmy Binks, and the legendary F.S. (Freddie) Trueman. I sat up against the boundary rope inside a packed Old Trafford and saw wickets fall like ninepins all day. On a turning wicket it was mesmerizing for both batsman and fans alike to watch the skills of the spin bowlers as they bamboozled the batsmen. Sixteen wickets fell as I watched, 12 of them to spin bowlers.

If the weather was nice, after Sunday Mass my friends and I would trek up to Altrincham and the area around Dunham Park. We would catch the electric train from Oxford Road, and the journey to Altrincham was always a big adventure. It was an escape from the inner city and we loved the wide open green areas. Many a Sunday afternoon was spent swimming in the murky waters of the River Bollin. There is an old water mill in Dunham Park whose large water wheel was always a source of fascination to me. Dunham Hall in all its magnificence was always eye-catching, and most absorbing to us young city urchins. Whenever we could, we would 'scrump" apples and pears from trees in the surrounding farms, and many were the times that we were spotted and chased by farmworkers. But they were extremely happy, carefree days, and safe days too.

If the weather was bad we would stay at home, and most of the enjoyment came from listening to the radio. Sunday afternoon programmes on the BBC's Light Programme were always entertaining: The Huggets, The Goon Show, The Navy Lark, Educating Archie (the only radio programme I ever knew that starred a ventriloquist and his dummy!), Jimmy Clitheroe, PC 49, Down Your Way, Journey Into Space, Dick Barton – Special Agent – all programmes that instilled a love of radio in me. Radio has always played a large part in my life, and I do not travel anywhere today without one. It stimulates the imagination as well as being an outlet for keeping you up to date when other media outlets are unavailable.

My last week at St. Augustine's arrived, and I didn't want the Friday to come. But come it did, and I didn't handle it too well. By this time Mr. Hammond had taken over as headmaster from Mr. Callaghan, who had retired at Easter time. He assembled the school over in the hall at the Cavendish Street school, and one by one the boys who were leaving were called out by name. My name was called and I walked the length of the hall and out to the front, where the school teachers and the headmaster were standing. Mr. Hammond shook hands with me and presented me with a small bible. What did get to me though was that as I turned to leave, Mr. Avery, who had been the sports master throughout my time at 'Gussie's, got hold of me and embraced me. His words got to me as he wished me all the best, and tears flowed from my eyes. In moments like that I am always emotional, and always will be. I suppose I was coming to terms with the realisation that I was actually leaving everybody I knew, everyone I had grown up alongside. My life was going to change, and in a big way.

The week after I left St. Augustine's I was back there to climb aboard the 'charra' for the trip to the Princess Dock in Liverpool as we began our journey to Skerries. The coach ride to Liverpool took us along the East Lancashire Road, and this in itself was an adventure. There were no motorways back then, and the 35 mile journey took well over an hour to complete. We descended into Liverpool and were soon at the entrance to the Princess Dock. Behind us stood the tall Liver Assurance building with the two Liver Birds standing erect on top of its towers. We went inside the passenger hall, and through the windows we could see the vessel, the Leinster, which would take us across the Irish Sea to Dublin. To us, it seemed like a great ocean liner.

Just after 11pm Leinster slipped her moorings, moved through the small locks, and then out into the River Mersey. Several ships lay out at anchor, and one I can always remember was a huge big B&I vessel, all white apart from two black funnels with two broad white rings around them. As we sailed past it, I saw it was named the Oxfordshire, and later in life I learned it was in fact a troopship. The Leinster bobbed and weaved its way out of the Mersey estuary and into the Irish Sea. The decks were crowded with kids, from other schools as well as our own, and there was a feeling of great excitement amongst everybody. We watched as the lights along the coastline started to recede – by this time it was early morning. The vessel ploughed on in the darkness.

Just a couple of hours later the Leinster started to roll, pitching up and down. By now most of the kids on board had consumed large amounts of pop, crisps and biscuits, and as the ship began to roll so did their stomachs! From being full of excitement and verve, they were now beginning to feel quite sick. It was the same for many of the adults as well, especially those who had been drinking in the bars, including our teachers. Most of the party from 'Gussie's were in an area of reclining chairs, and as the sea got rougher a horrible stench of sickness permeated the whole vessel. I recall it so vividly even today. I was affected myself, throwing up as I hurried towards the toilet area on the deck. It was a really rough crossing, the only time in my life I have been sea sick. I have sailed across oceans, sometimes in heavy seas, but nothing I can recall was as bad as that journey across the Irish Sea that night. Fortunately, as the dawn came, the seas began to subside, and as it got light we crowded the decks, straining for sight of the Irish coast. At last it came into view, and the Leinster inched its way into the River Liffey estuary, and towards its berth on Dublin's North Wall.

Once disembarked, suitcases in hand, we were marched to the Catholic Co-Cathedral in Dublin's centre to celebrate Mass (it was a Holy Day of Obligation). After Mass, we walked to Dublin's rail terminal and took a small electric train for the 45 minute journey to the little seaside village of Skerries. Upon arrival at the little railway station, we congregated on the platform, formed up in twos and walked the mile or so to our holiday accommodation at what was loosely termed, the 'holiday camp'.

The accommodation comprised wooden huts, and inside were dormitories that contained bunk beds along either side of the room. There were toilets and washrooms as well, but in today's society, the whole place would be described as 'less than basic'. For us kids though it was an exciting adventure and we didn't notice anything to spoil our two week holiday. In adjacent huts there were kids from other schools in Manchester, and opposite was a large building that housed a large dining room, kitchen and congregational hall. Each school had to provide a kitchen party to help with the cleaning up after meals, and washing up plates and cutlery. Kids didn't like it when they were selected to do it, but it was no real hardship.

Adjacent to the buildings was a large flat field, ideal for football, cricket and (for the girls) rounders. Over the next few weeks friendships were forged and rivalries made on that field. Some days we were taken on excursions to Glendalough, the Wicklow Mountains, and Dublin. Most of our time, though, was spent playing on that playing field. On some evenings, the dining room was turned into a makeshift dance hall and the teachers on duty would become dance instructors for the evening. The girls of course loved it, but it was a hard task trying to get the boys involved! Most of them thought being taught ballroom dancing was cissy-ish!

The two weeks' holiday was over, and it was back to Manchester. We all hoped and prayed that the sea crossing would not be rough, and our prayers were duly answered. The Irish Sea on that particular evening was so calm and tranquil, and most of the kids slept the journey away until the boat reached Princess Dock in Liverpool just after six in the morning. After claiming our suitcases we were hustled onto a 'charra', and made our way to a large café on Scotland Road where a hearty breakfast was provided for us. Fully sustained, the 'charra' made its way back along the East Lancashire Road, and finally to its destination in York Street. As I collected my battered old little brown suitcase, both Mr. Fay and Mr. Gibbons, two of my former teachers, came to say farewell and wish me well at my new school. For me it was the end of the first real chapter in my young life, and as I trudged the short distance from York Street to my home, I felt lost, as though a door had been shut behind me, leaving me all alone.

We were now into the last week in July, and just a few days after I returned from Ireland I again went to the Galleon swimming pool. Sure enough, a large number of the United lads were there enjoying themselves. They were just as friendly as they had been the year before, and they cavorted with the kids in the pool, but this time there seemed to be a larger number of them. Duncan and his girlfriend, Molly, were amongst them, and I just couldn't take my eyes off him. His smile was so infectious, and he set off laughing when he saw me. "You get everywhere – do you never go home?" he teased me. Bobby Charlton was once again playing the role of the Pied Piper as he led a line of children up to the ice cream booth, and supplied them with ices. The ball appeared, and they would play head tennis in the pool. Wilf McGuinness, Eddie Colman, Billy Whelan, David Pegg, Tommy Taylor and their friends all made up a happy crowd sat up on the grassed area. So much happiness, smiles and laughter.

United players on a visit to a sergeants' mess at a British military barracks in West Berlin in early August 1957 while on pre-season tour. From left to right: Johnny Berry, Jackie Blanchflower, David Pegg, a mess member, Alex Dawson, Tommy Taylor and Mark Jones. Photograph courtesy of Ken Winterbottom.

United skipper Roger Byrne with the General Officer Commanding Berlin. Photograph courtesy of Ken Winterbottom.

United players David Pegg and Mark Jones share the company of a mess member. Photograph courtesy of Ken Winterbottom.

Eddie Colman talks to an attentive mess member.

Photograph courtesy of Ken Winterbottom

Shamrock Rovers, September-October 1957

Although the end of the 1956/57 season had been tinged with the twin disappointments of defeat in the FA Cup final and European Cup semi-final, United had finished as First Division champions for the second successive season. This meant that come the start of the 1957/58 season, they would once again be challenging on three fronts. As the players left for their summer break, there was certainly a renewed optimism throughout the Red half of Manchester.

I took ill the week before the 1957/58 season began and there was a fear that I might have polio. At this time there was a horrible health scare in the country, with an outbreak of polio, especially amongst children. To be stricken with that disease was a terrible thing because it completely incapacitated you, and you were more or less doomed to spend the rest of your days in an ugly and unsightly contraption known as an 'iron lung'. I was full of fever and vomiting violently, so as a precaution, I was admitted to Manchester Royal Infirmary on Oxford Road. Fortunately for me, things turned out to be okay, and I was only there for a couple of days. It was found that I had just picked up a viral infection, more than likely from the River Medlock! Sometimes we would go down and play on the river and make rafts, and several times I had fallen in, though my parents were never aware of this. All sorts of rubbish used to find its way into that river back in those days, most of it from the surrounding factories, so the water was really polluted. However, it was certainly a worrying time for my parents.

United's first game of 1957/58 season was away to Leicester City at Filbert Street on 20 August. United put Leicester City to the sword, winning comfortably 3-0 in front of 40,000 fans, with Billy Whelan scoring all three goals. I listened to the second half on the radio. United opened their home campaign just four days later on 28 August against Everton. Because I had been so ill my parents forbade me to attend. However, being the United-daft little sod that I was, neither wild horses nor a virus would stop me from going, and so in mid-afternoon that

Wednesday, I slipped out of the house and walked to Old Trafford! The buzz and excitement of a new season was there for all to see. A large crowd of just over 59,000 saw United again dazzle with a performance that destroyed a good Everton team by 3-0, with Dennis Viollet, Tommy Taylor, and an own goal accounting for them. Upon reaching home after the game, I sheepishly went into the house and received the mother and father of all bollockings for not doing as I had been told. So much so, that my Dad, forbade me to go to the derby game against Manchester City at Old Trafford the following Saturday. I was heartbroken, but Dad said I needed to be taught a lesson.

The next few days were purgatory for me, and as I walked about I was the most miserable little beggar that you could have ever seen. No amount of pleading with my Dad seemed to work, and I resigned myself to missing what I thought was the most important game of the season. Come Saturday morning, I had a face like a robber's dog! Soulless, leaden and not pleasant. I did my errands for Mum, took my younger sister to the Saturday morning matinee at the Grosvenor picture house on All Saints, and then Mum sent me to Armistead's bakery on Rusholme Road for pies for lunch. I still had a long face when I returned, and settled into a chair close by the radio. I must have looked really miserable, sad, and a sorry sight. So much so that Mum eventually took pity upon me and relented. She dipped into her purse and handed me the money to go to Old Trafford.

I was gone like a shot, running all the way up to All Saints to catch the 49 bus. I got to Old Trafford and found huge queues along United Road, so I made my way around to the back of the Stretford End, found the junior entrance, paid my sevenpence, and made my way down the terracing to the picket fence behind the goal. The first three derby games I had watched saw three defeats for United, but the previous season had seen United break the jinx by winning both the home and away fixtures. Over 63,000 packed into Old Trafford that Saturday afternoon to watch United demolish City by 4-1, with Berry, Edwards, Taylor, and Viollet scoring the goals. Three matches played, ten goals scored and only one conceded – United were top of the league once again. Our young team had certainly begun where they had left off the previous season, and our hopes and expectations rose even higher.

The following week the draw for the first round of the European Cup was made, and United came out of the hat with the Irish part-timers of Shamrock Rovers from Dublin. The first leg was to be played at Dalymont Park in late September, with the return leg at Old Trafford during the first week of October. For Billy Whelan, it was to be a return to his home city, and one that he looked forward to so much. But before those matches, there was league business to attend to.

On the evening of Wednesday, 4 September, United had a return game, away at Everton. It was also the day that I started at my new school. That morning, I assembled in the school hall, together with all the other first year 'newbies', resplendent in the new uniform that Mum and Dad had worked so hard to provide for me. I was anxious and very nervous. There were lots of strange kids, strange teachers and an expectation of progress that I hadn't come across before. I was put into the form with my new classmates, and it was strange to find that quite a few of them spoke with 'funny' accents, coming from places which I thought were miles away – Royton, Oldham, Stalybridge, Ashton-under-Lyne and Stockport. It was stranger still to discover that they didn't follow either United or City, and that a lot of them only played rugby. This wasn't for me, I thought!

My mind drifted all over the place that day, with my main thoughts being on how United would do that night at Goodison Park – concentration was at its lowest as far as education was concerned. At four o'clock it was time to make my way home, and this was when the trepidation set in. The school was within walking distance of my house, so before I left the school building, I took off my school blazer, cap and tie; I rolled them up, and placed them into my new school bag. I knew exactly what lay ahead of me on my walk home – I was going to have to fight for my life! Kids from the area where I grew up had an intense dislike for boys who had made it to grammar school. They would lie in wait for them as they made their way home, and ambush them; fights were commonplace. That first day was no exception, even though I tried to be clever and take a circuitous route home. Lads who had been mates just months before, were now waiting to give me a hiding, and sure enough, as I cut around Mansfield Street, there were three waiting for me. There was provocation, and finally the first punch was thrown. Fortunately I was able to evade it, throw a few of my own, then set off like the clappers out of harm's way. I got home with little damage done – but over the next few years, it wasn't always like that.

Over 72,000 crowded into Goodison Park that night to watch a magnificent exhibition of all that was good in English football. Nobody left that ground without satisfaction, as the game ended in a 3-3 draw. It had ebbed and flowed, with terrific goals from both sides, United's scorers being Berry, Whelan and Viollet. The following Saturday saw United entertain one of the promoted clubs, Leeds United. They had the great John Charles in their team, and this would be the only time that I would see him play in the flesh. He made little impact that day as United went nap, winning 5-0 with goals from Berry (2), Taylor (2) and Viollet. Just two days later the Babes played at Bloomfield Road, Blackpool, and the sea air had great effect on them as once again they hit the back of the net regularly, winning 4-1. In the opening six games, this young team had scored 22 goals and conceded just five, taking 11 out of a possible 12 points – the league was already ours, nobody could stop us on this form!

As I have mentioned before, Bolton Wanderers were always a bit of a thorn in United's side. For some reason we always seemed to struggle against them, and Saturday, 14 September 1957, was no exception. It was a game that I travelled to Burnden Park to see. Along with all the other United supporters, I had took the 'Special' from Victoria Station, alighting 45 minutes later at Bolton's Trinity Street station. Leaving the station we made the short walk to Burnden Park, and packed the large terrace behind the goal at the Railway End. Everybody was in great spirits, with high expectations of our Babes in their current form, but how mistaken we all were. Whether it was over-confidence, given the previous six results, or whether it was Bolton's performance that day, I don't know. But what I do know was that United came down to earth with a pronounced bump, being quite emphatically drubbed by 4-0! It was a jolt to the system, and it was a very subdued trip back to Manchester for the United fans.

The following Wednesday, 18 September, United were at home for the return fixture against Blackpool. After the previous week's thrashing of the Seasiders most United fans thought that once again the game would be a mere formality, and that United would steamroller the men in tangerine. Once again, though, things didn't go according to plan and Blackpool, orchestrated by the diminutive Ernie Taylor, were two goals ahead early into the second half. United threw the kitchen sink at them, and with just over ten minutes left, Edwards broke from midfield and fired a 20 yarder past George Farm in the Blackpool goal. Blackpool then infuriated the United crowd with time-wasting antics for the remainder of the match, and the main villain was none other than little Ernie. From positions all over the pitch, he would fire back passes to the goalkeeper, some from 40 and 50 yards out, and then Farm would take his time in clearing the ball. Try as United did, they just couldn't break Blackpool down again, and when the final whistle blew, they had tasted defeat for the second game running.

With the first leg of the European Cup just a week away, were United having a mini crisis? All would be told in the next match, at home to Arsenal. That afternoon I was at Old Trafford to watch United return to form, winning comfortably by 4-2, with Billy Whelan (2), David Pegg and Tommy Taylor scoring the goals. The buzz in Manchester gathered momentum from that Saturday afternoon, and what we had all been waiting for since the end of the previous season, was almost upon us – European Cup football. United travelled to Dublin to meet Shamrock Rovers, and for Billy Whelan, the young and gifted United inside right, it was such a special occasion, as he returned to the city of his birth. Billy was such a quiet and unassuming lad, but what a player! On Wednesday, 25 September Dublin was alive, throbbing with the excitement and anticipation of United's visit. The match of course was a complete sell out, and Billy was inundated with requests for tickets from family and friends alike. United had left out Eddie Colman, who had picked up a knock in the game against Arsenal, and they lined up: Wood; Foulkes, Byrne; Goodwin, Blanchflower, Edwards; Berry, Whelan, Taylor, Viollet and Pegg.

United did not disappoint the fans that afternoon, and Billy put on a performance as he opened the scoring after just half an hour. The Irish part-timers made a game of it in the first half, but after the break United's superior quality and fitness began to tell as they moved their counterparts around at will. Ten minutes after the break the game was over to all intents and purposes: first, Billy grabbed a second goal on 51 minutes, as he waltzed through a bemused defence, and then on 55 minutes big Tommy Taylor powered in a header from a David Pegg cross. The Irish fans, in a no lose situation, applauded United's fine play. Shamrock tired dramatically as the game entered the last quarter of an hour, and in the last 10 minutes United scored three more goals, through Tommy Taylor, Johnny Berry, and David Pegg. So it was 6-0 at the final whistle, and the fans rushed onto the ground to congratulate both sets of players. Billy Whelan was mobbed as he left the field and it took him about ten minutes to reach the sanctuary of the dressing room. As a tie it was all over, as nobody could envisage Shamrock pulling back such a deficit. The festivities after the game were so cordial and there was a special bond formed between the two clubs.

United returned to Manchester, where the following Saturday they faced a hard game against the team that was vying with them for the top spot in the First Division – Wolverhampton Wanderers. Stan Cullis and his team were desperately trying to knock United of their perch, and there was a lot of jealously towards United from the Midlands club. Cullis had been upset some years earlier when United signed Edwards from under his nose as he tried to copy Matt Busby's youth policy. In 1953, the first year of the FA Youth Cup, United's youngsters had trounced Wolves in the final, 9-3 on aggregate. The following year, United's kids triumphed again over Wolves, although it was a little closer – 5-4 on aggregate. Wolves had played some prestigious friendly matches against great Continental clubs like Honved of Hungary,

Moscow Dynamo and Spartak Moscow, and had come out on top. But this was prior to the start of European competition, and Cullis always had a bee in his bonnet about it. He was desperate to win the First Division title, though when Wolves did become champions, in 1958, and 1959, their subsequent European campaigns left them with red faces.

United had to make several changes for the trip to Molineux. Roger Byrne had picked up a knock, so in came Wilf McGuinness; Eddie Colman was still out, so Freddie Goodwin kept his place; Dennis Viollet and Billy Whelan had also taken knocks and were replaced by Johnny Doherty and Bobby Charlton. United didn't fire at all, and went down to a 3-1 defeat, with Doherty scoring United's goal. There was much crowing from the Molineux crowd, as that result took them to the top of the league, and they weren't slow to let people know about it.

The home leg against Shamrock Rovers took place on Wednesday, 2 October. The result of the first leg definitely affected the attendance, as only 45,000 fans turned up. United had some of their wounded back, in Roger Byrne and Eddie Colman, but big Dunc had taken a knock at Wolves, so Wilf McGuinness moved up to his normal position at left half. John Doherty was also injured at Wolves, and Billy Whelan was still unfit, so Colin Webster was drafted in. Dennis Viollet returned at inside left in place of Bobby Charlton. So United lined up: Wood; Foulkes, Byrne; Colman, Blanchflower, McGuinness; Berry, Webster, Taylor, Viollet and Pegg. With a commanding 6-0 lead from the first leg, the game was over before it started, and within six minutes Dennis Viollet put United 1-0 up on the night. We thought that we were in for another landslide of goals, especially as just 15 minutes later David Pegg made it 2-0, but the Irish lads stuck to their task and there was no more scoring before half-time. The crowd were buoyant as the Beswick Prize Band marched around the pitch under the floodlights. Shamrock shocked United upon the restart by actually scoring through a little fellow named McCann, but any thoughts of a victory were quickly swept away as Dennis Viollet scored his second goal to make it 3-1 on the hour. But fair play to the part-time Irish lads, who didn't wilt, and

262

who made it 3-2 with a goal from Hamilton with 20 minutes left. United were cruising, to be honest, and the rest of the game petered out at that score. Shamrock took a lot of heart from a very good performance.

We now awaited the draw for the next round, and when it came United were drawn to travel to Eastern Europe for the first time in the competition. Our opponents would be a team named Dukla, from Prague in Czechoslovakia.

Dukla Prague, November-December 1957

The autumn of 1957 was a carefree, buoyant time for Manchester United fans. We had watched the team make a decent start to the season and brush aside the Shamrock Rovers in the first round of the European Cup. After being league champions in the previous two seasons, expectations were running high, not only among the fans, but also inside the club. The expectation was that a third consecutive title could be achieved, and with it the FA Cup and European Cup. The young team of Babes had come close to achieving the treble the previous season, and was determined to go further this time around.

At the start of October, United were fourth in the First Division behind the surprise joint leaders, Nottingham Forest, and Wolves. Forest had just been promoted from the Second Division and had made a great start to the season, particularly in away from home where they had won four out of five matches. Forest and Wolves each had 15 points, and in third place were West Bromwich Albion with 14 points, one more than United's tally with ten games played. Defeats to Bolton, Blackpool and Wolves had set United back a little, but there was no doom or gloom around Old Trafford, nor among the Red half of Manchester. Everybody remained upbeat, knowing it would 'come good'.

At my new school I was finding life more than a little strange and difficult. There were far more kids attending this school, and competition both in the classroom and on the sports field were much fiercer than I had ever experienced before. It was like a double edged sword for me. Among my new classmates I was a poor kid from the inner city; I had no real place at the school, and was a target for their mischief. But outside school, in the area where I lived, I was 'one of them', a 'high school wallah'. Both situations caused me no amount of grief, and I was in trouble several times in those early days at my new school for fighting. Back in those days, initially I was very quiet and shy, and some kids took this to be a sign of weakness. However, once provoked I could more than look after myself, and I was quick to throw the first punch. Early on, it gained me something of a reputation, and this became another rod for my back as older kids in the new school would come looking for me. Those early days at grammar school do not hold the happiest of memories for me.

One place I found to bring me out of my shell was the school gymnasium. I loved the PE lessons, and I liked the gym master, Eddie Hirst. Eddie was a hard taskmaster, but he was fair, and as long as you gave of your best he was happy. The one thing that I wanted to do was to play for the school football team. I set my heart on it. At my previous school I'd experienced two years of playing in the school teams, and I was something of an automatic selection. This, though, was going to be an entirely different kettle of fish. There was so much competition, and from kids who certainly didn't lack confidence.

The school football trials were held in mid-September at a place called Greenbank Playing Fields, which was in Levenshulme. The master in charge of the team was a wonderful guy named Renee Travers (who was actually a scout for United), and he was assisted by an Irish teacher named Fred Leyden. Those lads who had put their names down for the trial were given two red bus tokens to get to and from Greenbank, and on arriving there I was amazed to find that we actually had changing room facilities. My previous school had played at Hough End on Princess Parkway, where we would get changed in the open air behind the goal. Many was the time that people on the buses passing by on Princess Road got more than a flash of bare arse, no matter how much we tried to conceal it.

On the evening of the trial I had decided that I was going to have a change from playing in goal. Nobody knew that was where I played, as in the schoolyard I was always an outfield player. I fancied myself at right half, and tried to imitate Eddie Colman and his exaggerated body-swerve, and looking back it must have been really funny to watch. However, as the two teachers began selecting their teams, it became clearer and clearer that I wasn't going to get a start. The teams were almost complete when Mr. Travers announced, "We need another goalkeeper." There was no way I was going to be left out, so as quick as a shot, my hand was up in the air. And I was in.

Even now I can recall that trial game very clearly, and I did very well in it. So much so that I played the full game, which was unusual in school trials. I had confidence and I was more than a little brave for my own good. The trial over, it seemed as though I had even impressed some of my own classmates as there seemed to be a thawing in attitudes from some of them. The first game of the school season was just a week away, in a Manchester Catholic Schools Shield knock out tie. We had been drawn against St. Dunstan's from North Manchester, and the game was to be played at Cecil Avenue in Moston.

The week dragged, and I could not wait for the Monday when the team would be announced on the school notice board. My thoughts were all over the place that morning as I trudged along Ardwick Green to school, and a fear started to come over me as I thought, "What if I don't make it? How will dad react?" My stomach churned up all morning and things didn't get any easier when there was no sign of the team sheet during the morning break, nor at lunchtime. However as I entered the playground for the afternoon break, I could see kids crowded around the notice board, and I knew that the team sheet had at last been posted. At first, I was a little apprehensive, and approached the group around the notice board tentatively, my stomach still turning over. As I inched forward I felt elation as I saw my name pencilled in between the goalposts on that piece of paper. Even now, is hard to describe.

Once school had finished that day, I ran all the way home, and couldn't wait to tell my parents that I had made it. The following Sunday I felt even prouder as I was able to tell my Granddad that I had been picked for my new school. The excitement built up in me that week, and the night before the game I took out my football boots, and I lovingly coated them with dubbin, making sure they were comfortable on my feet. Cecil Avenue is still there today but I think houses now stand on the site of the football pitch. The football pitch back then had a hard coated, cinder surface, but it made no difference to me as I had played on some bad surfaces at 'Gussie's. We beat St. Dunstan's comfortably by 7-1, and it was the beginning of something new for me – playing in a team which was far superior to any side I had played for before. We had some very good players, and this was proved over the next month or so as we swept aside all the teams that faced us. I was so elated, as were my Granddad and my parents.

St Gregory's under-13s, 1957 – I am the goalkeeper in the centre of the back row

Saturday, 5 October saw Manchester United entertain Aston Villa. Fortunately for the Villains, Peter McParland, their Northern Irish international left winger was injured, and unable to play. United fans were still seething about his atrocious foul on Ray Wood in the previous season's FA Cup final, and the incident was still very fresh in their memories. United contemptuously dismissed Villa that afternoon, winning by 4-1. During the previous mid-week, as United had been playing in European competition against Shamrock Rovers, Wolves and West Bromwich Albion had both played league games. West Brom had drawn with Birmingham, and Wolves had demolished Spurs 4-0. As United were beating Villa, Wolves drew with Leeds United, West Brom beat Portsmouth, and Forest beat Spurs. The league was taking shape, and United were still in fourth position on 15 points, two points behind Forest and West Brom, and three points behind the leaders, Wolves. Wolves and West Brom had now played a game more than both United and Forest. It set things up nicely for Saturday, 12 October, when United travelled to the City Ground to play Forest in a league game for the first time since December 1938, when both teams were in the Second Division.

The game at the City Ground turned out to be a classic, an advert for all that is good in English football. It was an exhilarating display of attacking football from both teams, watched by Forest's record attendance of 47,654 fans. United had gone behind early in the game. They needed to draw on all of their reserves to hold a rampant and uninhibited Forest team. In the second half United began to exert a little more control, and gradually pushed Forest back. They equalised through Dennis Viollet, and ten minutes before the end Billy Whelan once again popped up to score the winning goal. But everybody went home satisfied as it had been such a tremendous game, and both teams took the plaudits in the Sunday newspapers. This win took United above Forest on goal average, and into third place. West Brom drew with Bolton, reducing their advantage over United to just a single point having played a game more. Unfortunately, however, Wolves were in a rich vein of form and had trounced Birmingham City by five that afternoon to maintain their three point advantage at the top.

The following weekend saw the Home International Championship matches played, with England away to Wales at Ninian Park, Cardiff. That same afternoon, United were at home to Portsmouth. In those bygone days, there was no cancellation of league games because players were on international duty – reserve team players had to be promoted to fill their places. At that time, a home game against Portsmouth was of little threat to United. Pompey were languishing towards the bottom of the league in 18th position, having won only one of their six away games. Even though United were deprived of Byrne, Edwards, and Taylor by England call-ups, their replacements being the young full back Peter Jones, Wilf McGuinness, and Alex Dawson, the consensus in the media was that United would be just too good for Pompey.

Making his debut for Portsmouth that afternoon was a long-legged, 19 year old beanpole of centre forward, who had just been signed from the Northern Irish club, Distillery, and who went by the name of Derek Dougan. I stood at the Stretford End, and saw Portsmouth totally dominate United throughout, with their young debutant scoring all three Pompey goals in a 3-0 win. Whether it was complacency on United's part, or whether Portsmouth just 'upped' their performance, I do not know, but I can recall that Dougan led United's defence a merry dance. He looked so ungainly, much like Peter Crouch does today, but here was a young player with an eye for goal, and for being in the right place at the right time. Over 38,000 fans left Old Trafford that afternoon with Dougan's name on their lips, and it was a glittering start to the young Irishman's career in England. Nobody was to know that Saturday afternoon just what an impact Derek Dougan was to have on English football in the following 15 years.

That result set United back again, and they dropped back to fourth place. Wolves had beaten Chelsea to increase their lead to five points, while West Brom drew with Leeds to go two points clear of United and maintain second place. Everton suddenly appeared in third place, one point ahead of United, having drawn with Burnley; they had played a game fewer than United and two fewer than Albion and Wolves. Forest, who lost at Leicester, dropped to fifth place. Things didn't improve for the Babes the following week, when they travelled to the Hawthorns for a crunch meeting with West Brom. Despite scoring three goals away from home, United conceded four! However, Wolves could only draw at Newcastle, while Everton lost at Preston, a result which put the Deepdale team into fourth position above United.

Something was not quite right within the team. Whether pressure and expectation were beginning to tell, we'll never know. Having won the title so easily during the previous two seasons, it may well have been that one or two players were coasting. With the season into November, and the Dukla Prague European Cup tie looming, they were going to have to tighten up, especially in defence. Busby never panicked, and on the first Saturday in November the team got back on a winning track by beating Burnley 1-0 at Old Trafford, with Tommy Taylor scoring the goal. Wolves and North End also won, while West Brom and Everton drew. Wolves remained out in front with a six point lead over the Reds; West Brom were still second on 22 points, while Preston, United, Everton and Arsenal followed, all on 19 points. It was tough going trying to peg back the lead that Wolves held, but the following weekend, 16 November, Wolves could only draw, as West Brom beat Villa, and United drew with North End at Deepdale 1-1, with Billy Whelan rescuing a precious point. United still had a game in hand on both West Brom and Wolves, but as things stood that evening, Wolves retained their six point lead over United, who were in third place, four points behind West Brom, but ahead of North End on goal average.

On the Tuesday afternoon following United's game at Deepdale I was playing in a school match against Ducie Tech at Fog Lane, Didsbury. We were unbeaten so far that season, having won all our games, and I was on top of the world as far as my own football went. Ducie were a very good school team with a big reputation in Manchester schools football. We were leading 2-1 late into the second half when their big centre forward broke through on his own. I advanced from the goal towards him, narrowing the angle and waiting to smother the ball if I got the chance. Sure enough, another touch and he'd pushed it just a little too far in front of him, and I was down like lightning clutching the ball. Unfortunately he followed through with a full blooded swing of his leg, and his boot came crashing down on my left forearm. The pain was intense, and I knew immediately that the arm was broken. Renee Travers took me to Manchester Royal Infirmary, and left me there while he went to my house to tell my parents. Mum came to the hospital and stayed as they put me to sleep under anaesthetic so they could reset the forearm. Football was now out of the question for the next three months. Little did I know what those three months were to hold in store.

I had to stay off school initially, but the broken arm did not prevent me from going to watch United at Old Trafford, nor from getting my ticket for the home European Cup tie against Dukla, which was now less than a week away. On Saturday, 16 November, I went to watch United play Sheffield Wednesday at Old Trafford, where the team scraped a 2-1 win, with Colin Webster, who was standing in for the injured Dennis Viollet, scoring both goals. It was also a day when United pulled a point back on both the Wolves and West Brom, as they had played each other that afternoon, drawing 1-1. Preston had also beaten Leicester City by 3-1, and had leap-frogged over United on goal average. Going into the European tie that week, Wolves were top with 27 points from 18 games, West Brom were second with 25 points from the 18 games, and North End and United were third and fourth respectively, each with 22 points from 17 games. The United fans were not worried as the team had a game in hand, and all three clubs above them still had to play United at Old Trafford – a rather daunting prospect for them.

After the game against Sheffield Wednesday, I hung around outside the main entrance for some time. Eventually the United players began to emerge from big wooden doors, and I asked each of them to sign the white plaster cast on my broken left arm. Little Johnny Berry was most inquisitive as to how I had come by the injury, as was David Pegg. David knew me, having seen me often at Old Trafford before and after games, and at the Galleon swimming baths in Didsbury during the summer months. Billy Whelan, Tommy Taylor, Bob Charlton and Little Eddie also recognised me. Nobody refused an autograph, and I only wish that I still had that plaster cast today!

Once again, European fever gripped Manchester as the game against the Czech champions loomed large. Not much was known about them, and certainly we hadn't heard very much about any of their players. Most of the fans were confident that United would go through easily.

However, looking back, the team had been conceding too many easy goals, and this fixture was a potential banana skin. The United players also knew little or nothing about their opposition, and they would see them for the first time when they played them. Mum and Dad allowed me to go to the match on what was a bitterly cold day. They had obtained a second hand duffle coat for me, and I was more than grateful for it as I made the journey to Old Trafford. I left home about half past four to avoid rush hour congestion on the buses, which would also be full of people going to the match. It was dark as I caught the 49 from All Saints, and by the time the bus reached Trafford Bar it was jammed full of people, some standing virtually nose to nose. The conductor had difficulty getting up and down the bus to collect the fares.

As the cold night drew in, the stars were already shining like glimmering crystals in the clear sky as the fans made their way towards the ground. There was a muted murmur, which in the next hour would become ever louder with incessant chatter as the fans multiplied in numbers, accompanied by the sound of feet marching on the stone cobbles. Back then, there were none of the vendors' stalls outside the ground that you see today, and there was no souvenir shop at all. Newspaper sellers were in abundance, though, and you could hear their pitches as they shouted out the name of the newspaper they were offering, the Evening News or the Evening Chronicle (or the 'Chron' as it was known). I made my way round to United Road, across from the two towering chimneys that stood in Glover's Cables site. White smoke billowed straight up into the night sky as I took my place in the short queue that had begun to form outside the juniors' gate.

At 5.45 a huge cheer went up from around the outside of the ground as the floodlights were switched on. At six o'clock the gates were opened, and another cheer filled the air. The steady clicking of the turnstiles could be heard as fans were ushered inside, along with the cries of the programme sellers, and the smell of Oxo and Bovril lingered in your nostrils as the little stalls inside the Popular Stand did a brisk trade. I collected my programme and made my way through the tunnel which led to the terracing inside the ground. I emerged overlooking the half-

272

way line, directly opposite the players' tunnel on the other side of the ground. I walked around to the Scoreboard End and took my place against the white picket fence, immediately behind the centre of the goal.

The ground filled steadily as Jack Irons, the United mascot, began his walk around the pitch, perennial cigarette in his hand. The Beswick Prize Band started to set up just opposite the Main Stand and players' tunnel. A big roar went up on the Popular Side as a man with an artificial leg, dressed in a red shirt and white shorts, began sprinting up and down the touchline. The band played, the crowd grew in size, and the expectation, anticipation and eagerness to see United do well, added to the atmosphere. Some 60,000 were in the stadium at twenty past seven, as the teams marched out from the tunnel. As was the usual in those days, after the preliminaries the United team went to the Scoreboard End. The usual trio of Colman, Blanchflower and Edwards were over to my right in front of the Popular Stand, and were joined by the young United mascot with the white number 6 on the back of his red shirt. The forwards fired balls in at Ray Wood, as Roger Byrne and Bill Foulkes passed a ball up and down the touchline in front of the Old Trafford Paddock. United were without the still-injured Dennis Viollet that evening, and lined up: Wood; Foulkes, Byrne; Colman, Blanchflower, Edwards; Berry, Whelan, Taylor, Webster and Pegg.

Dukla proved to be a very stubborn and obdurate team, and were very physical with it. They strangled the game in midfield, and were very difficult to break down. This wasn't going to be easy, and there would be no repeat of goal feast against Shamrock Rovers. The Czechs were very disciplined and organised, with plenty of gamesmanship in their locker. At half-time there had been no breakthrough, and we had seen nothing of a threat from Dukla at all – surely they were not going to sit back in the second half? Unfortunately, that did seem to be their plan. United now surged forward towards the Scoreboard End, but with an hour gone the game was still deadlocked. Both Berry and Pegg were seeing plenty of the ball, as Bill Whelan sprayed the ball into their paths. Taylor and Webster were making runs, but the final ball was just not falling for them. A toe poke here, a body in the way there, a hoofed and hurried clearance – it just didn't look as though United were going to have any luck at all. Then, on 63 minutes, David Pegg got the ball out on United's left hand side, and as the big Czech full back made for him, he played in a hopeful first time cross. The ball ballooned into the air off the approaching full back, and Tommy Taylor challenged for it, succeeding in knocking it down into Colin Webster's path. The little Welshman gleefully slammed the ball past the keeper and into the back of the net. The deadlock was broken, United had the lead, and a huge roar of relief erupted from the crowd.

Dukla now had to come out of their defensive shell if they wanted to get anything from the game. They did so, and they began to leave more room between their midfield and defence, which United began to exploit. Roared on, United began to exert even more pressure. In the 75th minute United won a corner over on their right, and Johnny Berry whipped it in low, around thigh height. It zipped into the area between the penalty spot and six yard line, and suddenly there was a blur of movement as big Tommy Taylor threw himself headlong in front of his marker to connect with the ball. It flew beyond the keeper into the net – 2-0 was a nice lead to take to Prague. And things got even better just two minutes later as Whelan robbed a Czech player in midfield, saw Pegg making a run inside, and delivered the most telling of balls to him. The young Yorkshireman hit the ball first time into the back of the net. It was 3-0 to United – and so it stayed until the final whistle. As the fans streamed out of the ground everybody was confident that three goals would be more than enough to take United through to the quarter-final. They still had to negotiate the second leg in Prague, but the players were confident that they would progress. There was no doubt about it, the fans wanted to meet Real Madrid in the semi-final, and I think that was players' choice also. They wanted their revenge. Both the team and the fans were still smarting from the previous season's defeat by the Spaniards, and they wanted to rectify it – the sooner the better!

The Saturday after the Dukla home game, United had to travel to St. James's Park in Newcastle for a potentially tricky league game. Viollet was still unfit, and Berry had taken a knock in the European game, so Scanlon came in for him and Webster continued at inside left. Almost 54,000 saw the Magpies go down to a 2-1 defeat with Duncan Edwards and Tommy Taylor scoring as United claimed the two points. Wolves beat Manchester City 4-3, West Brom beat Sunderland 3-0, and North End beat Bolton 3-0 to leave the top of the First Division unchanged.

On the last Saturday in November United had a home fixture with Spurs. Ray Wood had taken a knock at Newcastle and was replaced by 17 year old David Gaskell. Berry was still unfit so Scanlon continued at outside right. Tommy Taylor had also taken a knock so Colin Webster moved to centre forward, with Bobby Charlton coming in at inside left. Busby had one eye on the following week's second leg European Cup tie in Prague, and was taking no chances with players reporting these slight knocks. United hit Spurs for three that afternoon, with Pegg scoring twice and Whelan once. Unfortunately, young Gaskell made a couple of elementary mistakes as his nerves showed, and this helped Spurs score four times. It was a big set back, and one that already had Busby thinking about changing the make-up of his young team. West Brom drew that afternoon so United had missed the chance to claw back some of their advantage. Preston had also drawn, and moved a point in front of United, but the worrying thing was that Wolves had won again, beating Burnley 2-1, stretching their lead to seven points. Busby saw it as a missed opportunity, and certainly didn't want Wolves' lead getting any wider.

United flew off to Prague on the Monday morning in good spirits. However, Jackie Blanchflower had picked up an injury in the Spurs game and was unfit. Little was the popular Irishman to know at that time that he had played his last first team game in United's famous red shirt. Mark Jones came back into the team after a lengthy absence, but there was little to choose between the contrasting styles of the two centre halves, and the return of Jones in no way weakened United's young team. Mark Jones was the epitome of the old English centre half

– he was a 'stopper'. No airs and graces, very strong in the tackle, outstanding in the air, and tough as teak. He also had pace and read the game well. It is my opinion that he would have challenged very strongly for Billy Wright's England place. Blanchflower on the other hand was more diminutive, but had a great football brain. His anticipation and timing were second to none and, having been a forward, his ability to dribble and pass his way out of trouble was a joy to watch. For a smaller player, he also had great ability in the air, thanks to his timing.

Berry was also unfit so Scanlon continued in his place. Taylor was back, however, and he resumed at centre forward with Webster moving to inside left at the expense of Bobby Charlton. The game was played on the Wednesday afternoon of 4 December 1957, and United lined up as follows: Wood; Foulkes, Byrne; Colman, Jones, Edwards; Scanlon, Whelan, Taylor, Webster and Pegg.

The game was played at the Strahov Stadium in Prague, and was probably the poorest performance by a United team in the European competition so far. They never really functioned and fell behind to a goal from Dvorack just after the quarter hour. United also squandered a hatful of chances during the game, and when the final whistle blew, with the score still 1-0 to Dukla, Busby was not a happy man. He didn't lambast them after the game, but in his own mind he knew that if performances didn't improve he was going to have to make some big changes if they were going to challenge for all three honours.

As fans, we were just so happy that another European challenge had been met successfully, and we waited with eagerness for the quarter-final draw. We were still buoyant, still had great faith in the youngsters and what we believed they could achieve, and we had no doubt in their ability to overcome the seven point deficit in the league. The European Cup draw was made, pairing United with Red Star Belgrade from Yugoslavia. This team we did know something about, as they had already played in England and we knew that they had some wonderful players. This tie was going to be no easy task, with the first leg to be played at Old Trafford in January, 1958. The Christmas period, which included a derby match at Maine Road, was going to be a crucial period in United's bid to win a third consecutive title, and they had also drawn Workington Town away in the 3rd round of the FA Cup. The treble was definitely on as far as we were concerned.

Red Star Belgrade, the First Leg

The United performance in the second leg game of their European Cup tie against Dukla in Prague had disappointed Matt Busby. On the journey home he had much to ponder. Although the team were through to the European Cup quarter-final, and were in the top four in the First Division, he knew that they were not playing to their full capabilities. Some games had been lost through silly individual errors, and a lack of concentration. Attendances at home games were also fluctuating, and this was causing concern in the boardroom. At the beginning of the season, home games were pulling in 50,000 or more, but as the season progressed towards the mid-way point, attendances had begun to drop significantly below the 40,000 mark. Approaching the Christmas period, people had little spare cash to hand, and it was the norm that gates tended to be well down.

The Saturday after the Dukla match, United played Birmingham City at St. Andrews. On paper this should have been a fixture that a team of United's calibre should have negotiated easily. Birmingham were in 15th position going into this match. They had a few internationals in their team, including Merrick, Hall, Smith, and Kinsey, but they were also an ageing team. United made one change to their team that had played in Prague, with Albert Scanlon making way for the return of Johnny Berry at outside right. But for the third time that season United scored three goals in a game and still failed to win. Despite Dennis Viollet scoring twice and Tommy Taylor adding the third, Birmingham were able to match them goal for goal, and the game finished at 3-3. Busby was again disappointed that his youngsters had not been able to win the match. In a hard fought game just over the way at Molineux, Wolves beat Preston 2-1, and their lead over United at the top of the table had now increased to eight points. Even though United still had a game in hand, they would have a huge task in retrieving that kind of deficit. West Brom had also drawn with Blackpool, and remained four points clear of United. Busby looked at the situation seriously.

My broken arm was healing and I was back at school. I had taken on a delivery job for a pet shop which was situated at the bottom of Rusholme Road, just facing Ardwick Green. David and Jean Wyman were lovely people, and when they gave me the job they were happy to adjust my working hours so I would be able to go to Old Trafford. The shop used to supply what was basically ground horse meat, used as dog food. Most of the local companies had no alarm systems and used German Shepherd dogs as guard dogs. They would order the dog food over the telephone, Jean and David would make the orders up, and I would make the daily delivery. I could make that round even today, as I remember it so well. The deliveries would be in two white canvas bags, which were quite a weight by the time I had put one over each shoulder. As it was winter, and cold in the early evening, Jean would make sure I had a flask of Oxo with me when I left the shop to make the deliveries. I would stop several times along my route to drink from the flask and warm my young body. The route took about two hours to complete, for which I was rewarded with five shillings a week, most of which went to my mother.

I enjoyed this job immensely, as I got to know a lot of people, and the banter used to be great with them. They quickly found out that I was United daft and they would pull my leg and tease me a lot. A lot of them would have threepenny bets with me on the outcome of United's results, and the money from my winnings, I kept for myself. It was quite profitable as we came to the end of 1957 and into 1958, as you will see. I'd begun to settle more at school but I'd missed playing football so much. Unfortunately, during my absence the school team had been beaten for the first time that season, but that was in an open cup competition. My plaster cast was removed from my arm, and replaced by a light elastoplast-type covering. I was still having to put up with a lot of crap from other kids, though. The schoolbag, which my parents had worked hard to get the cash to provide, was slashed to pieces one lunchtime. We used to leave our bags on the windowsills of the school buildings as we played football in the schoolyard, and obviously a few cretins had taken advantage of this. My goloshers (or gym shoes as they would be called today) were stolen from their place in the cage in the gym, and subsequently, I had to do PE classes in my bare feet as my parents could not afford to replace them. I found out which kids were responsible, and took retribution upon them one by one, cornering each of them when they were on their own. With one of them I did more damage than intended because I broke his nose with my forehead and this resulted in my mother having to go in and see the headmaster, as there was talk of me being expelled. The headmaster's name was Joe Rocca, and he was the brother of Louis, the famous United scout.

On 14 December, United met Chelsea at Old Trafford, and were at full strength. Just under 37,000 people attended this game to see United stutter, losing 1-0. Alarmingly for both Busby and the United fans, Wolves had beaten Sheffield Wednesday that afternoon, 4-3, and had now increased the gap between themselves and United to a formidable 10 points. Fortunately, West Brom had been on the wrong end of 5-1 thrashing at Luton, and the gap to them in second place was still four points. Preston also slipped up at Arsenal, by 4-2, to stay in third place, level on points with United in fourth. For those of us that were present at Old Trafford that afternoon against Chelsea, little did we know that we were seeing Ray Wood, Johnny Berry, Billy Whelan and David Pegg playing for the last time in a first team shirt.

Matt Busby had to act, as it was already beginning to look as though Wolves had one hand on the First Division title. I doubt that anybody at that time (including the two local sportswriters, Tom Jackson and Alf Clarke, who were really close to what was going on inside Old Trafford) had any inkling as to what was about to happen. The following Saturday, 21 December, United had another home game, this time against Leicester City. As I trudged through my pet food round I had my leg pulled mercilessly by the customers. However, in mid-week, Busby startled the football world by paying a world record fee of £23,500 for the Doncaster Rovers goalkeeper, Harry Gregg. Gregg had played for Northern Ireland against England at Wembley just a few weeks before, and had given an astonishing performance that was largely responsible for Northern Ireland upsetting all the odds by winning 3-2. The Irish fans were so delighted by their totally unexpected victory that at the final whistle they flooded onto the field and lifted Gregg shoulder high, then carried him to the Wembley tunnel. Gregg was a flamboyant goalkeeper, and very unorthodox for the time. He had tremendous agility, and Busby was to comment later that he signed Gregg because he thought the team was in need of a continental style goalkeeper. Looking back, I feel sorry for Ray Wood because he had not really played badly despite the stuttering run that the team was going through at the time.

The signing of Gregg stimulated more United fans to attend the game against Leicester City, and just over 41,000 were there. I doubt if any of them could have forecast the changes that were made that afternoon, and there was gasps when the team was announced. Out went Wood, which everybody knew would happen, but also dropped were Johnny Berry, Billy Whelan, and David Pegg. Even today, I still find that astonishing, because United's problems had not been in attack. In just 26 games so far that season, in all competitions, they had scored 65 goals – but they had conceded 39. Into the team came a really exciting young right winger, 18 year old Welshman Kenny Morgans. He'd been a star in the reserve and youth teams, and was a delight to watch. He was a bagful of tricks and had great pace. Bobby Charlton came in at inside right – he had played in four first team games that season, without scoring a goal, though in the reserve team he had been scoring goals for fun. Charlton had enjoyed a decent run in the first team the previous season, after making his debut in October 1956, and had even made the FA Cup final team at Wembley because Dennis Viollet was unfit. Albert Scanlon came into the side to face Leicester at outside left. Albert was 22 years old, a local boy from Hulme who had made his debut in 1954, and had made more than a few first team appearances. He was lightning quick, and packed a terrific shot in his left foot.

That Saturday I took my place behind the Scoreboard End goal because I wanted to get a good look at Harry Gregg. As Roger Byrne led the team out I was transfixed by this broad, twine-toed man in the green jersey making his way towards the goal. The little boy who was

United's mascot at that time, and who wore the number 6 on the back of his red shirt, went around the players, handing out sticks of chewing gum. As he approached Gregg in the goal he stopped, and it was as though shyness had got the better of him. Roger Byrne saw this and came trotting across; he took the lad by the hand and called to Harry Gregg, who came over and took the gum from the mascot. I often wonder whatever happened to that young boy, who was no more than six or seven years old at the time.

It was probably the best game for Gregg and Morgans in which to make their United debuts, as Leicester were known as a yo-yo team back then. When they came to Old Trafford that day they were lying second from the bottom of the league. Gregg had little or nothing to do in a game that United won comfortably, 4-0, with Bobby Charlton and Albert Scanlon each opening their season's accounts with a goal, and Dennis Viollet weighing in with the other two. Young Morgans had played well too, and everybody was happy as they left the ground. Wolves had won again but West Brom had lost 3-1 at Newcastle so the gap to second place was now only two points, with United and Preston, (who also won that afternoon) still having a game in hand. However, unobtrusively, the blues from Maine Road had slipped into fifth place behind United and Preston, and had the same number of points! This was going to make the derby game at Maine Road just a week later, more than a little tasty!

It was Christmas week, 1957, and I so looked forward to Christmas morning. I knew what I was getting for my present and I couldn't wait to get my hands upon it. Mum and Dad had bought me a signed copy of Matt Busby's new book, *My Story*, and I got up that Christmas morning and stared for hours at his inscription and signature on the inside page – "Best Wishes – Matt Busby". It had cost them ten shillings, a lot of money for our family in those days, so I treasured that book. On that Christmas morning my Mum had to prize it out of my hands and chase me off to Mass. Needless to say, I didn't hang around the church once Mass was over; I just wanted to get back home to the book. Christmas 1957 holds much nostalgia for me, and it tugs at my emotions whenever I think of it. It was to be the last time in our lives that we would sit down as a complete family for Christmas dinner – my parents, my brother and sister, and myself.

Matches were played on Christmas Day in those days, and this year United were at home to Luton Town. After Christmas dinner I was off like a rocket to Old Trafford, where I again took up a position behind the Scoreboard End goal. Luton were well placed, in 6th position, just a point behind United, but just over 39,000 watched United win comfortably by 3-0. It was a game that that featured another Duncan Edwards 'special'. Deputising in goal for the Hatters that afternoon was a keeper named Bernard Streten who was standing in for Ron Baynham, an England international. Streten was getting on a little, and was almost completely bald, which gave the United fans behind the goals much merriment. Edwards scored with a shot from around 25 yards that was hit with great power, and although Streten made a terrific effort to stop it, diving across his goal and getting a hand to it, the sheer force of the shot brushed the goalkeeper's hand aside as the ball thumped into the back of the net. Bobby Charlton also got on the scoresheet again, along with Tommy Taylor. That Christmas Day was a good one for United as Wolves and West Brom did not play, so United had won their game in hand. Meanwhile, City lost at Burnley, and Preston drew 4-4 at home to Sheffield Wednesday. As the fans made their way home that dark, cold afternoon, United were up into second place, level on points with West Bromwich Albion, and eight points behind the Wolves.

There was another full fixture list on Boxing Day, and normally the Christmas Day fixtures were reversed. So on 26 December 1957, United went to Kenilworth Road to face Luton again. Kenilworth Road hasn't changed too much over the years, and it was the small, compact ground that is now. It was a game that United should have won, but ended up drawing 2-2 with Tommy Taylor and Albert Scanlon scoring the goals. Harry Gregg got a lot of flak from the sportswriters after this game because of his habit of wandering outside his goal area when play was in the other half of the pitch. Sometimes he would be found around the edge of the centre circle in his own half. Fans weren't used to this, and it caused them palpitations – something which the press took up on. Today, I don't think too much would be made of it, but back then it was unusual to see, and it was a habit that Busby got Harry to drop. Wolves lost at Spurs that Boxing Day, so United had clipped another point off their lead, which was now down to seven points. Unfortunately, West Brom beat Birmingham 5-3, and leap-frogged back into second place.

On 28 December 1957 well over 70,000 fans crowded into Maine Road to watch the derby game. City were just a point behind United and there was everything to play for. It was a humdinger of a game, with no quarter given or asked. City had been very much United's whipping boys for the previous couple of seasons, but had played themselves into some good form, and were trying to overtake United in the league. Harry Gregg again came in for criticism because of his wanderings, but they had nothing to do with the goals he conceded in a game that finished 2-2. Bobby Charlton scored with a thunderbolt of a drive that Bert Trautmann, City's big German goalkeeper, never got remotely close to. Dennis Viollet scored the other goal for United, and most fans agreed as they left Maine Road that a draw was a fair result.

It is fascinating to look back at that last week of 1957. Between 21 and 28 December, United played four league games in just seven days, something that managers and players would be up in arms about today. Then it was an accepted part of the game, and for the most part the players just wanted to get out there and play. On that last Saturday in 1957, Wolves won up at Sunderland, and thus restored their eight point lead, West Brom trounced Burnley 5-1, and went another point in front of United, and Preston won at Portsmouth to push United back into fourth place as the New Year beckoned.

The first Saturday of 1958 saw a break from the league as the FA Cup entered its 3rd round. United had been drawn away to Workington Town of the Third Division (North). It was a potential banana skin for United, as the weather was bitterly cold and the pitch was hard and frost-bound in areas. Borough Park was a compact little ground, but it was jammed to capacity as 21,000 hardened souls filled every space available. United turned in a thoroughly professional performance that afternoon and didn't give the Cumberland team a sniff of an upset. United's clever forwards and dominant half backs kept Town on the back foot, and Dennis Viollet claimed all the goals in a 3-0 victory.

On the Monday I rushed home from school at lunchtime to listen to the 4th round draw on the old radio. United came out of the bag with a home draw, paired with the East Anglian club Ipswich Town from the Second Division. The tie was to be played on Saturday, 25 January 1958. Little was I to know as the draw was made that this would be the last game I would ever see my beloved Babes play.

School had restarted that Monday morning, and I was called in to see Mr. Travers, who looked after my school team. He asked how the arm was, and I showed him the light strapping, but I told him that it was coming off later that week. He said my team had a junior Catholic Cup tie with St. Wilfrid's from Hulme the following Saturday morning, and asked if I thought I would be okay to play. He needn't have asked! The plaster was removed on the Wednesday, and the doctor cleared me to play active sport. Saturday could not come quick enough, and I willed the week to pass by. On the Thursday afternoon, the team sheet was put on the notice board, and I rushed towards it full of anticipation. I looked for the name of the goalkeeper, and my stomach turned over – the selected keeper wasn't me, but a big lad named Phil Johnson who came from Moston. The disappointment hurt, but then somebody pointed out to me that I was on the team sheet, but at centre forward! I couldn't believe my eyes. Apparently, Mr. Travers had seen me kick around in the school yard, and decided to play me as an outfield player. I was quite happy to be honest, because deep down I always fancied myself playing out of goal. When I told my parents, they were pleased, but Dad did say he had mixed feelings for me.

Saturday came, and I made my way up to Levenshulme, and Greenbank playing fields. All sorts of things were going through my head as we kicked off, and my concentration wasn't good. The match was a disaster for the team and for me personally. We lost 6-0 against a team that normally we would have been able to beat. Centre forward just wasn't for me, I was all over the place and hardly got a touch of the ball. When I did I was lost and clueless, and more often than not had it taken away from me. At half-time we were four goals down, and Mr. Travers moved me back into the half back line. That also met with no success – despite my attempts at playing like Eddie Colman, even with the exaggerated body swerve. I was, in truth, an embarrassment, and liability to my team. It was to be my last excursion in schoolboy football as an outfield player.

I was in a depressed mood after that morning's performance as I trudged along my pet foot round in the early afternoon. United were away at Elland Road in a game they would surely win. United had trounced Leeds at Old Trafford by 5-0 early in the season, so surely this game would not present problems for them. I finished my work and made my way home. At five o'clock the old wireless spluttered into life as the music *Out of the Blue* introduced the weekly *Sports Report* programme, hosted by Eamon Andrews. I listened anxiously as the news reader read out the results. You could tell the result by the tone of his voice, and as soon as he said "Leeds United 1," I knew the game had finished as a draw. And so it was, with Dennis Viollet snatching an equalising goal for United to earn a point. Fortunately Wolves had also drawn at home to Luton, so had not increased their lead at the top. Unfortunately, Preston had beaten West Brom at Deepdale, pushing the Black Country side back into third place, with United fourth. City had also drawn, at Forest, so they had been unable to make up any ground on United.

The day after the Leeds game, I was once again up early to queue for my ticket for the European Cup quarter-final first leg against Red Star Belgrade, a game which was being played the following Wednesday. I had lost my partner-in-crime, Brian, after I moved schools, and we didn't see very much of each other after that. I was also free of the burden of having to get tickets for the priests, which was quite a relief.

Once again the queues were long, but the reward at the end of them was something you couldn't put a price on.

Red Star had quite a reputation and, as I said, were at last a club that we knew about. They had some really good players in their team, players like the goalkeeper Vladimir Beara who was arguably one of the finest goalkeepers in the world at that time. Mitic and Popovic were international wing halves, full of guile and craft, whilst in between them was a rock of a centre half named Spajic. However, the biggest danger to United would come from the three inside forward players, Sekularac, Tasic and Kostic. This trio was supremely gifted, lightning fast and could finish with deadly accuracy. This would be a huge test of United's resolve.

The weather was not too good in Manchester in the days leading up to the game. The Red Star team arrived in Manchester on the Monday afternoon and must have wondered what they had flown in to. It was dark, murky, bitterly cold and inhospitable. On the morning of the match, I went to school as normal, but as usual my mind was never on what I should have been doing. Fog began to descend on the city, and by lunchtime it was quite thick. When the school lunch break arrived, I decided I was going to have half a day off! I was out of school like quicksilver, never saying a word to anybody. I trudged through Ardwick Green Park in the murkiness, smelling the grime in the fog, and feeling the cold dampness in the air. I went into Wyman's pet shop and told Jean a white lie. I said that we'd all been let out of school early because of the fog, and that the school wanted the kids to get home early and safely. I don't know if she really believed me, but she thrust a mug of hot tea into my hands. She began cutting up the horse meat and mincing it, and began wrapping the orders to be put in my two delivery bags. I devoured the tea and then skipped up Rusholme Road through the gloom to Taylor's chip shop. Alf Taylor was a United fan, and as he wrapped my threepenn'orth of chips he said he didn't think the game against Red Star would be played that night. My stomach turned over. I couldn't envisage not going to the game – how was a bit of fog going to affect a football match?

I returned to the pet shop, collected my two bags and my flask of Oxo, and off I went on my rounds: Dewsbury and Brown, the mineral firm; the Grove Hotel; the Church Inn; Raleigh Motors; Noble's Rubber Company; Bolger's Scrap Yard; The White Hart Hotel; Mazel's; the fire station; the Gog and Magog; and Champion Motors. The banter was always the same, especially with the pub landlords. I gave as good as I took, and as usual we placed our bets. They were all of the same opinion however, that the match wouldn't go ahead in the fog. I began to have serious doubts for the first time as I got back to Wyman's in late afternoon. Dispensing with my bags, I was off to All Saints to catch my bus for Old Trafford, first calling at home to collect my heavy topcoat.

The buses were full of people going home from work and people heading to the match. It must have been around half past five when I reached the top of Warwick Road, where there were more people around at this time than normal. I suppose that people had set off early to make sure that they got to Old Trafford in good time. The floodlights were already switched on as I walked towards the ground, and the fog swirled in the glare of those brilliant lamps. Queues had already formed outside the turnstiles, and I made my way around to United Road. There wasn't long to wait as the turnstiles were opened early, and fans streamed into the ground. Inside I bought my programme, and went up the tunnel to the terracing on the half way line. At this point my heart sank – you could hardly see a thing, and from where I stood both goal areas were invisible. How on earth could they play in those conditions? I didn't go down to the picket fence at the front, as I normally did. I reasoned that I would be able to see better this evening if I stayed up towards the middle of the terrace, and so I climbed onto one of the crush barriers. The fog was teasing; it would thin out so you could just about see both goals, then it would thicken again, so you could only see the area around the half way line. It was difficult to see the far side of field and the Main Stand. Fans began filling the ground, but it was a rather muted atmosphere to begin with. The Beswick Prize Band could be heard playing, and there was a lot of chatter from the adults around me. The consensus was that even if the game did start it would probably be abandoned later on.

Around seven o'clock our spirits were lifted when the fog seemed to thin a little, and we could just about make out the people on the far side of the stadium. We could also just about see both goals, but it was still very murky. The band marched around the pitch and at twenty past seven the teams appeared from the tunnel. At first it was just a ripple, and then as people realised that the teams were out, it developed into a huge roar. On that cold, damp and foggy night, Wednesday 14 January 1958, we were about to see our talented young team of Babes play at Old Trafford in the European Cup for the last time. United lined up as follows: Gregg; Foulkes, Byrne; Colman, Jones, Edwards; Morgans, Charlton, Taylor, Viollet and Scanlon. Harry Gregg and Kenny Morgans were making their European debuts that evening. Red Star's line up was: Beara; Tomic, Zekovic; Mitic, Spajic, Popovic; Borozan, Sekularic, Tasic, Kostic and Cokic.

Roger Byrne and Rajko Mitic, the two captains, could be seen in the centre circle shaking hands, and then Roger tossed the coin. I am almost certain that Mitic won the toss because the referee blew his whistle and signalled for the teams to change ends. Back in those days, when United came out of the tunnel they always went to the Scoreboard End, and always preferred to attack the Stretford End in the first half. (This changed in 1959/60 after renovations to the Stretford End, when United's more vocal support began to congregate in that area.) Several fans, on seeing the teams change ends, voiced their fears that this was a bad omen. Over 60,000 were inside Old Trafford that night, but I am being honest when I say that hardly any of us saw all of the game. In the modern game, in such conditions the game would never have gone ahead. The fog played havoc with our view, as it descended, then lifted slightly, then thickened again. It was difficult to follow the game. When play was on the far side of the field we could hardly see a thing, and were taken along by the roars from the other side of the ground. What we could see of the game was giving us palpitations as the Slavs took the game to United, and pinned them back in their own half. As was had been feared, this was no easy game, and many had misgivings about it. Our fears were justified when, on 37 minutes, Red Star took the lead through centre forward Tasic. I can't tell you how it was scored because the plain truth is that I couldn't see it, and neither could most of the people around me. What we did see was the blue shirted Red Star players congratulating each other as they made their way back to their own half.

Once again, United's young team had a mountain to climb. Red Star had controlled the first half from what we could see, and Sekularac and Kostic were causing problems for Edwards and Colman. United were getting little or no impetus from midfield. Apart from Real Madrid, I don't think that there is any doubt that Red Star were the best team United had ever met in the competition. During the half-time break some fans even voiced their hope that the referee would abandon the game. As the teams came out for the second half, the conditions hadn't improved at all. As the second period began it looked as though United had begun to keep more of the ball. We could see players driving towards the Stretford End, but often could not really tell who they were. Whether the Slavs tired or not, we'll never know, but the second half was totally different from the first. Bobby Charlton had started to drift around more, and Beara pulled off three or four magnificent saves from some pile drivers that came his way. Nevertheless, Red Star had some good defenders, and they seemed to be holding firm as the minutes began to tick away.

With just under half an hour to go, Charlton equalised. Again, I can't describe the goal from my own point of view, as I couldn't see it. However the roar that went up from behind the Stretford End goal was more than enough to tell us what had happened, and that roar had a ripple effect as it travelled around the ground and as people realised United had scored. As the match entered the last quarter of an hour, the fog began to lift somewhat, and visibility was the best it had been all night. You could now see both goal areas. With just nine minutes left, and United pressing, Beara fumbled and the ball broke loose. There was an almighty scramble inside the six yard area; bodies dived in, and the ball rebounded off several legs before little Eddie Colman, of all people, lying on the ground was able to poke out his right leg and deflect the ball over the line and into the back of the net. The roar that erupted was deafening, and once he got up Eddie cavorted about like a schoolboy. He was engulfed by his team mates, and their smiles told a story. The next nine minutes passed uneventfully, and when the final whistle went, there was relief all around the ground. Red Star had provided a stern examination, and going to Belgrade three weeks later was probably going to be the stiffest test that United had faced in Europe – and I include the games against Madrid in that statement.

Once more, the Babes had stood up to an enormous challenge, and had come through it with dogged determination, much will power and great skill. Would this be the turning point in their season? The Saturday after the Red Star game United had to face their arch rivals and nemeses, Bolton Wanderers, at Old Trafford. Did our lads still believe they could achieve the treble? The next few weeks would be critical to their quest, with some huge games on the horizon.

As I left Old Trafford that dank, foggy evening, I could have no inking at all as to what the next three weeks held in store, and how they would affect me, and many thousands like me, for the rest of our lives.

Red Star Belgrade, the Second Leg

After the 2-1 first leg win over Red Star Belgrade on that foggy night of 14 January 1958, Manchester United had to wait for three weeks before the European Cup quarter-final tie could be resolved. The second leg would be played in Belgrade on 5 February 1958, and it would be the most difficult European adventure, in terms of travel and distance, that the club had yet to undertake.

Of course, we could not know at that time just how significant the next three weeks would be in the future of a club that had already skirted with the dangers of foreclosure on two occasions in its history. Since the end of World War Two, with the foresight of a great chairman, and a staff that fully supported his vision, United had laid the foundations of what was fast becoming a dynasty in British and European football. The appointment of Matt Busby as team manager was certainly the catalyst that brought Chairman Gibson's initial dream to fruition. Busby had shown great vision selecting his own backroom team. The appointment of Jimmy Murphy as second-in-command was the real master stroke, and Murphy's role in the formulation and emergence of the club's youth policy should never be forgotten, nor understated.

Without doubt, the fiery but genial Welshman played as important a part in Manchester United's history from 1946 to 1970 as Sir Matt Busby. While there is not a shadow of doubt that Busby was 'The Boss' – Jimmy was the man who worked with all the young players from the moment they arrived at the club. His presence was enormous, on the training ground and at Old Trafford, and he worked so hard in tandem with Matt Busby to achieve the goals they had set. From the moment those youngsters became Manchester United players, they were all well aware of just who Jimmy was. He was the man who eventually molded them into the players that they were to become. Hours and hours were spent on the training ground, bollocking them, cajoling them, urging them, willing them, pleading with them, trusting them, but most of all, teaching them and toughening them for a life in

292

professional football. He had a fierce bark, but deep down he loved working with all those youngsters, and there developed a special bond between them and him. Even today, as the players that passed through his hands move into their old age, they speak of him with reverence.

Jimmy was in charge the inaugural youth team set-up in 1952-53, and it says so much for his hard work that for the first five years of the FA Youth Cup competition, the teams that he fielded were unbeatable. Their record of five successive FA Youth Cup triumphs has never been equalled, nor (I suggest) will it ever be. Fuelled by the special talent of Joe Armstrong's scouting team, there was a never-ending stream of talented youngsters coming into that youth team from all over Great Britain and Ireland.

The people of Manchester, in the three weeks leading up to United's game in Belgrade, were gripped by European 'fever', with talk of the treble once again. The game against Red Star in Belgrade had now become just as significant as the battles against the Spanish teams the previous season. With United holding such a slender first leg lead everybody was again asking, "Can they do it?"

The Red Star game at Old Trafford had been hard fought and there were bumps and bruises to be tended to the following day. The next First Division fixture was on Saturday, 18 January 1958 at Old Trafford, against those old foes, Bolton Wanderers, who had ended United's great start to the season by beating the Reds 4-0 at Burnden Park in September. United were inconsistent after that. They found themselves playing 'catch-up' in the league, chasing Wolverhampton Wanderers. Prior to the Bolton game at Old Trafford, United were in fourth position, eight points behind the Wolves with 26 games played. There were just 16 games left to pull back that deficit.

On the Thursday before the Bolton game the sports sections of the morning newspapers led with the announcement that Matt Busby had been appointed as manager to the Scottish international team. It was a great honour, not only for Matt himself, but also for Manchester United

Football Club. It was recognition for his sterling work in making United Britain's leading football club at that time, with the Busby Babes having captured the hearts and minds of football followers throughout the nation. Busby's appointment with Scotland would take in the 1958 World Cup, to be held in Sweden in the summer. It was noted that at the World Cup Matt Busby could well come up against his number two at Old Trafford, Jimmy Murphy, who just a few months before had taken up the appointment as the Wales international team manager. For the only time in Britain's football history, all four home nations had qualified for the World Cup finals, and we looked forward to the summer with great interest.

Saturday morning, 18 January, arrived and it was bitterly cold. After doing household chores early in the morning, I made my way down to Wyman's pet shop earlier than usual, as I was off to the United v Bolton match immediately after I had finished deliveries. The banter with the customers was good natured as usual, and those that had bet with me on the outcome of the Red Star game the previous Tuesday evening paid up their threepenny bits! Some thought that after the game later that afternoon I would be returning my gains, so we decided on 'double or quits'. I was so happy as I walked the route.

Deliveries complete, I was off to Old Trafford, with a certain amount of trepidation because we were playing Bolton. I wanted so badly for United to win because in the three and a half years I had been attending first team matches, United had only beaten Wanderers once in seven attempts. My desire was also fuelled by the fact that the skipper of my school team was a huge Bolton fan, and he never failed to rub it in my face whenever they put one over on United. We would walk the school yard together each day talking about football and our rivalry between us over our teams was intense. I smile as I recall that boy now because he went on to play for Manchester United, making one appearance in the first team.

Since Matt Busby had shaken up the team in mid-December, they had gone on an unbeaten run in all competitions. They had won one and drawn three away games, and won all three home games. They had an impetus going, but Bolton was going to be a test. The 41,141 fans who braved the cold weather that afternoon were treated to a football feast, as United were rampant and destroyed Bolton by 7-2! Oh, what a performance as they ran the 'Trotters' legless. Bolton's goalkeeper, Eddie Hopkinson, was on the small side for a keeper, but he was nonetheless a very capable player. That afternoon, though, he was shell-shocked. He left the field having conceded more goals in a single league game than at any other time in his career.

It was a performance that must have had Busby chuckling because everything seemed to fire that afternoon. Bobby Charlton hit a hat trick – two were absolute screamers from over 20 yards out that Hopkinson never even saw. Dennis Viollet chipped in with a brace, and Albert Scanlon netted the sixth with a simple tap in. However, at 6-2 down and the game almost close to the final whistle, you could have forgiven Hopkinson thinking that his afternoon was over. In the dying minutes as United attacked with gusto once more, there was a melee in the Wanderers penalty area and the eagle eyed referee spotted a defender's hand push the ball away – penalty kick.

How must Eddie Hopkinson have felt as he saw who placed the ball onto the penalty spot? It was none other than Duncan Edwards. Tom Jackson wrote in his match report for the Manchester Evening News 'Green 'un' that evening, "I've little doubt that England's 'keeper Eddie Hopkinson will not face a fiercer shot than that which registered United's seventh goal this afternoon. It was hit with such power that it was past the Bolton custodian before he could even move his feet." That says it all really.

As I made my way out from the ground, I stopped, along with a few hundred others, as below the old scoreboard, and waited for the final score from Bloomfield Road, where Blackpool were playing Wolves. It was agonising as first West Brom's score went up – they had beaten Sheffield Wednesday, 3-1. There were cheers when the Preston North End result appeared – a 3-3 draw with Spurs at White Hart Lane, so that was a point pegged back on them. The minutes ticked away and then suddenly a huge roar erupted below that old black and yellow scoreboard as it showed below the letter D, first a 3 and then below it a 2 – Blackpool had beaten the Wolves by 3-2! The gap was now down to six points, and the great thing from United's point of view was that all three clubs above them, Wolves, West Brom, and Preston, still had to come to Old Trafford. The title race was on, and United fans knew it!

The Monday after the Bolton game I couldn't get to school quickly enough. But the lad I was looking for was conspicuous by his absence – that is until just before the bell went for classes to begin. We saw each other at the mid-morning break and I had my pound of flesh out of him. I do have to say though that he was absolutely smitten by the performance of Edwards that Saturday. In case you are wondering who that lad was, it was Wilf Tranter who went on to play for United, and who made one appearance against West Ham at Upton Park in 1964.

On Monday, 20 January 1958, it was announced that Jimmy Murphy would not be travelling to Belgrade for the second leg of the European Cup quarter-final. The reason was that Wales had a home World Cup qualifying tie against Israel at Ninian Park, on Tuesday, 4 February – the day before United's game with Red Star. Murphy's absence from United's travelling party would turn out to be of utmost significance in the weeks, months and years ahead.

For the next week I was a happy soul on my delivery rounds, collecting my bets. The customers revelled in the banter with me, and in reality most of them were actually United fans. I had begun to settle more at school and had started playing football again after the broken arm. The trial with me playing at centre forward for the school team had been a disaster, and it was a relief to me to find myself back in goal for the next game, against Nicholl's High School from just around the corner in Ardwick – a local derby. It was played on the morning of 25 January 1958, and we won comfortably 4-1. I rushed back to Wyman's for my delivery round immediately after the game was over, as I wanted to get

296

to Old Trafford for the afternoon's FA Cup tie with Ipswich Town. Jean Wyman used to chuckle about my enthusiasm for United, and when I returned to the shop after completing the deliveries, she asked me for a favour. She had a neighbour whose son was United daft, even though he was only seven years old, and Jean asked if I could obtain some United players' autographs for him that afternoon – it was a request that I relished.

I recall that afternoon with great sadness and a very heavy heart. Going up to Old Trafford on the bus, I was full of excitement and expectation, and the adrenalin flowed as it always did whenever I went to a first team match. The Babes were my heroes, as far as I was concerned they were a huge part of me. For the past three and a half years I had watched them make their transitions from young boys into young men. I was no different from thousands of others, youngsters just like me and adults as well. We had watched as United embraced everybody's lives, and as youngsters we were growing up alongside them. We all felt so much a part of it. The players, the manager, the staff were all very much part of the local community. There was no distance between them and the fans – they were just young working class boys who loved to play football for the club that had given them the chance to progress to the very top of the first class game. No airs and graces, no pretentiousness, no big egos – feet firmly planted on the ground. Manchester United was just one big happy family.

I was a little later than normal getting to Old Trafford, and the crowd was much larger than expected. I entered by the juniors' entrance in what is now United Road, and made my way to a place behind the goal at the Scoreboard End. After the shellacking of Bolton the previous week, most fans expected a goal feast against Ipswich Town that afternoon. It wasn't too many years before that they had resided in the old Southern League. They had a young manager in his first season with the club, who had once graced the First Division with Spurs and who was a cultured England left back. It was none other than Alf Ramsey, who just eight years later would lead England to a World Cup triumph. Also returning to Old Trafford that afternoon was a former

Manchester United manager, Scott Duncan, who had been in charge at Old Trafford just prior to the war.

It had snowed earlier in the week and as the game started there were small snow piles all around the touchline, placed there by the ground staff who had swept the pitch clear. In goal for Ipswich was Roy Bailey, father of Gary who played his part in United's Cup successes in the 1980s. The expected goal feast didn't happen that afternoon, and United did no more necessary to progress into the 5th round of the FA Cup. A crowd of 53,550 saw United take the game at a slower than normal pace, and with a brace of goals from Bobby Charlton, they won easily by 2-0. Since coming into the team in mid-December the likeable young Geordie had scored nine times in as many matches.

Immediately after the final whistle, I made my way to the main entrance. As usual there was a horde of kids waiting for the players to emerge. It was dark and it had become colder. We could see the steam, and hear laughter and banter, coming from the open windows of the dressing room. We waited patiently for our heroes, who began to emerge from around half past five. Mark Jones, with his inevitable trilby on, and pipe in mouth; Harry Gregg; Roger Byrne, always in a hurry to get away; Tommy Taylor, Bobby Charlton, and Kenny Morgans; little Eddie Colman; Albert Scanlon and Dennis Viollet. With the exception of Roger Byrne, all the players stopped and signed our books and bits of paper, before they disappeared towards Warwick Road. The big fella and Bill Foulkes must have left via the old ticket office, as we didn't see them at all. My abiding memory of those few minutes is of little Eddie who came out through those doors with a group of friends. He was happy, chirpy, bubbly, chatting to his friends as he signed away. So full of fun was that young boy, and then he was gone, just like all the others, off into the distance and darkness, and out of our lives.

I look back on that day with mixed emotions. We were not to know that this would be the last time that we would see them in the flesh. To have witnessed their smiles and their happiness is something that I will always treasure. They had their whole lives in front of them. So many dreams to aspire to, so much vibrancy, so much to live for, so much to give. I had a book signed with a good few signatures, and on the Monday afternoon, I handed it over to Jean Wyman. She was so pleased, as it would make her neighbour's son such a happy young boy when she gave it to him later that evening.

On the Tuesday, 28 January 1958, Manchester United announced their travel plans for the forthcoming trip to Belgrade. When they had played the game against Dukla in Prague in early December 1957, the return journey had been beset by problems. United used scheduled airline services in those days, but because of fog there were long delays in Prague, and eventually the United flight was diverted to Amsterdam. Walter Crickmer, the club secretary, had to run around organising the travel required to get the team back to England in time to fulfill their First Division fixture with Birmingham City at St. Andrews on 7 December. They made the journey by sea from Amsterdam and arrived in Harwich in the early hours of Saturday morning. From there they went by coach directly to Birmingham, arriving just a few hours before kick off. It probably helps understand why United didn't fire on all cylinders that afternoon, coming away with a 3-3 draw. Not wanting a repeat episode, especially with the mouth watering clash against Wolves at Old Trafford coming immediately after their scheduled return from Belgrade, United announced that for the trip to Belgrade they would charter their own aircraft. They chartered an Elizabethan aeroplane from British European Airways, so would not be tied to rigid airline schedules. This decision was to have catastrophic ramifications.

On Friday afternoon, 31 January, United left London Road station in Manchester, and travelled to London where they would stay overnight at the Lancaster Gate Hotel before playing Arsenal at Highbury the following afternoon. The players, management, and directors were all in high spirits as they headed south. The team had gelled, and was playing some wonderful football. They had not been beaten since mid-November. United knew that they had a monumental task in trying to overhaul the lead that Wolves had established in the league, but they were confident that they could achieve this. The season was approaching its most exciting and important time – they were chasing a third consecutive championship, were in the 5th round of the FA Cup, and had the second leg of the European Cup quarter-final less than a week away.

On the Saturday morning, 1 February, there was a good deal of activity inside United's hotel. It was established later that morning that Mr. George Whittaker, one of the club's directors, had been found dead in bed in his hotel room. It was another event that would have significant implications for the future of Manchester United Football Club.

Travelling with the United party that day was a fan who was a close friend of Matt Busby. His name was Willie Satinoff. Satinoff was a successful businessman, who had made his money in the 'rag trade' in Manchester. He was a devoted family man, and his main leisure pastime was following Manchester United. He was a fanatical supporter and had travelled widely, to league games and throughout Europe, with the official Manchester United party. It was well known in Manchester sporting circles, and especially amongst the press boys, that Willie was on the verge of becoming a Manchester United director. Louis Edwards was around the scene in those days, but was looked upon more as a 'hanger on' than anything else. George Whittaker disliked Louis Edwards, and had thwarted him a number of times when he attempted to become a board member. It was Willie Satinoff who was the firm favourite.

As a mark of respect for Mr. Whittaker, United wore black armbands at Highbury, and a minute's silence was observed before the kick-off. I doubt very much whether anybody who entered that famous old ground that afternoon could have imagined the game they were about to witness. Here is an abridged description of the game by Geoffrey Green[2]:

> *At Highbury, Manchester United gained quick ascendancy. After only ten minutes they snatched the lead through their powerful wing half Duncan Edwards. A neatly laid-off pass from Viollet found Edwards a few yards outside the penalty box. In this position he was irresistible. His shot was driven too powerfully for Kelsey to handle and United were one up. The goal was typical of Edwards' shooting power.*
>
> *Next, on the half hour, United were two up with a goal that was a model for the quick counter-attack. At one moment Gregg was saving superbly under the United crossbar; seconds later, straight from the clearance, Scanlon sprinted seventy yards down the left flank and Bobby Charlton crashed in the centre with all the explosive power that was to become his hallmark.*
>
> *United's magnificent performance was, of course, a team effort, but the contribution of their wing halves stood out above all else. There can have been few pairs of wing halves with more contrasting styles and appearances as Edwards and Colman, but both shared a belief in the old dictum that attack is the best form of defence. Each complimented the other to perfection; the one the aggressive dreadnought, the other the pocket Napoleon; they prompted and prodded the forwards into unceasing action. As the rhythms and directions of the attack were changed in midfield, the attack itself blossomed in response. Morgans, Charlton, Taylor, Viollet and Scanlon moved like one man.*
>
> *A third goal was to come before half time. Scanlon crossed from one wing, Morgans returned the ball from the other and Tommy*

---

[2] Geoffrey Green in *There's Only One United: The Official Centenary History of Manchester United*, Hodder and Stoughton, 1978, pp 68-71.

Taylor slotted the ball past Kelsey in the centre to complete a goal of symmetrical precision. At half time the rest of the game looked to be a formality.

The second half did indeed look to be a formality, but football was then a good deal less predictable than it is now. For it was an era when even the payers with the technique and know-how of 'putting up the shutters' invariably lacked the inclination to do so when the alternative was to move on yet again with attack. The unexpected was in store. With half an hour left, phase two of the game exploded on the crowded scene. In a dazzling space of two and a half minutes, Arsenal were level. One moment United were free-wheeling to victory, the next they were hauled back to level-pegging.

The goals tumbled out against a solid wall of noise. The breathless recovery was started by Herd, when he volleyed in a clever lob by Bowen. Gregg could only have heard that one. In another minute the score was 2-3, as Groves headed down Nutt's centre for Bloomfield to score. The cheers were still ringing as the match became all-square. Nutt's cross was low and precise and there was Bloomfield, diving forward to glance the ball into the net off his eyebrows. Highbury was a big top spinning madly; the stands nearly took off in the pandemonium.

Having turned the game on its head, Arsenal burst every blood-vessel to push home their initiative. At that point Bowen had become an inspiration at wing half; Tapscott, Herd and Groves threatened danger every time the stylish Bloomfield threaded the ball through to them with pin-point passes.

Where others would have sagged and died, United, however, as so often over the years, refused to wilt at the crisis. They trimmed their sails, steadied the boat with a firm hand on the tiller and rode out the storm. Step by step over the last twenty minutes they took charge again like champions. By sheer force of character and will-power they superimposed their skill to dominate events once more.

A flowing passage between Charlton and Scanlon saw Viollet, an exceptional player before the Munich crash, head the ball sharply past Kelsey to give United a 4-3 lead. Yet another sinuous attack by Colman and Morgans sent in Taylor to score a remarkable goal from an acute angle. Even then Arsenal refused to admit defeat. Tapscott, always a great competitive spirit, burst clean through United's middle to score from a clever opening by Bowen and Herd, and a see-saw match of nine goals finally drew to a close with the score at 4-5.

By the end the thermometer was doing a war-dance. Spectators and players alike were breathless as the teams left the field arm in arm. They knew instinctively that they had created something for pride and memory. Yet, in the event, the match was to become an obituary.

It was the last time most spectators were to see the great Duncan Edwards. He had made his debut for United at the age of fifteen; at eighteen he was the youngest player to win an international cap. He was a player of immense stature; the embodiment of all that was best in professional football. Jimmy Murphy, assistant manager at Old Trafford, felt that he was 'the one player who, had he survived, would have made the rebuilding of United so much easier'. Beside Edwards, four others [who played at Highbury] were killed: Tommy Taylor, a remarkable centre forward who, with his unselfish running off the ball anticipated the like of Hurst at a time when the battering-ram role of the centre forward was only just beginning to lose ground; defenders Roger Byrne and Mark Jones, and the midfield player Eddie 'Snake-hips' Colman, of whom Harry Gregg said, 'When he waggled his hips, he made the stanchions in the grandstand sway'.

The teams that day were:

Arsenal: Kelsey; S. Charlton, Evans; Ward, Fotheringham, Bowen; Groves, Tapscott, Herd, Bloomfield, Nutt.

Manchester United: Gregg; Foulkes, Byrne; Colman, Jones, Edwards; Morgans, Charlton, Taylor, Viollet, Scanlon.

Let that game stand as an epitaph for a side that the gods loved too much.

We now know, of course, that this would be the last time this dashing young team would perform on the English stage. The 63,000 present at Highbury that day were left with the memory of a beautiful young team, a wonderful bunch of young men and a team that played the game in the right way and in the right spirit. They had witnessed a marvellous and historic game of football between two great clubs.

As the train headed back north that evening, the players were elated. Although they had conceded four goals, Busby didn't seem to be too concerned. What was worrying him most was that his skipper, Roger Byrne, had picked up a strain and initially was thought doubtful for the Belgrade game the following Wednesday. The players were in high spirits, and eventually arrived at London Road station just after ten thirty in the evening. For the married men it was off home to their wives and families, but the single lads wanted a night out, so went into Manchester city centre to explore the nightlife. They found themselves in a club named The Costa, where they were unaware of the presence of a fair-haired boy from Aberdeen, sitting just opposite them. The lad would play such an important part in reviving Manchester United's fortunes in the coming years, writing his own name into the folklore of the club. For the time being, however, he was a promising player with Huddersfield Town, and his name was Denis Law.

Early on Monday morning, 3 February, the players gathered at Old Trafford to take the coach to Ringway Airport for their charter flight to

Belgrade. Their departure was delayed because, uncharacteristically, Mark Jones was late. It was a misty, foggy morning, and at Ringway their departure was delayed for at least an hour. The players broke off into their various groups, some playing cards, others just having a brew. The spirit amongst them was good, especially after the win at Arsenal.

There were no Manchester United directors on the flight as they were all committed to attend Mr. George Whittaker's funeral on Wednesday, 5 February – the day of the match in Belgrade. In their place, and representing them, was Mr. Willie Satinoff, who was obviously much more than just a fan, a description which belies the importance and significance of his presence on that trip to Belgrade. The flight to Belgrade took just over six hours, with a re-fuelling stop en route at Munich. As the plane approached Belgrade there was snow and poor visibility. It circled the city a few times before it managed to land safely. Looking back, it is rather ironic that the records show United's charter flight to have been the only aircraft that managed to land in Belgrade that day.

Entering the airport arrivals hall, the players were surrounded by pressmen and photographers from news agencies all across Europe. The media interest in the forthcoming game was immense. By the time the party reached their hotel, The Majestic, it was early evening and already dark. Their rooms were on the fourth floor, and the players were surprised but not alarmed to see armed guards on each floor. Much to their disappointment, the evening meal at the hotel was cold. Some of the players had taken their own supplies and so retired back to their rooms to supplement what they had eaten.

After dinner, a number of the players decided to have a walk about in the city. They donned their overcoats and off they went. It was a culture shock for all of them. Their eyes opened wide as they witnessed the poverty, and long queues at all the shops. Tommy Taylor stared in disbelief, pointing out that a number of people were wearing shoes made from old car tyres. They came across what they thought was a skating rink, which upon closer inspection was found to be a small park lake that had frozen over. Tommy Taylor and Jackie Blanchflower decided to give it a try while the others stood back and watched. The management team would have had palpitations had they witnessed what these two international players were doing! After the skating episode, some of the players did a little late night shopping and bartered with chocolates, cigarettes and toothpaste, instead of using cash.

Upon arrival in Belgrade it had been rumoured that the game was in danger due the pitch being frost bound. But Red Star officials assured United that the pitch would thaw out in time for the Wednesday afternoon kick off. On the Tuesday afternoon the United party, along with the press lads and the aircraft crew, went to the stadium, where and the players trained. With the air crew was a steward, Tommy Cable. Tommy was a United nut and he had managed to change duties with the person originally selected to serve the United flight. He just wanted to fly with United and see the game. The surface of the pitch was still hard and under a covering of snow and there were patches of ice. Roger Byrne took a fitness test and declared himself fit to play. The party returned to the hotel, and trainers Tom Curry and Bert Whalley got busy with the players' boots, making sure that they had studs of the correct length for the conditions.

The players were still in great spirits, and that evening they decided on a visit to the cinema. Much to their surprise, as they entered the cinema, the first two rows were cleared of people and the United party were given preference. The players felt sorry for those poor people that had paid their hard-earned money, though they may not have been able to understand the film, which was in English. With the film over, the players retired back to their rooms at the hotel and had an early night – the following day was going to be a huge test for them. Back in Manchester, we were all nervous and anxious about how this game would go.

Wednesday 5 February dawned, and several of the players slept in. At lunchtime they had a light snack, then were told of the team selection and briefed by manager Matt Busby in one of the hotel's dining rooms. As they boarded the coach for the stadium, there were hundreds of singing and dancing Red Star fans outside the hotel. It was the same all the way to the stadium. The stadium was packed to capacity, many of the spectators being servicemen. The pitch was still not in the best condition, but from the very first whistle United had decided to take the game to Red Star. Within two minutes United were rewarded. Red Star had an attack broken down just on the United 18 yard line and the ball was swiftly played up the channel on the right hand side of the pitch. Tommy Taylor had moved wide to collect the ball just inside his own half. Turning quickly, he was away down the right as the Slav defenders retreated. Dennis Viollet made a run inside Taylor, and as the big Yorkshireman bore down on goal, he slipped a short ball inside to Viollet who made no mistake in putting it past Beara and into the net. The goal should have given United more breathing space, but they continued with their strategy of attacking the Slavs, and after 14 minutes thought that they had increased their lead when Charlton had the ball in the net only for the goal to be ruled out for offside.

The Austrian referee was spoiling the game, as he whistled so often. It frustrated the United lads, who only had to go near a Red Star player to be pulled for a foul. The game was stop-start, and even the most innocuous of challenges was penalised. Big Duncan Edwards vented his feelings to the referee only to find himself booked for his audacity! But on 15 minutes Bobby Charlton picked up a loose ball in central midfield just inside the Red Star half. He drove forward until he was some 25 yards out, and let fly with a blockbuster of a shot that hardly got off the ground. It was hit with such venom that once again Beara got nowhere to it. Leading 2-0, 4-1 on aggregate, the tie was virtually over and the Slav crowd was silenced. It got even better just two minutes later when on 17 minutes, after United had been awarded a free kick, there was a melee in the Red Star goalmouth. The ball fell to Edwards who miscued a shot which rebounded from Beara to Bobby Charlton who made no mistake from such short range. With United 3-0 up, 5-1 on aggregate, after just over a quarter of an hour, things couldn't get better. To all intents and purposes, this tie was over.

For the remainder of the first half United were content to play the ball around, keep possession, and keep it safe at the back. The Red Star team looked demoralised and downhearted as they made their way to the dressing rooms at half-time. But whatever was said by the Red Star management team in their dressing room during that break, it certainly had an effect! Within two minutes of the restart inside forward Kostic had pulled a goal back, and then just 10 minutes later there came an incident that is still talked about today. Bill Foulkes was marking Zebec tightly, and the ball was played into the young Slav's feet. He was blatantly backing into Foulkes, and as he did so they both went tumbling inside the penalty area. The United players were furious when Keitl, the referee pointed to the penalty spot. It was a very suspicious decision, but one that allowed Kastic to score. Red Star were back in the game at 2-3, and 3-5 on aggregate, with over half an hour still to go.

United had to fight a hard rearguard action now, and for the remainder of the game Edwards and Byrne marshalled their defenders magnificently. They did breakaway on a few occasions, and after carrying the ball some 40 yards or more, young Kenny Morgans was unlucky to see his shot rebound off the inside of a post and out to safety. The Yugoslavian fans were now very noisy and as the minutes ticked away they upped the atmosphere. Somehow United hung on until in the very last minute, when Harry Gregg had to come racing out to the edge of his area to smother a through-ball destined for the feet of Sekularac. The big Irishman made sure that he got there first, but the impetus of his dive took him outside of the area and he was penalised. From the free kick, Kostic lifted the ball over United's wall and into the net to make the score 3-3, and 4-5 on aggregate. The crowd were in raptures, but unfortunately for them the referee blew to end the game almost as soon as play had re-started.

Tom Curry and Bert Whalley ushered the players off the pitch as some of them were bombarded with lumps of ice from the disappointed Red Star fans. Once inside the dressing room there was relief. United were through, and could now look forward to the semi-final draw. Busby's reaction was one of elation, and his words to the players were, "Well that's another one out of the way, and we're there again." Afterwards, when the players met the press, and were asked about the second half, Roger Byrne told them, "We had to stop tackling because the referee was blowing up for anything and everything. We had to be careful and keep our composure. We just dared not go in." But the Red Star players were generous in their praise for United after the game, and admitted that the best team over the two legs had won through.

The United party returned to the Majestic Hotel, and after a few hours rest they made their way down to one of the state rooms, where a reception was hosted by the British ambassador. There was a great deal of respect and camaraderie between the two sets of players, and as the evening wore on they just wanted to get away and enjoy themselves. Matt Busby had told Roger Byrne, the United skipper, that he would allow the players to leave the reception once the formalities and presentations were complete. As midnight approached the younger players were getting itchy feet, so Roger wrote on a napkin, "You promised the boys that they could leave once the formalities were over. Permission to go?" The napkin was passed to the top table, and upon reading it Matt looked down Roger's table and nodded his assent. Before they left, the Yorkshire trio of Tommy Taylor, Mark Jones and David Pegg gave the diners a rousing rendition of *On Ilkley Moor Baht 'At*. Then Roger rose and assembled his team together, and led them in a rendition of Vera Lynn's famous war time song, *We'll meet Again*.

Sadly, that was never to be. The players slipped out of the Majestic, and into the snow and darkness. For the majority their careers, their European adventures, and their journeys through life, were just a few short hours from ending.

Munich – 6 February 1958

Although I was just 13 when the tragedy of Munich happened, my memories of that time have never dimmed. The tragedy happened on a Thursday afternoon, and I can remember that day vividly. It was cold and bleak, and some areas of Manchester experienced snow that afternoon. It was dark before four o'clock in the afternoon. After school, I had trudged down Ardwick Green, schoolbag on shoulder, and crossed Downing Street into Rusholme Road. On the corner of that junction was Wyman's pet shop, from where I would start my dog food delivery round. My spirits that day were so high following United's marvellous performance in Belgrade the previous day. Following the 3-3 draw with Red Star, many United supporters were hoping the team would be drawn to play Real Madrid again in the semi-final of the European Cup. Revenge was sought for defeat at the same stage of the previous season's competition.

As I walked my delivery round, the banter with the customers was terrific. They all knew I was United daft, and they pulled my leg as they paid their debts to me from our threepenny bets on United's results! The first time that I had any foreboding, any sense that something was wrong, was when I walked down Store Street, under the long railway arch beneath London Road (now Piccadilly) station, and out onto London Road itself. I used to deliver to a Wilson's pub named The White Hart, on the corner of Whitworth Street, facing the fire station. There was a newspaper man there every night, selling the Evening News and the Evening Chronicle. As I crossed over to his side of the road, he had just finished putting up a poster with the headline *Stop Press – United Plane Crashes at Munich*. The Stop Press was a column on the right hand side of the newspaper's front page which contained a late headline for any breaking news that had not been in the wires before publication time. It looked as though the newspapers had been run through a Gestetner machine to add these headlines after the newspaper had actually been printed. I hurriedly paid my tuppence for the Chron, but all it said was "Manchester United's Plane has crashed at

Munich Airport – more to follow in later edition." At first, people assumed it was something minor, and nothing to worry about. As I got further down London Road, and into Downing Street, news had started to filter through about the crash on the wireless. The publican at the Old Gog and Magog was the first to tell me that there had been fatalities, although he couldn't say who they were. It was almost six o'clock in the evening by the time that I got back to Wyman's, but Jean and David knew nothing of the unfolding tragedy. I ran all the way up Rusholme Road, to my home in Royle Street, where I found my father sitting besides the fireplace with tears streaming down his face. He'd arrived home from Henshaw's Blind School, close to Old Trafford, where he was training to be a joiner after losing his sight, and he had heard the news on the wireless.

More news was filtering through, and we sat together for the next few hours as the names of those lost became confirmed: from the team Roger Byrne, Geoff Bent, Eddie Colman, Mark Jones, David Pegg, Tommy Taylor and Billy Whelan; from United's staff Walter Crickmer, Tom Curry and Bert Whalley; the Manchester newspapermen Alf Clarke and Tom Jackson; and from the national press Don Davies, Archie Ledbrooke, Henry Rose, Eric Thompson, George Follows and Frank Swift. Tommy Cable, a steward with British European Airways and a member of the crew; Bela Miklos, a travel agent; Willie Satinoff, listed as a supporter, but who in reality was much more.

News trickled through intermittently. The hours passed. It was as if we were all in a trance, as though time had stood still. Mum was at home, my sister was at home, but there was little or no conversation. We just sat there in the dim firelight, listening, waiting and praying. As the evening grew late news of the injured became clearer. Kenneth Rayment the co-pilot was critical (and would not survive). Matt Busby was critical and was not expected to survive, and it was the same for Frank Taylor, one of the travelling journalists. Duncan Edwards, Jackie Blanchflower and Johnny Berry were also described as critical.

Others were described as survivors – Albert Scanlon, Dennis Viollet, Bobby Charlton, Ray Wood, Harry Gregg and Bill Foulkes; Peter Howard and Ted Ellyard, who were newspaper photographers; Captain Thain, and crew members Rosemary Cheverton, Margaret Bellis and George Rodgers; Mrs Miklos, the wife of the travel agent; Vera Lukic and her baby; and Bato Tomasevic, a member of the Yugoslavian Embassy in London, who had travelled as a liaison officer with United.

There was no mention of Kenny Morgans – he was actually found some four hours after the crash by two German journalists who had returned to the wreckage looking for a canister of film which they had put on board the plane.

A heavy sadness enveloped the whole house. For me, a 13 year old boy, it was unthinkable that I would not be seeing my heroes play Wolves at Old Trafford in a vital league game the following Saturday afternoon. I cried so much that evening, and went to bed hoping it was all a horrible dream, and that I would awake to find that all was well. Unfortunately, when I did awake, I was to find out about the harshness and reality of life. Dad didn't go to work that morning, nor did hardly anybody else in the city. The reality was there before us in the morning editions of the newspapers and in the news bulletins on the wireless. There were pictures, stories and tales of heroism, but the stark actuality was the decimation of a team of wonderful young boys, loyal United backroom staff and the cream of the British sporting press.

The atmosphere in the city during the days that followed was surreal. A great pall of mourning was omnipresent. Adults openly shed tears. Each day I cried so much, and I could not eat. I had no interest in play or doing any of the things that young boys do, so much so that Mum had to keep me off school for some time. In hindsight I know I was suffering from shock, and years later my parents agreed that this was the case. I'd known a number of the United players and, as I have described, I had played with them during the summer months at the swimming pool. They were my idols, my heroes. During the previous three and a half years, I'd hardly missed a match at Old Trafford – in effect, I'd been growing up with them. It was beyond my comprehension that I wouldn't be seeing Tommy Taylor, David Pegg or Billy Whelan again – players I had got to know. If there was a light, it was that Duncan had survived, and there was optimism about his recovery.

A few days after the tragedy, the coffins bearing the bodies of those who perished returned home. On a cold, wet, dark evening a long convoy of black hearses brought them from Ringway Airport back to Old Trafford, where they were placed in the gymnasium beneath the Main Stand to remain overnight before being released to their families. Huge crowds lined the routes, and I stood in Warwick Road with my Mum as those vehicles passed by. Not a sound could be heard except the rumble of tyres on the cobbled road, and the quiet sniffles and sobs, as people's emotions got the better of them.

Funerals were held in the week that followed, and still the air mourning was palpable throughout the city. Attention became more focused on those who had survived, and on the daily bulletins about Duncan's recovery. Jimmy Murphy had travelled out to Munich and had returned to Manchester with Harry Gregg and Bill Foulkes. Matt Busby had told Jimmy to keep the flag flying at Old Trafford, and he now had to go about the business of putting a team together to play Sheffield Wednesday in an FA Cup 5th round tie on the evening of 19 February. The FA had allowed the club to postpone the tie the previous Saturday, because of the funerals that had taken place earlier that week. To get the patched up young team away from a grief-stricken Manchester, and away from media interest, Murphy took his players away to the Norbreck Hydro hotel in Blackpool.

That second week after the tragedy, Duncan's condition began to fluctuate. Professor Georg Maurer, who had worked so hard at the Rechts der Isar Hospital in Munich, had said that any lesser mortal than Duncan would never have survived, given the injuries that he had suffered. Oh! How I wanted him to live!

On 19 February I attended the first game after the tragedy with Mum and her friend from Ardwick, Mary Donohue. Although it was a 7.30 evening kick off we got to the ground at four o'clock in the afternoon, as we wanted to be sure of getting in. It was no surprise that there were already long queues outside each turnstile. It was a bitterly cold afternoon, with a very clear sky. The turnstiles opened early, and people flooded into the ground. We stood on the Popular Side, on the half way line, underneath the old shed, with the Glover's Cables factory immediately to the rear of the stand. There was a muted murmur as the ground began to fill – it was eerie, not like a normal match day at all. People spoke softly to each other, and there were still tears of sorrow shed as people contemplated the loss of so many young boys.

As the old steam trains drew into the station on the opposite side of the ground, the clouds of smoke came over the top of the Main Stand, making it look as though a fog had descended inside the ground. The programme was unique, and has since become a collector's item: United's teamsheet bore no names at all, just 11 blank spaces. At a quarter to seven it was announced that the gates were closed – Old Trafford was jammed packed full, a far cry from my previous visit on 25 January, when I had watched my beloved Babes beat Ipswich Town 2-0, in the 4th round of the FA Cup. At seven o'clock came the announcement we had been waiting for - the United team for the match, and even today I can hear that announcer's voice: "In goal, Harry Gregg; number two and captain, Bill Foulkes; number three Ian Greaves; number four Freddie Goodwin; number five Ronnie Cope; number six, and please welcome our new signing from Aston Villa, Stan Crowther (there were gasps when this was announced); number seven Colin Webster; number eight, another new signing, Ernie Taylor; number nine Alex Dawson; number ten Mark Pearson; number eleven Seamus Brennan.

Ernie Taylor had been signed from Blackpool the previous week. It was a great signing because little Ernie was so gifted and experienced, having played a full career with Newcastle United and Blackpool, winning the FA Cup with both clubs. Stan Crowther's signing was the

314

surprise, as it had taken place just an hour before the kick off, and had been specially sanctioned by the FA. Stan, who was a member of the Aston Villa side that overcame the Babes in the 1957 final, had played in a previous round of the FA Cup that season for Villa, and would under normal circumstances have been 'cup-tied'. He is still the only man to play for two different teams in the same season in the FA Cup.

The roars of the crowd suddenly erupted like a giant geyser as Bill Foulkes led United out from the players' tunnel. Wednesday's skipper that night was Albert Quixall, who was to join United the following year. Recalling the moment he emerged from the tunnel at the head of the Wednesday team, Albert said the wall of noise that met them was like nothing he had heard before. In effect, poor Wednesday were on a loser whichever way the game went – public opinion was dead against them, and God knows what would have happened that night had they won the game. As it happened, roared on by the crowd, United won 3-0. Towards the end of the first half, United got a corner on the left hand side at the Scoreboard End, and Seamus Brennan whipped in an in-swinger, which Jim Ryalls, the Wednesday keeper, could only help into the net. Shay scored again in the second half, and then big Alex Dawson scored near the end. The atmosphere was electric throughout the game and roars could be heard all over the city. Even the people who were locked out of the ground earlier that evening did not go home, but stayed outside the ground. To win that match 3-0 was beyond people's wildest dreams, and as the crowds filtered out and the ground emptied, there was a kind of eerie silence again on the way home. People had expended so much nervous energy in the preceding five or six hours, they were absolutely drained.

Sadly, the elation and jubilation of the Wednesday evening was to turn to tears once again on the following Friday morning. I can recall my Mum coming upstairs to my bedroom, waking me with gentle shakes, and telling me quietly that Duncan Edwards had died in the early hours of that morning. Once more, my world was shattered. The one player I idolised more than anybody else was now gone. No more would I witness the boyish exuberance of the man, as he emerged from the tunnel taking those great bounding leaps onto the pitch. No more would any of us hear him shout to his colleagues just before a match started, "Come on lads, we 'aven't come 'ere for nuffink!" The Giant was gone, and the Legend had just begun.

I used to find it difficult to talk about the tragedy, especially as I went from adolescence into manhood. There is no doubt that it left a big scar on me and, to be honest, hundreds of kids like me. I was difficult to control for a while, and both Mum and Dad were so worried that mentally something had happened to me. As I said earlier, in hindsight they both realised that they were having to deal with somebody in deep shock. Even my schoolteachers voiced their concern to my parents, as I became disinterested, difficult, very introverted, and was only happy out on the sports field. I would play 'wag' (truant) from school, and walk all the way to Weaste Cemetery just to stand in front of Eddie Colman's grave, as his was the only one that I knew how to get to. I wrote lots of things about the team, and the players as individuals, and I only wish I still had that material today. It was a macabre pattern of behavior, but I had known a number of those boys, and I was grieving. For a young boy, it was hard to come to terms with, losing heroes that I absolutely adored. At that age, knowing that I would never see them again had a profound effect upon me. I was United 'daft' in the truest sense of the word.

I think the main reason the tragedy affected so many people in the way that it did, was because those players, the staff and the press men were all part of the local community. In those days there was a very close proximity between players and fans, club and local community. It is hard to relate to today, and younger readers may find this unusual, but all those players were just ordinary, everyday guys. There were no prima donnas, there was no pretentiousness. They were 'stars', yes, but in the nicest possible way. They were literally 'the boy next door', just lads who happened to have the gift of football talent, and the good fortune to play for the club they really loved – Manchester United. They were so accessible to everybody. If you waited long enough after a match you could travel home with one of them on the bus; you could meet them in the shops, and always at The Locarno in Sale on Saturday evenings after home games. I have a few mates in Sale who are a little older than me, but who have related to me tales of sitting with players in the Locarno: the United lads would have a lemonade on top of the table, but half of mild underneath it! Some of them would walk from Stretford to the city centre just to go to the cinema. They wouldn't travel on the bus because in their own words, "to do that was boring!" Many of them could be found in the local parks during afternoons throughout the week, watching school kids playing football, and there would always be banter and laughter with them. They always had the time of day for ordinary people, for the fans. They never lost sight of where they came from.

They had awakened the imagination of the British sporting public. Until the mid-1950s, football teams had an average age somewhere towards the late 20s. All of a sudden, here was this team winning their first championship with an average age of 22, playing the most outrageous brand of attacking football. Matt Busby's long-term vision had been proved right, and the doubters (and there were many of them) had been proved wrong. Matt, Jimmy Murphy, Bert Whalley and Tom Curry had schooled them in the correct way: the foundations of the club that we know today were laid by those great men in those years immediately after Busby's appointment in 1945. Like the players, the staff were also accessible, and Walter Crickmer would walk around the outside of the ground on a match day, chatting with the fans. For the big 'all ticket' matches, when fans queued for tickets from the early hours of Sunday mornings, Matt and Jimmy would find time to walk down the queue, while Walter would stand on the canal bridge on Warwick Road as if he was counting the fans. After tickets had been purchased at the turnstiles (yes, they were sold through the turnstiles!), it wasn't unusual to see players at the ground because they had been in for treatment to injuries or strains picked up the previous day.

It is also interesting to note that although it this was the era when a maximum wage of twenty pounds was in force, not many of those players, not even Roger Byrne, the captain, were on that amount as a flat rate. They used to get two quid for a win, and a quid for a draw! But you never heard the slightest moan or groan about money. Those lads just lived to play football, and would have played every day. They were unusual in some ways, because socially they were also a very close knit set of lads, and were all mates together. Byrne was a great captain and leader, and was Matt's mouthpiece in the dressing room. He was also the route to the boss for the players. Roger kept everybody in line. It is my honest opinion that Roger was being groomed by Matt to take over eventually as the next Manchester United manager after himself.

Such was the appeal of the Babes that more people wanted to see them, and attendances started to increase. The BBC had limited coverage of games around this time, showing clips of matches on Sunday afternoons, when those families that had television would invite the less fortunate kids around to watch the programme. This gave the team more exposure, and then came Europe, which really did capture the imagination. There is no doubt that all of England's football fans (apart from City's!) were really behind United in their push for the European Cup. The two epic games against the mighty Real Madrid in early 1957, further enhanced the team's reputation, especially after some dubious methods and tactics were used by the Spaniards in both of those games. The Babes were considered such great ambassadors for their club, their city and their country, and were held in such high esteem everywhere they travelled.

Even today I can get very emotional when talking about those times. And I'm certain that it's the same for most people who were around at that time. But in my opinion, these stories have to be told. The story of the Babes is such an important part of United's history – not so much the actual accident, but the story of those tremendous young men who lost their lives pursuing not only their own dream, and the dream of Matt, but the dream of all of the fans as well. Their memory and legend must never be allowed to die. They were an extraordinary group of young men, blessed with tremendous abilities, who conducted themselves impeccably, and played the game in the right way and in the right spirit – what we know today as 'The Manchester United Way'. It is why our traditions are so strong, why mediocrity is not accepted, and why those traditions have to be passed on from generation to generation. It is why so many clubs are jealous of United now, because we have always been there at the forefront, and they cannot compete with our history. It is why Manchester United is the family that it is, because when you are born into that tradition, it is there for life. When United bleeds, we all bleed. We can disagree with each other, curse each other, fight with each other, but at the end of the day, we all agree on one thing – there's only one United!

The Aftermath – Murphy Battles On

When I look back at the events surrounding the period from Wednesday 5 February to Wednesday 26 March 1958, a time span of just seven weeks, it brings it home to me just what Jimmy Murphy achieved with his patched up team. Upon reflection, fifty years later, it is simply staggering. That team certainly deserves the accolade of 'Murphy's Marvels' or, even better as far as I am concerned, 'The Fourth Great Team'.

Without a shadow of a doubt, Murphy's heroic endeavours in that sad period of time deserve far more recognition than they have been given down the years. United defeated Fulham 5-3 in an FA Cup semi-final replay on that foggy, wet Wednesday afternoon at Highbury. It was hard to take in that for the second year running Manchester United had reached the FA Cup final, in circumstances so different from the optimism of the previous year. And in the trauma of those early weeks after the disaster, people seemed to forget that there was also a European Cup semi-final to negotiate as well. This would not take place until the week after the FA Cup final had been played on 3 May.

The 'new' team had acquitted itself so well in the weeks that followed Munich. For the most part they were not seen around Manchester at all, as Jimmy preferred them to be up in Blackpool, away from pall of mourning in the city. The weight on those young players' shoulders must have been an enormous burden for such inexperienced people to carry. When they trooped off that sodden pitch at Highbury on 26 March, it must have seemed that a little of that weight had been removed. By reaching the FA Cup final they fulfilled a promise that Roger Byrne, the late skipper, had made just a year before as he stood at the bottom of the steps at Wembley, watching the Aston Villa team collect the famous old trophy from the Queen.

In the weeks following the semi-final the pressure started to take its toll. The next two league games were lost, first at Hillsborough by a solitary goal, then in front of just over 16,000 spectators at Villa Park on the last day of March they lost 3-2. The first weekend of April was Easter weekend, and on Good Friday United entertained Sunderland at Old Trafford, and on the Saturday welcomed Preston North End. The team fought like tigers to eke out a 2-2 draw against Sunderland, with Bobby Charlton equalising with an absolute thunderbolt of a shot. For the Preston North End game, Kenny Morgans returned to first team duties just eight weeks after the disaster. There was a tremendous ovation for him when he ran out of the tunnel. Making his debut for United that day was a left winger signed from Portadown in Northern Ireland just a few days earlier – a man I was to meet many times in later years, Tommy Heron.

Morgans was just a mere shadow of him old self in that game and it petered out into a tame 0-0 draw. On Easter Monday United travelled up to Roker Park for the return fixture against Sunderland. The Wearsiders turned out in force, and over 50,000 fans saw United win 2-1 through a brace of goals from Colin Webster. This would be United's only league win of the season after the tragedy, out of 14 matches. Considering the circumstances, and the flimsy available resources, a return of four points from six in the three day Easter period was some achievement.

On 12 April 60,000 fans crowded into White Hart lane to see Spurs beat United by a solitary goal. The United team stayed down south, as the following Wednesday evening they played Portsmouth at Fratton Park. Again there was a good attendance as 40,000 fans turned up to see a real ding-dong affair that resulted in a 3-3 draw. United had to make changes from the game against Spurs, as Harry Gregg had picked up a knock, and 18 year old David Gaskell replaced him in goal. Freddie Goodwin and Bobby Charlton had also picked up knocks, so Crowther was moved to right-half and Wilf McGuinness came in at left half. Up front, Dawson came in at outside right, Morgans switched to outside left and Mark Pearson moved to his favourite inside left position. The changes freshened up the team a little as Alex Dawson, Ernie Taylor and Colin Webster all found the net. Each time United scored they couldn't hold onto their lead, but when the final whistle blew the fans had enjoyed a thriller, and the result was a fair reflection of the game.

Just three days later, Birmingham City were the visitors to Old Trafford, and they left with a 2-0 win. On Monday evening, 21 April, came the rearranged game against Wolverhampton Wanderers that should have been played on 8 February. It was an emotional night as another of the survivors, Dennis Viollet, made his return to football after recovering from his injuries. It was to be no happy return for Dennis as the league leaders outclassed United, strolling to an easy 4-0 win. I was really angry watching that game, for I hated Wolves with venom. I smile when I think about it now. Wolves had been the pretenders to the United's crown, and their manager Stan Cullis was always of the big opinion that his young Wolves were the better team, and that they never got the credit they deserved. To see United whipped so easily that evening hurt enormously and I could only reflect what might have been but for the tragedy. Incredibly, on the following Wednesday evening, 23 April, United had another home game, this time against the Geordies from Newcastle. This meant that they would play four league games in just seven days, something you could never envisage today. Dennis Viollet had picked up a knock on the Monday, but the good thing from United's point of view was that Bobby Charlton was back to replace him. Just 28,000 saw United take the lead that evening through young Alex Dawson, but once again they could not hold on to it. Newcastle equalized, and that's the way that it was at full-time.

Saturday, 26 April saw the last league game of United's season, at Stamford Bridge. There was a lot of speculation about the team selection for that game – would this be Jimmy Murphy's Cup final team, the final being just one week away? A spirited performance saw them go down 2-1 at the Bridge, with little Ernie Taylor scoring once again for United. The team that afternoon was: Gregg; Foulkes, Greaves; Goodwin, Cope, Crowther; Dawson, Taylor, Charlton, Viollet and Webster.

United returned to Manchester after the Chelsea game, and in the early part of the week they again went up to Blackpool. On the Thursday they moved down to London to prepare for the FA Cup final against arch rivals Bolton Wanderers. Jimmy had to deliberate and agonise over his team selection. Dennis Viollet had just two league games under his belt, and Kenny Morgans had seven games behind him. Morgans had been coming into some form, but had been left out for the Chelsea game, having played the previous seven games. Jimmy had to make a decision – Viollet's undoubted experience, even though he had no real match fitness, or Morgan's potential? In the end, Jimmy went for the line-up that had played at Chelsea, and there was bitter disappointment for the young Welshman.

It was also a bitterly disappointing time for me, as I desperately wanted to go down to Wembley for the final. My grandfather would be there, but going with him was not an option. Tickets as usual were as scarce as rocking horse crap, but I was determined to get one. The problem was that both Mum and Dad would not allow me to travel down even if I had a ticket. They absolutely forbade it, and it broke my heart. I came to understand why years later, but at that time I was inconsolable. Dad was blind and Mum feared that it was a journey too far for me to go alone. Unfortunately our home in Chorlton-upon-Medlock had no electricity, so we had no television. I had to compromise by going to my grandfather's home and sitting with his wife to watch that final in their old parlour that held so many happy memories for me.

Saturday, 3 May 1958 was a glorious sunny day, and the temperature was well into the seventies as kick off time approached. Just before the teams came out Ted Dalton, the United physio, helped Matt Busby take his place on the United bench. Matt was walking with the aid of crutches, and was greeted with fondness by both sets of fans. As soon as the Cup final hymn ended, both teams emerged from the tunnel. Bolton were led by their manager Bill Ridding and captain Nat Lofthouse, and United by Jimmy Murphy and skipper Bill Foulkes. United's shirts bore the crest of an eagle which in later years was to become the point of much speculation. Even I always thought that it was phoenix rising from the ashes, but recent research has established that the crest was definitely an eagle, taken from a small badge on the Manchester coat of arms, which had been redesigned around that time.

The game itself was never a classic by any stretch of the imagination, and as far as United were concerned, it was a non-event. United went behind as early as the third minute when bad defending allowed Lofthouse to steal in behind and score from just a few yards out. The game was a stalemate from then on, and I think the turning point came shortly into the second half when a tremendous shot from Bobby Charlton beat the Trotter's keeper Eddie Hopkinson all ends up – nobody was more surprised than the goalie when the ball rebounded off the foot of a post, and straight back into his hands. With time ebbing away, there came another moment of Cup final controversy. Dennis Stevens, the Bolton inside forward, headed speculatively towards the United goal. Harry Gregg palmed the ball upwards and turned to take the catch. Lofthouse came thundering in, charged Gregg in the middle of the back, and took both keeper and ball into the back of the net. Even back in those days it was an obvious foul, but astoundingly the referee gave a goal. Gregg was out cold for several minutes such was the severity of the impact, and when he did recover he was groggy right up until the final whistle blew. Jack Crompton, the United coach, has recently revealed that he bumped into the referee on holiday a short time afterwards. The referee, Mr. Sherlock, confessed to Jack that he had seen the controversial goal on television after the match, and felt he had made a mistake in allowing it to stand. Crompton, ever the gentleman, put the ref's mind at ease, saying he had no need to apologise for having made an honest decision as he saw it at the time.

That Bolton were the better team is not in dispute, and they deserved their victory, but the Lofthouse-Gregg incident has always left a sour taste in my mouth. Once again I was heartbroken after a game. I remember watching Lofthouse going up to collect the trophy, with tears streaming down my face. Again my memories took me back to just a few short months before when Babes had made mincemeat out of this same Bolton team, trouncing them 7-2. It just seemed so cruel and unfair. United's patched up team had given their all, but I think that it is true to say that Wembley that day was a bridge too far for them. The exertions of the previous 12 weeks certainly took their toll. They were not disgraced by any means, but when it came to it they had nothing left in their tanks – they were drained, physically and emotionally.

The following day the team arrived back in Manchester to a heroes' welcome, but it wasn't the same for Bolton. When they returned they embarked on a long open topped bus journey to Bolton, which took them through the United heartland of Salford, where bags of flour were hurled at them by United fans disgruntled about the Lofthouse incident.

Jimmy Murphy had to get down to work immediately after that final to pick the team up for the following week. The first leg of the European Cup semi-final was played on the Thursday against AC Milan. There had been some nastiness between United and Milan, as the Italians wanted the game played on the Wednesday, but the authorities acceded to United's request for another day's recovery from the FA Cup final. Nobody gave United a chance, including some of our own fans, and this was reflected in the attendance, as only 44,000 turned out for the game. United played in a changed strip of all white that evening and Bill Foulkes led them out of the tunnel with Cesare Maldini (Paolo's father) leading out the Italians.

United had to make changes from the team that had appeared at Wembley just five days earlier. Unfortunately for United, Bobby Charlton had been called up to play for England in a friendly match against Portugal at Wembley the evening before this game. Today this would be unthinkable. He would also miss the return leg in Milan the following week as the England team flew to Belgrade to play a friendly against Yugoslavia which took place the following Sunday. For Charlton, it was a harrowing experience to have to fly back to that city, and to return to the stadium where he had played just three months before with his great friends who had been lost in the tragedy.

Mark Pearson replaced Charlton, and Kenny Morgans returned in place of Dawson. The Italians had a star-studded team that apart from Maldini also included Nils Liedholm, who would captain Sweden to the World Cup final just a few weeks later. They boasted Juan Schiaffino, an Argentinian, who was a wonderfully talented inside forward, a flying left winger named Cucchiaroni, and a solid no-nonsense defence, at the heart of which was a giant sweeper named Bergamaschi. United faced a mammoth task.

The opening exchanges were fairly even, but gradually the Italians began to take charge. It was no surprise when in the 24th minute Schiaffino got behind the United defence to open the scoring. They seemed to settle for it for a while and they allowed United to become more dominant. With the partisan crowd urging them on United took charge, but it looked as though the Italians would cope. That is until a fine piece of opportunism by Dennis Viollet, showing some of his former self, saw United equalise to go in at half-time on level terms.

The second half saw United, prompted by Ernie Taylor, throw the kitchen sink at the Italians. They attacked in waves, and the Italians stooped to all sorts of tricks to slow the game down and waste time. It was even worse than the Real Madrid home tie the year before. United pegged away, and Ernie Taylor's passing was a joy to watch. For me, this was probably his finest performance in his short time at United. Given his age, he stood out like a beacon, and the young players around responded in kind. The game was approaching the final ten minutes, and just as it looked as though it was going to be stalemate, United were awarded a penalty at the Stretford End. The smallest man on the field couldn't get hold of the ball quickly enough. The Italians besieged the referee, but he stood firm. Little Ernie stood with the ball on the spot, waited for the goalkeeper to take his place on the line, calmly placed the ball, turned, took a few paces back, turned again, and waited for the referee to blow the whistle. Then he strode forward and smacked the ball straight down the middle, as the goalkeeper dived to his right. The ball thumped off the underside of the crossbar and into the back of the net. United were ahead and Old Trafford erupted. The

Italians could not believe it, and though they went chasing an equaliser, it wasn't to be – United had won 2-1.

Whenever I look back on that game it always amazes me what a great achievement it was. It said so much for the character and will of the players, but also of Jimmy Murphy. The return leg was to be played at the San Siro in Milan the following Wednesday, and the win had given not only the players, but the fans and the nation as well, a glimmer of hope. Could this team do the impossible and reach the European Cup final? We all hoped that they could.

Because of the disaster, United obviously opted not to fly to Milan. Instead they travelled over land. The first leg of the journey took them by rail from Manchester to Harwich, where they caught the ferry for the Hook of Holland and then went by rail to Milan. The United party left what was then London Road station early on the Sunday afternoon. I went to see them off, buying my one penny platform ticket so that I could get closer. The players and Jimmy were assembled in the station cafeteria when I arrived, and they were busy signing autographs. We followed them out from the cafeteria and onto the platform where they boarded the train. The players assembled at the various windows and the steam engine whistled loudly as the train slowly inched away from the platform. The players waved, we all waved back and wished them well, and there were a lot of tears amongst the fans. Lots of memories came flooding back of happier times.

The journey to Italy was long and arduous, and the team did not arrive in Milan until late on Monday evening. It wasn't any kind of preparation, but what could United do? The San Siro was teeming with 80.000 vociferous Italians when the teams took to the field on the Wednesday evening. Both sides were unchanged from the previous meeting. For United it was a hard, hard task, especially as Schiaffino wiped out their lead inside three minutes. It was backs to the wall stuff, but they held out until half-time. Seven minutes into the second half the referee awarded a penalty for some unseen offence, and the United defenders were most unhappy about the decision. Nils Liedholm stepped up and sent Harry Gregg the wrong way as he rolled the ball into the goal. The tie was now over, to all intents and purposes. The Italians took command, and scored again in the 67th minute through centre forward Danova, and Schiaffino got his second goal in the 77th minute to complete a 4-0 rout. United's lads had given their all, but as at Wembley just ten days before, Milan was another bridge too far. They had nothing at all to be ashamed of. They had performed valiantly and had done the club, Manchester and their country proud. It was time for them all to go away and have a rest from the intensity of the spotlight that had been upon them for the previous three months.

And so the European trail had come to its end. It was to be six more years before United took part in European competition again. At that particular time, though, we just wondered whether they would ever get there again.

Those first two European campaigns will always hold such a special place in my heart. There were some marvellous moments and some terrific matches. The memory of seeing the first ever English team to compete in Europe; the memory of seeing the first ever home European tie, ending in a 10-0 win; the battle in Dortmund on an ice bound pitch; the win against Bilbao against the odds at Maine Road; the two memorable ties against Real Madrid; and the games against Red Star. I remember the dreams of a wonderful group of young men who were just so much a part of our lives, and who acquitted themselves so magnificently. I don't forget either the patched up team that took up their mantle, and performed so heroically in the aftermath of the tragedy. Even today, in moments of quiet solitude, I still remember. I still see them so clearly. I still see the happiness and joy which they gave to us all. I'll never forget, and neither will those of my generation who are still around today.

The Fourth Great Team

It is commonly accepted that during Matt Busby's tenure at Old Trafford, three great United teams graced that hallowed turf. First, there was the side led by Johnny Carey that won the FA Cup in 1948 and the league championship in 1952. Within a few short years the second great side, the Busby Babes, had arisen. Then, the third great side, the side of Charlton, Law and Best, won the European Cup in 1968, adding to two league championships in the previous three years.

But I consider that there was a fourth great team, one that is often forgotten, and much maligned. On 19 February 1958 a patched up team of two Munich survivors, two seasoned professionals signed in a hurry, five reserve team players and two players from the 'A' team took to the field at Old Trafford to face Sheffield Wednesday in a delayed 5th round FA Cup tie. Outside the ground, the thousands of United fans who couldn't gain admission, massed in silence, waiting as the events unfolding inside were relayed to them by fans shouting to them from the top of the terracing. Inside, 66,000 United fans could not realise that they were witnessing a resurrection of such consequence that it recruited devotees from beyond the city limits of Manchester, and created what is probably the world's greatest sporting institution.

Jimmy Murphy had worked tirelessly for the previous 13 days trying to put together this team of odds and sods. This was Jimmy's team. In the whole history of English football it would be hard to find a more inspiring story than that of Jimmy Murphy, and his achievement of getting Manchester United to the final of the FA Cup that year. It also has to be remembered that he played a huge part in taking them to the First Division runners-up spot the following year as well. It is sad, but in my opinion Jimmy has never been given the accolades that he so richly deserves for his part in the initial rebuilding of Manchester United. Throughout his long career, and his great service to Manchester United, he lived in Matt's shadow, but the debt that both the club and

Sir Matt Busby owed to him was enormous. Unfortunately, today's historians tend to underplay Jimmy's part in that rebuilding and revival.

Harry Gregg was in goal, and Bill Foulkes skippered the team from right full back. Both were survivors of that ill-fated day less than two weeks before. In the left back berth was Ian Greaves, a reserve who had played a handful of first team games, and who in later years enjoyed a successful career in club management. At right half was another reserve who had played a number of first team games, and who was also a Lancashire county cricketer, Freddie Goodwin. He also went on to have a fairly successful career in club management. At centre half was a reserve player with limited first team experience, Ronnie Cope. Big Ronnie should have been on the plane to Belgrade, but when Roger Byrne picked up a strain in the game at Arsenal the Saturday before Munich, Matt Busby decided to take Geoff Bent as cover, and leave Ronnie at home. Ronnie was angry and disillusioned by this, and he told Jimmy (who also didn't travel to Belgrade because of a commitment as manager of the Wales team) that he would be handing a transfer request in when the team returned. Although Ronnie played for United for a few seasons after the disaster, he was never the same player, and one can only reflect on what a burden the tragedy put upon him. At left half was a man signed from Aston Villa just an hour before the kick off, Stan Crowther. Stan was a really hard, tough, uncompromising player. I think Jimmy brought him in to add that little bit of steel to the team, and also to do a little 'minding' – making sure nobody took liberties with the youngsters. There is no doubt that Stan played his part in getting the team to that final, but very early the following season, he left to join Chelsea.

At outside right was a Welsh international whom United had signed from Cardiff City - Colin Webster. Webster was experienced, and had featured a number of times in the first team in previous season, without becoming a regular. He was a fiery, tempestuous player, but one who gave his heart and soul to the club. At inside right was Ernie Taylor. In my opinion, no praise is ever high enough to describe just what this little fellow did for Manchester United in those dark days after the tragedy. He was Jimmy Murphy's master-stroke. There wasn't too much of little Ernie, and he was also the wrong side of 30. Nowadays, he probably wouldn't even pass the medical, but what a ball-player! He had a tremendous spirit for such a little guy, and would get stuck in with biggest of them, and oh! could he pass a ball. Ernie was one of those players who could unlock defences with that one pass. His passes were laser guided with either foot, short or long, it didn't matter to him. He was termed in those days 'a tanner ball player' – nowadays they are as rare as wingers who can dribble. In the short time that he was at Old Trafford, he was a joy to watch. In some ways reminiscent of Eric Cantona, he cajoled, bollocked, but inspired those young players around him. I can recall games where despite what was going on around him – the atmosphere and passion in the stands, the frenetic passages of play – Ernie would suddenly stop, put his foot on the ball and point to the areas of the pitch where he wanted his young runners to go to. He used to say to them, "When I look up, all I want see are your arses disappearing upfield. Give me something to aim at." Ernie got them to Wembley. The following season, Matt bought Albert Quixall, and Ernie left for Sunderland.

At centre forward was a young boy with the physique of a bullock – Alex Dawson. He was a Scot, from Aberdeen, but he had played for England schoolboys because his father, a trawlerman, moved the family to Hull. Alex earned the nickname 'The Black Prince' because of his jet black hair, and craggy good looks. He was a real handful, though, and but for having to shoulder such a huge burden in the immediate aftermath of the tragedy, I think that he'd have gone on to greater things. He scored the third goal that evening against Wednesday. With the arrival of David Herd in 1961, Alex left for Preston North End, and featured in the 1964 FA Cup final, scoring for the losing side against West Ham United.

At inside left was a fresh faced Yorkshire teenager, Mark Pearson. That night was his debut – he hadn't even featured in a reserve team game. But he could play, and had wonderful ball skills. He was the original 'Pancho' Pearson, nicknamed by a journalist in 1958 because of his long sideburns (the same nickname was given to Stuart Pearson in the 1970s). Mark was fiery, and the following season was sent off at Burnley, prompting Bob Lord, the notoriously autocratic Burnley butcher and chairman, to call him a 'Teddy Boy'. Bob Lord never liked United, but there was an underlying reason for that. At outside left was the other 'A' team player, Seamus Brennan. Little were we to know on that emotional evening that ten years later, as a full back, he would help United win the European Cup. Shay was still so fresh faced then. When he ran out at Old Trafford that night, he couldn't have dreamed that 90 minutes later he would return to the dressing room a hero. He scored twice, one direct from a corner kick.

Yes, they were Jimmy Murphy's team, and for me were the fourth 'great' team produced during that great era between 1945 and 1968. It is certainly time that they were included in the roll of honour. Maybe they did lack the glitter and stars of the other three teams, but I'll tell you what – it would be very difficult to name another team who battled so overwhelmingly against the odds. More than that, I think it would be fair to say that they are largely responsible for the special link that exists today between Manchester United and our tribal following around the world.

Between 1958 and 1963, there was considerable movement of players both into and out of Old Trafford. The Munich tragedy had taken its toll, and in 1962/63, the club was almost relegated, finishing 19th in Division One. However, despite that lowly position, United were nowhere near as bad as the press made them out to be. There were games where they did fire on all cylinders, and were a joy to behold. The FA Cup seemed to spur them into another gear, and they reached the final where they beat the much fancied Leicester City 3-1 at Wembley, with vintage performances from two Scotsmen, Paddy Crerand and Denis Law. Denis had joined the previous August after an unhappy spell in Italy, and Paddy had come south from Celtic in January 1963. In September 1958, Matt had made Albert Quixall the costliest player in Britain by signing him from Sheffield Wednesday for £45,000. In 1960 he signed the tough tackling Maurice Setters from

West Bromwich Albion; in 1961 came David Herd from Arsenal, and Noel Cantwell from West Ham. Thus, six of the 1963 Cup winning team had been bought in – Cantwell, Crerand, Setters, Quixall, Herd, and Law. Busby had used his buying powers wisely, whilst quietly sowing the seeds of his youth policy once again. In 1964 the youth team once again brought home the FA Youth Cup, for the first time since the days of the Babes.

In the December of the 1963/64 season, two young Irish wingers made their debuts in the first team – Willie Anderson and a waif of a boy named George Best. Little were we to know, that dark December day, just what an impact young George would have on the game in the years to come. Also in that 1964 Youth Cup winning team were Jimmy Rimmer, Bobby Noble, David Sadler, John Fitzpatrick and John Aston.

In 1964/65 the championship came home again for the first time since Munich, and was won again in 1966/67. The team played a bright attacking style of football, and were a joy to watch. It was the team of Best, Charlton and Law – three players from the same side who were named as European Footballer of the Year during that period. The climax of the 1967/68 season saw United pipped for the title by arch enemies, Manchester City. However, City's achievement was eclipsed by the realisation of Matt Busby's golden dream when United lifted the European Cup for the first time, beating Benfica at Wembley 4-1 – just ten years after the Munich tragedy. The period between 1963 and 1968 was once described so eloquently by Michael Parkinson as "the period of Busby, Best, and Bachus!"

The Best Player I Have Ever Seen

"The best player that I've ever seen, the best footballer that I've ever played with, for United or England, the only other player who ever made me feel inferior."

Those are the words of one of the greatest players ever to grace the world football stage, one of the greatest ambassadors of the game, and most of all one of life's gentlemen – Sir Bobby Charlton. Who was the player that he was talking about? Well, he was a young man – just. He played at the top level of the professional game until he was only 21 years and 143 days old. But in that so-short career, he left such an indelible mark, both on football as a game, and in the memories of the people that were so fortunate to have watched him play.

It says so much about this remarkable young man that even now, almost 51 years after his passing, he is still talked about and remembered, not only by fans of the club for which he played and loved so much, and who cherish his memory so guardedly, but also by football fans throughout the British Isles, Europe, and the rest of the world. He was a household name by the time he reached his 18th birthday. He was indeed world class, a colossus, a giant in the truest sense of the word, a great, and he has become a legend. In the modern day, those words are bandied about and bestowed upon players so freely and so easily. But when they are used in this young man's profile, no other words could describe him more aptly. He is, of course, Duncan Edwards.

So much has been said and written about Duncan Edwards. Outside Manchester, the mere mention of his name can provoke argument, because some believe that Duncan's legend is based upon sentiment. The belief is expressed that he could never have been as good as is claimed. For some younger fans today, I suspect that they just can't accept that he was so good. It is difficult for them to believe that there was ever the perfect player. It must make them wonder just who this fantastic young man was. Could he have been as great as they say? Are the descriptions of him over-exaggerated? As I said, over the years, much has been written about Duncan, some of it true, some of it myth. Those of us who were around during his time and did watch him play, recognise the truth.

Was Duncan as good as they say? Without doubt! And he never even reached his full potential. That is a mind blowing statement because at the time that he passed, he'd already had some five years in the game at the very top level, including almost three years of full international experience. Could he have improved? Well in my honest opinion, if he had improved he would have gone on to eclipse even Superman! Duncan lived and breathed football and was arguably the most dedicated player that the game has ever seen. He looked after his body, lived the dedicated life of a professional athlete, and was solely focused upon one thing – playing football. Apart from his family and fiancée, nothing else mattered to him.

I was fortunate to have watched Duncan for the majority of his first team career, and I have so many memories of him. He was a wonderful human being as well as a great football player. Let me tell you a few things about him, and then about my memories of him.

Duncan was born on 1 October 1936, to Gladstone and Sara-Ann Edwards, in a little terraced house at 23 Malvern Crescent in the Black Country town of Dudley, Worcestershire. They were a typical hard working, working class family. His Mum used to tell the story about Duncan being able to kick a ball before he could even walk! His parents had a set of reins which they would tie around his waist, and whilst Gladstone would hold him upright, Duncan would kick the ball up and down their living room, much to their amusement.

He grew into a young giant for his age. He had a huge frame, and was much bigger than children of his own age. He loved to play football. His waking hours were spent playing the game whenever the opportunity arose, and if he wasn't actually playing football then he would dream about it. It was obvious to anybody watching this young man that he was so gifted and skilful where football was concerned. At the tender age of eight, he was playing in his school team against boys two and three years older than himself. By the time he was 11 years old, he was playing for his town team, and also representing Worcestershire Schoolboys, his county team – he was three years younger than his team mates.

Around that time Duncan wrote an essay at school in which he recalled a conversation between his father and uncle that took place in the living room of the Edwards home in Dudley. During that conversation, he had heard his father remark that England would be playing Scotland at Wembley Stadium the following Saturday. Duncan plucked up the courage to interrupt the conversation and ask, "Where is Wembley Stadium?"

His uncle told him that it was in London. Duncan then related to him how much he would like to play there. Little did he know just how soon his dream would come true. On 1 April 1950, at just 13 years and six months old, Duncan strode out from the tunnel and onto the hallowed Wembley turf in front of 100,000 spectators, wearing the shirt of England Schoolboys. He was representing his country, playing at left half, against the Wales Schoolboys team. He played in every England schoolboy international fixture for the next three seasons, and was even made England captain at just 14 years old. His record of playing in three successive seasons for England schoolboys still stands today, and he remains the youngest ever captain. I doubt very much if those two records will ever be broken.

Obviously, a talent such as this attracted a lot of attention. From the moment he became a schoolboy international, lots of the top professional clubs courted his parents in the hope that they would eventually land the signature of this remarkable young boy. All the big Midlands clubs, Wolves, Albion, Villa, Birmingham were prominent, as well as Arsenal, Tottenham Hotspur and Chelsea. A chance conversation between two old adversaries, as well as old army friends, was the beginning of the road to Old Trafford for Duncan. In 1950, Joe Mercer, then still playing for Arsenal, was doing some coaching with the England schoolboys team. After a game between United and Arsenal, Joe happened to remark to Matt Busby what a remarkable talent he had seen, and that in his opinion, "Young Edwards is going to be some player." This alerted Busby, and he sent for his trusted chief scout, Joe Armstrong. Busby was pleased to find out that United's scout in the Midlands, a Mr. Reg Priest, had already notified Joe Armstrong, and that he had been down to Dudley several times to watch young Edwards play. Joe Armstrong confirmed to Busby that Duncan was indeed "the boy wonder".

Busby and Jimmy Murphy went to see for themselves and in Busby's own words[3]:

"When I actually watched him for myself, what everyone had told me about him was so true. It was more than obvious that here was a young boy who was going to be a player of exceptional talent. He was so easy on the ball, perfect first touch, two footed, perfect balance, legs like oak trees, and the perfect temperament to match. We had to have him, but there was always one thought at the back of my mind. Would Duncan ... want to play for his local side, which was Wolverhampton Wanderers? I had no need to worry, because as soon as I met with him, he told me that he thought that Manchester United were the greatest team in the world, and as soon as he was old enough, he only wanted to sign for us."

For the next few years Priest and Armstrong kept a close watch on the situation. One particular weekend, Reg Priest found out that Bolton Wanderers were going to make a concerted effort to sign Duncan. The thing was, Duncan had a cousin, Dennis Stevens who had already signed for Bolton, and they were using this as a lever in the hope of

---

[3] From *Duncan Edwards: A Biography*, by Iain McCartney and Roy Cavanagh, Temple Printing Ltd, 1999.

persuading young Edwards to sign for them. Reg Priest informed United what was going on, and advised them to get somebody down to Dudley immediately. Busby and Jimmy Murphy slipped unobtrusively into Dudley and at 2am on the morning of 1 October 1952, a bleary eyed Gladstone Edwards came downstairs to answer the knocking on the front door of his home. Stood there, outside in the darkness, were Matt Busby and Jimmy Murphy. He invited both men into the living room, and called Sara-Ann. For the next hour the four of them talked about the possibility of Duncan joining Manchester United. Gladstone told both of them that the decision would be left to Duncan as to which club he would like to join – unbeknown to him, Sara-Ann already knew the answer, as Duncan had confided in her the previous morning.

Gladstone called Duncan, and this giant of a boy arrived in the living room wearing his pyjamas, rubbing the sleep out of his eyes, and immediately upon recognising Matt Busby said, "Mr. Busby, there's only one club that I want to play football for, and that's Manchester United. I'd give anything to sign for them."

It was as simple as that. He had followed the exploits of the Manchester United team that had won the FA Cup in 1948, the First Division championship in 1952, and who had also finished runners-up in the league on four other occasions. Their brand of football had captivated him. He was a Manchester United fan! A few minutes after meeting Matt Busby, Duncan was a Manchester United player, and a few days later he left the family home for digs in Stretford and a career in professional football.

Upon his arrival at Old Trafford Duncan was quietly introduced, and within weeks it was apparent that here was somebody truly remarkable, with a special talent. The coaches reporting to Busby stated that there was absolutely nothing that they could teach this kid. Jimmy Murphy was amazed at the talent this young boy had, so natural and gifted in everything that he did. Nothing fazed him, not the surroundings, his team mates, nor opposing players; he just had the perfect temperament. In no time at all Duncan had been promoted into the reserve team, where his performances belied his years. Even at this youthful age, he had a superb physique. Players of his own age looked under nourished compared to him! But for a big lad he was exceptionally quick over the ground, he could turn either way with a devastating body-swerve; he had two great feet, a tremendous shot in either foot; he was exceptionally powerful in the air, so strong in the tackle, but most importantly, for one so young, his positional play was flawless because he read the game so well. It also soon became apparent that he could play in any position, and still be the most outstanding player on the park!

Just six months after his arrival at Old Trafford, the day that he had lived and dreamed about arrived. On Saturday, 2 April 1953, at the age of 16 years and 185 days, he appeared from the players' tunnel at Old Trafford, wearing the number 6 shirt for Manchester United's first team. United's opponents were Cardiff City in a Football League Division One match.

My earliest recollections of Duncan are of seeing him play in a reserve team game at Old Trafford early in 1953. It was astonishing to see this young giant playing amongst men. In hindsight, it was his age that first attracted me to him, and him becoming a favourite of mine. United's reserve team wing halves in the second half of that season were two really young players: Jeff Whitefoot, who was even younger than Duncan when he made his first team debut, and Duncan himself. After his first team debut, Duncan hardly appeared in a reserve game again, although he did play in the youth team and won a winner's medal in the inaugural season of the FA Youth Cup.

In 1953/54, his reputation started to gain momentum, and even though he was just 17 years of age, he appeared for the England Under-23 team against Italy, in Bologna in the very first England Under-23 game. He had already started to earn rave notices with his outstanding displays in United's first team. In those days, there were some really outstanding players around, with huge reputations. They meant nothing at all to Duncan – even at such a young age, he just eclipsed them with the power and polish of his own performance.

The late Jackie Milburn used to tell the story of the day he first came up against Duncan. He recalls standing beside him early on in the game him, when Duncan told him, "I know that you are a great player Mr. Milburn, and that you have a big reputation, but it means nothing at all to me. Today I am not going to allow you a kick at the ball." This was from a 16 year old boy. It wasn't arrogance, or egoism, it was Duncan's inherent self-belief in his own ability. As Jackie said, "The thing was, Duncan was absolutely true to his word, I hardly did get a kick throughout that game and United won 5-2. I just could not believe how mature this young kid was, and what ability and self-belief he had."

His reputation had already started to grow, but it never went to his head. He had his feet firmly planted on the ground. Duncan knew he was special, I don't think that he ever doubted that. He just loved to play, and be it in the first team or the youth team, he gave each game the same commitment. His appetite for playing was voracious. Jimmy Murphy recalled another game, this time a youth team match early in the stages of the competition against a well known London team. From the very start of the game, there was a loud mouth sitting behind Jimmy who kept baiting him by shouting, "Where's your famous bleedin' Edwards then Murphy? Where's this bleedin' so-called superstar?"

Jimmy just gritted his teeth and said nothing until about twenty minutes into the game. A tackle was won in the centre circle, and the tackler was away with the ball and moving towards goal. Several of the opposition players tried to get within touching distance of him, but this boy was just too strong. From fully 30 yards from goal, he unleashed a tremendous shot that hardly got off the ground. Before the home goalkeeper could move, it was past him and nestling into the back of the net. Jimmy just smiled, turned around, looked the loud-mouth straight in the eye, and said, "That's bleedin' Edwards!"

The youth team was formidable in the first years of the Youth Cup competition, and nigh on unbeatable as they won it in the first five years of its inception. I can recall a semi-final against the Chelsea youth team – Ted Drake had also put together a really good team of youngsters in 1954/55, and the first leg had been drawn at Stamford Bridge 2-2. In the return leg, played at Old Trafford on a Saturday morning in front of 30,000 spectators, Chelsea held the upper hand, at half-time and led 2-1. In the second half, Edwards moved up to centre forward. Within minutes of the re-start, Terry Beckett floated over a cross from the right, and there was Duncan powering into the area, soaring above everybody, to thump the ball with his head past the goalkeeper and level the tie. Sometime later there was a corner to United on the left hand side at the Scoreboard End. Bobby Charlton floated it towards the penalty spot, and once again Duncan's timing and power got him there before anybody could react, and another bullet header was planted into the net. He then moved back to left half, and his influence on the young kids around him made sure that they were never going to lose that tie.

Duncan Edwards trains alone inside a misty Old Trafford in 1957.

He was such a wonderful young boy. In those days, United's players used to make their own way to the ground for home games. Duncan used to have an old Raleigh bicycle, and this was his mode of transport for getting to and from the ground. I would stand on the railway bridge and wait for him as he would come wheeling down what was then Warwick Road (now Sir Matt Busby Way). Once across the bridge he would turn left and free-wheel down to the old ticket office, with a stream of kids (me included) chasing after him. He would alight from his bicycle, prop it up against his leg, get all the kids to line up, and he would stand there signing the books and bits of paper before taking a piece of string out of his pocket, securing the bike to a drain pipe, and disappearing inside to the dressing room. It was the same ritual in reverse after the game: out he would come, line up the kids once more, sign every book and bit of paper, before untying the bike and climbing on it. Then he was off, back up Warwick Road, and to his digs in Stretford.

He also had a sense of humour. In 1954, together with Albert Scanlon and two other players, he went down to the Tyldesley and Holbrook sports shop on Deansgate. In those days the players were issued with vouchers by the club so they could buy their football boots, and the club had an agreement with a retailer for the exchange of the vouchers. The two types of boots that were popular in 1954 were the Hotspur and the McGregor. The McGregor was the all-singing, all-dancing football boot of its day – no instep bar, no bulbous toe cap, and this was the boot that a lot of the players preferred. The younger players were delighted that the club would pay for their footwear, even though they only got one pair of boots per season!

Tyldesley and Holbrook was very much 'the' sports shop in Manchester. Cyril Washbrook, the Lancashire captain and England batsman, had an interest in the business, and used to work in the shop out of the cricket season. Washbrook was a feisty character, and one of the old school – a strict disciplinarian as some of the old Lancashire players would tell. He could frighten people by his manner towards them and a lot of people would find him very overbearing. On this particular day, Duncan, Albert and the other two young players went to the shop with their vouchers. Albert and the other two duly handed over their vouchers to the autocratic Cyril, and in turn received boxes with the McGregor boots inside.

While Duncan was being served the other three browsed in the shop, but minutes later there was a commotion at the counter and Washbrook was raging. Red-faced, he was shouting, "You can't have them, you can't have them. Will you people tell him that he can't have them!"

Albert and the two others looked at each other enquiringly. They hadn't a clue what it was all about. Washbrook was getting angrier as Duncan stood his ground against him. Washbrook said, "I'll call Mr. Curry and he'll tell you that you have got to have McGregor boots."

Duncan very calmly replied, "I don't want McGregor boots. I want what I asked you for." Albert thought Duncan was after the Hotspur brand, but also thought that to be unusual. Washbrook picked up the telephone, called Tom Curry at Old Trafford, and explained that he was having trouble with one of the young players who would not have the McGregor boots. Tom replied, "Who is it? Put him on the phone. I'll sort the bugger out for you! What's his name?"

Washbrook replied, "His name is Edwards, Duncan Edwards."

The phone went silent, and then Tom Curry told Washbrook, "Oh! Yes, give him whatever he's asking for. It's fine, it's okay. He can have what he wants."

Duncan duly walked out of the shop with two tennis rackets, a dozen tennis balls and what we used to term, a pair of goloshers (gym shoes)! Albert and the other two lads were gobsmacked.

In April 1955, Duncan was selected to play for the full England side against Scotland at Wembley, so becoming the youngest player ever to play for his country at senior level, at the age of 18 years and 183 days. It was unheard of in those distant days, when teenagers just weren't considered good enough, nor experienced enough, to play for England. Duncan had already represented England at schoolboy, youth, under-23 and 'B' team level. He took to international football like a duck to water, and once selected was never left out of England's team again. In the Autumn of 1955, England went to Berlin to play the then world champions, West Germany at the Olympiastadion in front of 100,000 spectators. For the first 20 minutes of the game, the Germans gave England a torrid time, but then Duncan made a tackle midway inside the German half, winning the ball. His acceleration took him past two startled German defenders, and from 20 yards he just bombed the ball into the back of the net before the keeper could move. Even today, the

Germans remember him by the nickname that they bestowed upon him that day – 'Boom-Boom'.

The following winter, 1956, the Brazilians arrived at Wembley, testing the water for their assault on the World Cup finals to be held in Sweden in the summer of 1958. Most of the players the Brazilians used in Sweden played in that game at Wembley. They were outclassed by an England team that won 4-2, missing two penalties in the process. Tommy Taylor led their defence a merry dance, but Duncan eclipsed the man who was to be their big star in Sweden – Didi. Didi was made to look more than ordinary, and believe me, this fellow was up there with the best of them. Edwards won 18 caps in total, and scored 5 international goals. There is no doubt in my mind that he would have played for England for a very long time but for fate. I also believe that England, and not Brazil, would have lifted the 1958 World Cup, but for Munich, and but for the cruel loss of Jeff Hall, the Birmingham City full back, to polio. The very heart was ripped out of an extremely good England team.

In 1955/56, Matt Busby's famous Babes came of age and lifted the championship by a margin of 11 points. United suffered a shock defeat in the FA Cup 3rd round against Second Division Bristol Rovers at Eastville, by the astonishing scoreline of 4-0. Recently, I asked a friend who lives in Bristol to recall this fact to an old friend of his who was actually at the game. His response was, "Aye, we won 4-0, but you have to remember that Edwards didn't play in that game." That was the esteem in which Duncan was held in by the British football fan.

From late 1955 to late 1957, Duncan had to serve his National Service, and did so in the Royal Army Ordnance Corps. He hated having to do time in the services, but like most young men of the time he took it on the chin and just got on with it. In 1956/57 he picked up another championship winner's medal, and also appeared in United's losing Cup final team against Aston Villa. That final was the only time that he came close to losing self control on the football pitch, having been horrified by the vicious assault by Villa winger Peter McParland upon

Ray Wood in the United goal. Coming in the opening minutes of that game, it effectively put Wood out of the match with a fractured cheekbone and reduced United to ten men. As McParland lay on the ground Duncan strode over to him, but then held back before the red mist descended. He was scrupulously fair, and expected nothing less from opposing players.

My abiding memory of him during that season's European campaign was not from any of United's victories, but in the semi-final second leg against that great Real Madrid team. Although that game was drawn 2-2, United were eliminated by 5-3 on aggregate. Over the two legs, the Spanish champions had employed some dubious tactics, and United were on the end of some very suspicious decisions from the referee in the away leg in Spain, twice having what seemed legitimate goals ruled out for offside. As he came off the field that evening at Old Trafford, I could see the hurt and dejection etched in his face. He had run his socks off that night, but even his superhuman efforts were not enough to pull of an almost impossible victory. It hurt him, you could see that.

The last time I saw him play was on Saturday, 25 January 1958 in a 4th round FA Cup tie at Old Trafford against Ipswich Town, which United won by 2-0. His last appearance in England was on 1 February 1958, against Arsenal at Highbury. It was fitting that it was an absolute classic of a game, which United won 5-4, with Duncan outstanding, scoring early on with one of his specials. The result was of little importance in retrospect – football won that day. It left a lot of fans with the memory of a truly outstanding young footballer who performed in a truly outstanding young team. His last appearance for United was on 5 February 1958 in the Army Stadium in Belgrade in the 3-3 draw with Red Star, and again it was fitting that he gave another outstanding performance. On a treacherous pitch, he floated and glided with grace and power. In the second half, when United's defence was on the rack, he tackled like a demon, and marshalled everybody superbly. Again he was the outstanding player on the pitch.

Duncan was very reserved off the field, almost to the point where he was shy and retiring. He just lived for football and would have played every day if he had been allowed. Oh yes, he knew that he was gifted, and he knew that he was special, but it never put an edge on him. He didn't feel any different from his team mates. For his age he was so mature, and nobody took liberties with him. Bill Foulkes tells a tale from a game against West Brom in 1957[4]:

"Duncan could drive the ball accurately over vast distances with either foot, he could coax short passes through the eye of a needle, he could send an opponent the wrong way with the sweetest of swerves. For all that, though, what really took the breath away was his sheer power. He was awesome in the air, and on the deck people would just bounce off him. West Bromwich Albion's Maurice Setters, later to become an Old Trafford team-mate of mine, was a formidably abrasive individual, and I recall him threatening Duncan, who was in the act of taking a throw-in. Maurice was positively bristling with aggression, but our boy shot him a contemptuous glance, stuck out his chest and poor Maurice was sent reeling. For all the apparent effort Duncan put into that slight movement, he might have been brushing off a fly."

How many players have played for England at senior level one week, and for their club's youth team the next? He was never in the media for the wrong reasons, and the only time that he ever got into trouble was one Saturday evening after a derby game at Old Trafford in 1955. City had trounced United 5-0, and as usual Duncan was on his way home on his bike. An overzealous policeman stopped him on Chester Road, and booked him for riding a bicycle without lights. On the Monday morning he was fined 10 shillings in the magistrate's court, and upon arriving at Old Trafford, Matt Busby fined him two weeks' wages for bringing the club's name into disrepute! He lived his life as the professional should. He conducted himself impeccably, looked after his

---

[4] From *United in Triumph and Tragedy,* by Bill Foulkes, Know the Score Books, 2008.

body, and just loved the club that he played for. He was an icon to young boys like me, and without doubt was the perfect role model.

Duncan Edwards leaves the field at half-time in a match against Arsenal in 1957. The United player to his right is Billy Whelan, and Dave Bowen, the Arsenal and Wales skipper, is on the extreme right.

He survived for almost 15 days after the tragedy. He fought, my how he fought to live. His injuries were so severe though, especially to his kidneys. Dr. Georg Maurer the eminent doctor and surgeon at the Rechts der Isar Hospital in Munich, where all the injured were taken and treated, said that any lesser mortal than Duncan could never have survived those injuries for as long as he did. His fitness, stamina and courage were unquestioned.

In the first few days after the tragedy, when Jimmy Murphy visited him as he lay there fighting for his life, his first words were, "What time's the kick off against Wolves on Saturday, Jimmy? I can't miss that one."

It must have broken Jimmy's heart to see his big champion lying broken and battered. There was a very close bond between those two men. Jimmy tells a few stories about Duncan against himself. In an England v Wales game at Ninian Park in Cardiff, Jimmy as the Wales team manager, was in the dressing room before the game giving his players instructions on how to combat the England side. When he had finished, Reg Davies, the Newcastle United centre forward piped up, "But Boss, you haven't mentioned this fellow Edwards – what do we do about him? How do you want us to play him?"

Jimmy looked Reg straight in the eye and said, "Stay out of his way son, stay out of his way. If you don't, you'll get hurt."

During the second half of that game, with England leading 4-0, Duncan had to collect the ball from close to the dugout so he could take a throw in. Seeing Jimmy in there he looked up and said, "Hey Jimmy, what time's the next train back to Manchester? You're wasting your time here!"

Jimmy exploded, "Wait till I get you back in Manchester on Monday, young man – I might make you into a half decent player!" Yes, there was a special bond between them.

Years later, in 1975, I was playing football for a club in Hong Kong, where one of my team mates was Reg Davies's son, Trevor. Trevor told me that after that international game in Cardiff, his father and Duncan had exchanged shirts after they left the field. When Reg's playing career finished he emigrated with his family to Australia, and began coaching out there. The Edwards shirt was, according to Trevor, his dad's most prized possession. In the late 1990s, on a family visit to England, Reg brought that shirt with him, and made the journey to Old Trafford, and presented it to the club's museum, where it remains on display today. It was a magnificent gesture by the Welshman, who could have made a lot of money at auction with the item. Sadly, Reg Davies passed away on 9 February 2009 in Perth, Australia.

Not long before the tragedy, Duncan became engaged to a young lady named Molly Leach. He also bought a car, even though he couldn't drive. Sunday mornings would see Duncan and Molly outside his digs, busily polishing that car! It was his pride and joy. It must have been heartbreaking for his parents, and young Molly, to listen to him as he lay in that hospital. He told his Mum, "I've got better things to do than lie here, Mum. We've got an important game on Saturday."

She reminded him that he also had a car waiting at home, and he replied, "Keep it on the road, Mum, keep it on the road."

At eighteen minutes past one o'clock on the morning of 21 February 1958, this giant of a young man succumbed to the terrible injuries he had received in the tragedy two weeks earlier. When the news broke in the city of Manchester later that morning, a great pall of mourning once again enveloped the people.

My memories of him never dim. I can still see him today as he comes bounding out from the tunnel, taking those giant leaps into the air, heading an imaginary ball. Standing in the middle of the pitch, expanding his chest and shouting to his team mates in that thick Black Country accent, "Come on lads, we 'aven't come here for nuffink!"

He was special all right. In some ways he was a freak, and I say that in the nicest possible way. He was the perfect human being, as well as being the perfect footballer with the perfect technique, the perfect temperament. The one player I have seen that really did have everything and who could play anywhere and still be the most outstanding player on the field. People often ask me today who I would compare with him. Well, the honest answer is, I haven't seen anybody come near to him. To try and explain I tell them, take a little bit of Bobby Moore, a little bit of Bryan Robson, a little bit of Roy Keane, and a little bit of Patrick Vieira – mix them together, and maybe, just maybe, you may just get a little bit of Duncan Edwards. Have a look at the websites www.duncan-edwards.co.uk and www.munich58.co.uk and read the various newspaper reports and testimonials about him. It will give you an idea of just how gifted this young man was.

There was a famous athlete years ago who used to proclaim, "I am the greatest, I am the greatest." Well, unfortunately I have news for him: even he got it wrong. You see, 'The Greatest' was a 21 year old wing half who played for Manchester United and England, and who in my opinion was the most complete player the game of football has ever witnessed. Dear Dunc, I say it so often, the years roll by, but your memory never dims, and your legend will live on forever. Rest on in your sleep and peace, and thank you for the happiness that you brought into my life.

Duncan Edwards played 177 first class games for Manchester United and scored 21 goals. He also won 18 full international caps for England and scored 5 goals.

Epilogue: They Were My Heroes

1958 to 2008, a period of 50 years. To some, it may seem like an eternity. However, on Wednesday, 6 February 2008, when I and thousands of Mancunians from my era closed our eyes in those silent moments of reflection and remembrance, that 50 year period was recalled in just a fraction of a second. A kaleidoscope of memories flooded back. It was a bitter-sweet, but moving experience.

To be in Manchester and to follow Manchester United in the 1950s was a wonderful experience. Matt Busby had arrived when there was no ground for his team to play on, when training facilities were non-existent, when money for the transfer market was less than adequate, and the players in the team which he had inherited had lost six years of their careers to a little matter called the Second World War. Undaunted, he met the challenge head on, and as the years passed he built a club that became a family unit.

Busby embraced everybody into that family: players at every level within the club: staff; groundstaff; scouts; tea ladies; laundry ladies; and even the fans. He made people belong. Remembering his first tentative steps as a young professional player arriving in Manchester in the late 1920s to play for Manchester City, he was to tell that wonderful writer, Arthur Hopcraft (in *The Football Man – People and passions in Soccer*):

"To begin with I wanted a more humane approach than there was when I was playing. The younger lads were just left on their own. The first team players hardly recognised the lads underneath. There never seemed to be enough interest taken in them. The manager sat at his desk and you probably saw him once a week. From the very start, I wanted even the smallest member think he was a part of the club."

That he succeeded is beyond dispute.

The club in the 1950s was vibrant with youth. It was such a wonderful place to be around. Everybody was so approachable. The Babes captured the hearts of fans wherever they played. They were stars, yes, and they knew it. But their feet were firmly planted on the ground.

The period between September 1950 and February 1958 gave me so much pleasure, as I grew up alongside this young team, watching them develop and mature. I shared their highs and lows – I laughed when they won, and was heartbroken whenever they lost a game. It seemed as though my happiness would go on forever – but that wasn't to be.

I can still recall with great clarity that late Thursday afternoon in Manchester when the news began filtering through that there had been an accident at Munich. That memory never leaves me. The news that there had been fatalities made me experience, for the very first time in my life, that awful, gut-wrenching, churning feeling of loss. It was incomprehensible that I would never again see the young men who had become my idols. The sense of shock and loss is just so hard to describe. It has stayed with me throughout my life, and I would imagine it is the same for all my contemporaries. Even now, as I enter my old age, I still get so emotional about those dear young people. I have suffered loss and also tragedy in my lifetime, and I have been able to cope with it. However, the loss that was suffered at Munich is still there, and it never goes. That gut-wrenching, devastating feeling whenever I think back to that sad day will never, ever, go away.

At my home in Houston, Texas, I have a video about the lives and careers of the Busby Babes. There are often times, now that I am in the twilight of my life, and especially when I am on my own, when I'll sit down and watch it in quiet reflection. It takes me back to those heady days of such carefree happiness. There are some wonderful moments in that tape which bring the memories flooding back; wonderful memories of a tremendous group of young people, who had time for everybody. Players who caught the bus on home match days and who would happily join in the banter with the fans who were going to watch them; players who gave up their time and their energy so willingly to the community; players who always remembered where they had come from; players who never became detached from who they were; players who just loved the game of football and who would have played every day if they could. No moans about tiredness or fatigue or the number of games that they had to play – they just wanted to get out there and perform.

The last part of the video relates entirely to the accident, and both Bill Foulkes and Harry Gregg relate their memories. It's when I see this that my own hurt really begins, and it all floods back.

As I have often stated, I can never forget the pall of mourning that affected Manchester on that afternoon and evening, and which carried on into the next few weeks. Seeing the curtains of people's houses closed for a week or more as a mark of respect. They even had pictures of the team put up inside those windows. Men and women were weeping, and showing their grief so openly in public. I'll never forget the exact moment when I heard that big Duncan had passed away or the hurt and sadness that hit me so hard again.

Sadly, in the blink of an eye, it was all gone. The effect that it had on fans of all ages was plain to see for weeks, months, and even years afterwards. On some of the days, I played truant from school and would walk to Old Trafford, and just hang around the stadium all day. In my young head it made me feel closer to them. I still half expected to see some of them coming out of the players' entrance after their training had been done. I still expected to see their smiling faces and hear them tease each other again. Often I would stand outside that entrance, the tears streaming down my cheeks as I recalled times when I had spoken to them, laughed with them, and had my hair ruffled by them. I often stood by the drain pipe by the old ticket office, and remembered the many times that I had watched the big fella tie his bicycle to that pipe with the piece of string he always had in his pocket. It hurt so much knowing I would never see him again, and I'm not ashamed to say that I wept openly. Whenever I think of him today, that still happens.

They were just so different. I would stand and think of Eddie's cheeky chappy smile – that big black duffle coat that he always seemed to wear. I'd recall the gentleness of Mark Jones, and also of Billy Whelan, who I always had difficulty in understanding when he spoke. The trio that was Tommy Taylor, David Pegg, and Bobby Charlton. All three of them so happy, full of smiles and inseparable. Little Johnny Berry, Dennis Viollet, Bill Foulkes, Roger Byrne, Jackie Blanchflower and Ray Wood - the married lads who always seemed to want to get away quickly and get back home. The enormity of the loss was just so hard to take in, and even today it still is.

Other days I would meander along to Salford, and into Weaste Cemetery where Eddie had been laid to rest. At first his resting place was just a mound of earth with floral tributes upon it, and I would stand there for an hour or more willing him to be with me, smiling and joking. I was never the only one person there, as many other people would be visiting as well. The black headstone inscribed with gold lettering appeared some six weeks after the disaster and that brought home to me the permanency of Eddie's passing. Everything seemed so unfair and so hard to take. How could they have gone just like that? How could they have left us with no goodbyes? It was, and always has been, one long and continuous heartache.

There was a tidal wave of sympathy which built up in the immediate aftermath of the disaster, and it has been said by many a misinformed person that because of this Manchester United were able to expand their fan base dramatically. I personally do not agree with that. Yes, gates rose substantially immediately after the disaster, and even into the following season. But between 1960 and 1963 they dropped significantly, and in those three seasons the average gate hovered around 32,000. The real fan explosion began with re-birth of the club after winning the FA Cup in 1963, and the advent of the glorious era of Matt's third team which included Crerand, Stiles, Best, Law and Charlton. It was in 1967 that the average gate exceeded 50,000 for the first time since 1958/59. It is certainly my contention that it was at this point that the press first started to become aware of United's expanding home and international support. The attraction of fans to Manchester United was due to the exhilarating style of football they played, and the aura of Sir Matt – nothing more, nothing less.

Other clubs, and their fans, have used Munich as an excuse to criticise Manchester United, and they still do. They used to say that United cashed in on the sympathy, and would get special treatment from both the FA and the Football League. Nothing was ever further from the truth. I have yet to see any evidence of that ever being produced. There was a lot of jealousy within the game, and there were, in my opinion, certain clubs who would have revelled in the complete demise of Manchester United. Within weeks of the disaster, a number of well known First Division clubs did try to lure Jimmy Murphy away from Old Trafford.

Colin Schindler in his book *Manchester United Ruined My Life* stated: "Manchester United used to be supported by people who lived in Manchester. But after Munich, United were supported by people who couldn't find Manchester on a map." That kind of statement always gets under my skin. The facts don't support what he is saying. There is a whole lot of rubbish generated by journalists and media people who weren't even around at the time of Munich, who have picked up on hearsay stories, and embellished them for their own ego. One even accused United of, "wallowing in the misery of Munich, and using the disaster as part of the branding of the club". It is utter nonsense.

If only people would only take time to check out the facts – but then again, that is too easy. It is like the proverbial rolling stone that gathers moss as it rolls along. These stories are always the same. Whether people like it or not, Munich is a part of Manchester United's history. I would always argue for anybody to show me concrete evidence that the club ever exploited it commercially. If anything, the real truth is that the club is always in a no-win situation – damned if they do, damned if they don't – especially where the treatment of the survivors and their family dependants are concerned.

What it boils down to is jealousy – success does breed it. People should remember that in the 1950s it was a regular occurrence for many United and City fans to attend each other's matches. Fans just wanted to watch football. But in the 1960s that culture began to change. Lancashire at that time housed over one third of the clubs in the First Division: United, City, Everton, Bolton, Blackburn, Burnley, Preston and Blackpool, and there was already a health rivalry between their fans. In the early 1960s there were new kinds of social freedoms that began to emerge, especially among younger people. Young fans began a more vocal and identifiable allegiance to their clubs. The old fan culture was replaced by a culture of passionate one club loyalty, and that has led to the extreme tribalism between fans that we see today.

I have to admit that I do yearn for those old days, even though I know that they will never return. It is why I am the nostalgic old sod that I am today. I enjoyed such happiness in those early years, and such a sense of belonging. It was such a wonderful and fulfilling experience, and one that I wish with all my heart that our young fans could experience today. The club was tied by its umbilical cord to its grass roots support. Sadly over the years, that cord has gradually been severed, and I feel such sadness about that.

Whenever I return to the heart of my memories I remember the Babes with so much affection. They were my first love, and always will be. Michael Parkinson asked Sir Matt Busby the question, "If they had survived, what do you think they would have achieved?" I watched the great man as he paused to give his answer. His face betrayed the feelings that welled up inside him, and there was the hint of a small tear in his eyes. Emotionally, he responded, "I think that if they had entered it, they'd have even won the Boat Race."

I agree with that statement because believe me they would have taken some stopping.

At the end of my video about the Babes, Harry Gregg comes out with some wonderful words about the young players with whom he played for so short a time: "They say that they were the best team that we have ever seen. Well, maybe. They say that they may have gone on to be the best team that we have ever seen. Well – again, maybe. However, there is one thing that is for certain – they were certainly the best loved team that there has ever been."

Such a powerful statement, and that love came from the humility of those dear boys, their sportsmanship, the way they lived their lives, and the respect they gave to their opponents whilst never fearing them. Although the hurt is there whenever I think of them, I do think of a group of young men who always had smiles upon their faces. They were such a happy bunch, and such fun to be around. They never considered themselves anything special, and as Wilf McGuinness once said, "We were just a great bunch of pals who happened to play football."

I miss them just as much today as I did when I first became aware of the horror of what had happened on that sad, fateful day. Whenever I return to Old Trafford, before a match I close my eyes, and I can still see them. It is so easy for me to see Roger Byrne leading them out from the old tunnel, taking two taps of the ball up into his hands and then ballooning it up towards the Scoreboard End goal. I see Big Dunc emerging from that same tunnel, taking two giant leaps as he strides onto the pitch, heading an imaginary ball. I see the big smile of Tommy Taylor as he fires in balls at the goal, and the triangle of little Eddie, Mark Jones and the big fella moving the ball around in front of the Popular Stand. Those memories will never leave me.

On 6 February 2008, there was no other place in this world that I would have wanted to be than at Old Trafford. To be there, and to pay my respects to a wonderful group of people who gave me, and thousands just like me, so much happiness and pleasure, and who lost their lives pursuing not only their dreams, but also our dreams as well.

Sleep on in peace dear boys. Your memory and legend will never die, and you will always live on as the definitive heartbeat of our great club. That's why I am, and will always remain, Forever a Babe.